PASSPORT TO ANYWHERE

PASSPORT TO ANYWHERE

The Story of Lars-Eric Lindblad

LARS-ERIC LINDBLAD

WITH JOHN G. FULLER

Introduction by Roger Tory Peterson

Times BOOKS

Published by TIMES BOOKS, a division of
The New York Times Book Co., Inc.
Three Park Avenue, New York, N.Y. 10016

Published simultaneously in Canada by
Fitzhenry & Whiteside, Ltd., Toronto

Library of Congress Cataloging in Publication Data

Lindblad, Lars-Eric.
  Passport to anywhere.

  1. Lindblad, Lars-Eric. 2. Travel agents—
Norway—Biography. 3. Safaris. I. Fuller, John
Grant, 1913–   . II. Title.
G154.5.L56A36 1983   910'.92'4   82-40468
ISBN 0-8129-1068-0

Manufactured in the United States of America
83 84 85 86 87 5 4 3 2 1

In the pages of this book, I am able to mention only a few of the scores of others who helped bring about an operation that has carried over 165,000 travelers to many parts of the world that have rarely, if ever, been visited before by outsiders. For those I have not been able to name, my gratitude is nonetheless just as strong.

—Lars-Eric Lindblad

Acknowledgments

I think the best way to describe this book is to call it a conversational odyssey, a montage of reflections and impressions. It is not an autobiography, which would probably take twice the space. Nor is it a deep and ponderous survey of the world that I've had the privilege of exploring in depth for many years. It's what might be called a world sampler. What I've tried to do is to share my experiences—some bright, some sad, some almost tragic, and some more suspenseful than I wished—with readers who might want to experience many journeys to the ends of the earth with me. I've also tried to impart what I have learned in doing so.

There are so many people to whom I'm grateful that it is impossible to list them all. Without the continuing help of my first wife, Sonja, and my son, Sven, both of whom are major stabilizing forces in Lindblad Travel, it would be hard to keep our company on course.

To Esperanza, mother of my two daughters, Cristina, fifteen, and Ana-Maria, thirteen, I am much in debt for her help and guidance in the Antarctic, all of South America, and especially the Amazonas, in addition to bringing up two wonderful children.

Without the help of my present wife, Cary, the opening up of the enormous reaches of China and Tibet would have been almost impossible to accomplish. Thousands of visitors are now able to see the formerly hidden treasures of this region.

Contents

Illustrations follow page 146.

INTRODUCTION
by Roger Tory Peterson

If Lars-Eric Lindblad had lived in the year 1000, he probably would have set foot on the North American continent before Leif Ericson. Or, turning eastward, he might have reached China before Marco Polo.

The Viking wanderlust is dominant in his genes. Although he loves his home in rural Connecticut, he spends little time there. He is almost constantly on the move, taking travelers as intrepid as himself to the ends of the earth. He will undoubtedly be the first to take well-heeled tourists into outer space, where they can enjoy a cosmic view of our "Small Blue Planet."

To me the name Lindblad has become synonymous with adventure. Ever since I met Lars-Eric, twenty years ago, after I had shown my film of the Galápagos at an Audubon banquet, my life has not been the same. Sharing the same Viking instincts, I was soon helping him to scout some of the wild places that few people had seen.

I have lost count of all the Lindblad cruises and expeditions in which I have participated. Perhaps forty; fifteen of these to the Antarctic, usually as a guest lecturer. But on my first cruise I was grandly listed as "Expedition Leader." Our ship was the *Navarino,* chartered from the Chilean navy for cruises in the Antarctic. This naval vessel, converted for passenger use, was far from elegant by tourist standards—a super-annuated hulk, really.

That trip was a fiasco, although it started pleasantly enough. We proceeded past the Strait of Magellan, steamed through the Beagle Channel, and then turned southward toward Cape Horn. After dinner and a convivial evening in the lounge, we went out on deck to see fabled Cape Horn in the light of a full moon. Serene, beautiful. We retired to our cabins to rest up for the long crossing of the Drake Passage to the Antarctic Peninsula.

It must have been about two in the morning when the ship began to lurch violently, waking me from my dreams and sending my camera equipment to the floor. The Drake Passage has a reputation for its bad temper, but this, I thought, was even rougher than I had expected. Then I became aware that the engines were off. Why, I wondered, would we drop anchor way out here? Or could we? Too deep. A few minutes later Kevin McDonnell, one of Lindblad's lieutenants, burst into my cabin with the announcement that the rudder was broken. Worse than that, the manual steering system was locked, and if we couldn't free it we would have to send out distress signals. Fortunately we were well beyond the last islands, so there was no danger of dashing against the rocks. We would just drift.

Quickly putting on my parka I rushed to the bridge for more information. Only one passenger was on deck, a tall fellow from Amarillo, Texas, a railroad engineer who had signed up for this trip because he wanted to go to a place where there were no trains. A rather silent man, he had spoken hardly a word to me until this moment, when he intoned, ''This damned ship is going to sink!''

Well, it didn't sink. I proceeded to the bridge to talk with the captain, but I didn't get very far because he spoke no English and my Spanish was almost nil. However, within an hour the engines started up again, and with four men at the manual controls the ship was guided back to Puerto Williams, the southernmost Chilean naval base.

That morning our fellow passengers, unaware of what had happened, looked out at the wooded landscape of Navarino Island and exclaimed, ''We thought we had left here yesterday!''—and indeed, we had. But the trip was off. There was no way to make repairs or to install a new rudder within a week's time. Eventually we all flew home, but Lars made good his commitment by offering to take everyone the following year—on a more seaworthy ship.

It was because of the unreliability of chartered vessels that Lars decided to have his own ship, the *Lindblad Explorer*, which he had built to his specifications in Finland. It was strengthened for ice and had a swimming pool for more tropical latitudes. To many of his clients the *Explorer* became like a second home—a home away from home. Some repeaters adopted their favorite table in the dining room or their own special stool at the bar.

The *Explorer*, with the wandering albatross as its symbol, is not a typical cruise ship in which dancing, dining, and cabin hopping are the main thrust. Although the cuisine is superb and there is a bit of dancing when the seas are not too rough, the *Explorer* is more like a floating seminar. Naturalists, geologists, marine biologists, geographers, historians, and other specialists give their slide talks in the Penguin Room when the ship is at sea. No reasonable person is ever bored.

One third of the passengers, on average, are nature-oriented; not biologists, but possessing some empathy with natural things. Another fifty percent or more are intelligent citizens who wish to extend their knowledge of the world. Perhaps ten percent might be called "travel snobs" who have been almost everywhere and simply want to add new countries or places to their lists. One traveler in a hundred seems to be not with it (Lars says three in a hundred), scarcely knowing why he or she signed up or where he or she is. Such persons may confuse the two ends of the earth and, gazing out on the Antarctic ice floes, may wonder why there are no polar bears or Eskimos.

Although Lars-Eric Lindblad is linked in most people's minds with the *Lindblad Explorer*, oceanic travel is but a portion of his worldwide network of tours. Not only have his ships dropped anchor at hundreds of islands where no tourist had previously set foot, but he has also opened up hitherto unvisited areas in the high Andes, the Himalayas, and the frozen North, as well as the tropical forests and deserts. To pave the way, his contacts have included kings, presidents, and distinguished academics. Other entrepreneurs may try to copy his methods or poach on his terrain, but he is always a leap ahead.

Some environmentalists have questioned whether it is a good idea for wild places to be opened up to tourism. However, the evidence indicates that when people of influence go on tours and see things with their own eyes, they become a powerful force for the preservation of the places they visit. This has been demonstrated particularly in the Galápagos, the Seychelles, and the Falklands, as well as in the African game parks. Lindblad, a devout conservationist, believes that tours should be led by the best available talent, guides who not only interpret, but also instill in the traveler a code of behavior and a reverence for life. In fact, a roster of his tour guides and guest lecturers reads like a *Who's Who* of exploration, natural history, and the humanities.

Lars-Eric Lindblad will not send clients to a place he has not checked out himself. Nor would he fall into a trap, as did a less experienced friend of mine who organized a three-day birding cruise without first inspecting the fishing craft he had chartered. By advertising "double occupancy" he soon filled the boat. To his horror he discovered too late that "double occupancy" meant not two in a room, but two in a bunk—three bunks deep; seventy-two people in the same room! The accommodations were as minimal as those on a troopship.

In preparation for his Seychelles cruises, before he sent the *Explorer* into unfamiliar waters, Lars chartered an old tub of a boat, the *Iron Duke,* which had sailed the Indian Ocean for forty years. There was barely room in the cabin for the six of us—the captain, Lars-Eric, Tony Irwin of the Nairobi office, the photographer George Holton, Jimmy James of British Airways, and I. Indeed, our quarters were so cramped that I had to sleep, with my cameras, in a bunk so short that my feet projected into space. Even so, it was a month of idyllic island hopping, with frigate birds hanging under tropic skies and porpoises leaping in jade seas. On the long passage to isolated Aldabra, the island of the great tortoises, we were caught in a storm that confined us to our crowded cabin for three days while we waited for the turbulent seas to calm down. Later, when we ventured on deck, a huge wave nearly washed George Holton overboard, but he was saved by a line Lars had had the good sense to attach to the back of the boat.

I have many such memories of dicey incidents while scouting for Lars—such as the time my tent collapsed under an unseasonable snowfall in the Himalayas, or the situation I faced in the mountains of Ethiopia, when my mule walked onto a much too narrow ledge, stranding me on a thousand-foot precipice. Later that day, trying to get a picture of a troop of gelada baboons, I was charged by a big male, but instinctively I stood my ground and turned him away. My companion, Fernando Maldonado of the New York office, agreed with me that negotiating the highlands of Ethiopia was not for anyone over sixty. However, the revolutionary turmoil developing at that time precluded any tourism in that country for a while, anyway.

Lars, imaginative and resourceful, can find a solution to almost any problem. Once, after we had lifted anchor in the Galápagos, he was informed that the dock workers and seamen at our South American destination were about to go on strike. We were scheduled to disembark the following day and take off again with sixty people who had flown in from England, and twenty more from the States. By pulling strings, as only Lars knows how, he was able to have the strike postponed for two days until the *Explorer* was again at sea. That takes real power. Nothing short of a revolution or a volcanic eruption seems beyond his control.

And yet Lars can be defeated by the simplest of mechanical problems—such as fixing his camera when the film refuses to advance. But there is always someone around who can repair things in a jiffy. I recall the time in Peru when three of us—Lars, Esperanza Rivaud who ran his Buenos Aires office, and I—took off in a motorboat to scout the Chinchas, three small, rocky islands fifteen or twenty miles out in the Pacific, where cormorants, pelicans, and boobies assemble by the millions to breed. When we had lost sight of land, except for the snowy crests of the Andes, our 25-horsepower outboard motor conked out. Our Peruvian boatman could not start it, nor could Lars, nor I. We were helpless. But not Esperanza, who had an engineering degree. Using a couple of hairpins she quickly improvised something that solved the problem. Otherwise we might have drifted on the Humboldt current into the empty Pacific with little hope of rescue.

Quite unlike these exploratory probes, the expeditions and cruises that follow them are on the posh side and completely safe, featuring the excitement of new places but with all the comforts of home. Nor are they all nature-oriented. Some are, but increasingly such tours have been put into the competent hands of Sven-Olof Lindblad, Lars's son, freeing his father for the many other aspects of tourism—visits to primitive tribes, archaeological sites, castles, monasteries, ancient towns, and offbeat cities of cultural interest.

Lars-Eric's beautiful wife, Cary, who accompanies her husband on every mission, is the guiding hand behind The Intrepids, the travel club conceived and sponsored by Lindblad. I was named the first president, but inasmuch as I am more comfortable identifying birds than chairing meetings, I begged that my duties be put into more capable hands.

But I have said enough. Let the story of Lars-Eric Lindblad be told properly in the following pages. Like several other far-out Swedes I know, he is, in his own way, unique. There is no one else like him.

—Roger Tory Peterson

Passport to Anywhere

I

_A_NTARCTICA
Shipwreck

FROM the bridge, the pack ice appeared to be getting tighter. The white slabs, giant pieces of a frozen jigsaw puzzle, crackled against the reinforced bow of the ship. Ahead of us was Hope Bay, just off Bransfield Strait, and north of Erebus and Terror Gulf, appropriately named. Below that, some 200 miles to the south, lay the Antarctic Circle.

It was February 10, 1972. I was proud of the way the _Lindblad Explorer_ was behaving herself, down from Cape Horn, across the notorious Drake Passage, down to the Antarctic Circle, through a half-dozen research stations, and now back up to the tip of the Antarctic Peninsula near Hope Bay. It was a world of enchantment, a Disneyland of sculptured icebergs, glaciers that calved into the sea in front of our eyes. Thanks to the _Lindblad Explorer,_ I had been able to take touring groups farther south and farther north than any other passenger ships had ever ventured.

I was glad my colleagues and I had put so much thought into designing the 250-foot _Explorer,_ launched only two years before. Built to go anywhere in the world, she treats her ninety-plus passengers well. She is a snug and inviting vessel less than the length of a football field, cool in the tropics and warm in the face of a polar storm. She has a rudder

ice-knife, pilothouse deicer, double hull, bow thruster, and variable
pitch propeller.

But she is not a true icebreaker, and the pack ice was now crunching
against the bow. There were still channels, or leads, ahead of us, unsta-
ble rivers that often come to a sudden dead end. The water that showed
was smooth as a mirror: pack ice acts as a breakwater to bring a welcome calm to parts of the polar seas. The Antarctic summer morning
was tranquil, warm, and clear, with the temperature just a few degrees
below freezing. The sun turned the ice into a broken carpet of crystals
and diamonds—a perfect time to see Hope Bay and its penguin rookery,
where several hundred thousand of these exquisite birds packed the
shore and ice floes like ubiquitous headwaiters in boiled shirts, holding
their heads high in great dignity, but screeching in intolerable decibels.

On the foredeck, the passengers leaned over the bow rails to watch
the bow slicing the ice floes. Dressed in easy-to-spot scarlet parkas, the
passengers seemed to be foaming with impatience to scramble down
the gangway and go ashore in the Zodiacs, rubber outboard boats that
serve as our landing craft, sprightly little water bugs that challenge almost any kind of sea. Twenty feet long, they hold up to sixteen passengers, plus a pilot. The Zodiacs are essential for the type of adventure
travel we use the *Explorer* for, and for the other ships used by Lindblad
Travel all over the world.

On this February day, the view from the crow's nest showed that the
ice pack in the direction of Hope Bay was almost impenetrable. We
could, however, heave to and lower the Zodiacs to cruise through the
ice packs and skim close—but not too close—to the icebergs that towered over the floes. Not infrequently, the bergs could roll over with a
roar, crack with the sound of a gunshot, or spill a cascade of ice into the
sea.

Safe as the Zodiacs are, safety could never be taken for granted.
Only a year before, Dr. June Howard-Flanders of Connecticut had
gone ashore at Cape Hallett to feast her camera on the colony of
100,000 Adélie penguins there. In temperatures several degrees below
freezing, she filmed for several hours with Roger Tory Peterson, the
leading ornithologist, his wife, and other experts from our staff. Taking

the last Zodiac back to the ship in a rising storm, the intrepid group of photographers was drenched in minutes, and a large lifeboat set out from the *Explorer* to give them more protection from the green water that was breaking over the small rubber boat.

The transfer in the mounting waves was precarious enough; the attempt to secure the boat to the gangplank, dropped down from the *Explorer*'s main deck to sea level, was worse. The heavier boat bounced off several times in fruitless attempts, but all were eventually brought aboard. Dr. Howard-Flanders remembered that she was sure Roger Tory Peterson was going to slip into the frigid waters and drown. "All I could think," she said, "was that if this happened, what a loss it would be to the world of ornithology!"

We were already having our share of misadventures on our February 1972 cruise. Bertram Cox, an accountant from South Australia, had learned firsthand the trickery of the magnificent blue ice cliffs that range along the shore. Cox prepared to get some dramatic close-up views from the beach below as soon as he could get ashore in a Zodiac. He slipped and slid over the massed ice scattered on the shore, until he reached the base of a particularly high and beautiful cliff.

Suddenly, globs of ice about the size of basketballs began to fall around him. Then he saw a large overhanging ledge starting to crack and break off above him. He quickly but awkwardly scrambled clear, slipping on the ice and stumbling into crevasses as he did so. Just as he cleared the zone, he looked up to see several hundred tons of ice crumbling down on the spot where he had been standing. "It's funny," he said later, "my disappearance would have remained a permanent mystery, and my wife would not have known where to send a wreath each year!"

We had now filled four Zodiacs with a dozen intrepid passengers each, some of them in their eighties, and representing a cross section of professions, from doctors, lawyers, and business people to artists, writers, and teachers. There would be two shifts in the rubber boats to give everyone a penguin's-eye view of the scene. In the Zodiac I was handling, I could feel the excitement of the passengers as we swung close to ice floes where leopard seals were basking in the sun like enormous slugs spread across the ice. Overhead, the skua gulls were gliding across a cloudless aquamarine sky like minesweepers, seeking a disabled penguin for an early lunch.

We had to watch out for leopard seals. Along with killer whales, they are the most dangerous carnivores in the Antarctic. The only killer seal, they have been known to eat other species of the peaceable seal kingdom, to say nothing of attacking whales. Penguins are helpless before them in the water. As many as eighteen unsuspecting Adélie penguins were once discovered crammed into the belly of a single leopard seal. One Antarctic scientist from the National Science Foundation warns against any scuba diving in leopard seal waters. Man is hardly a match for this predator, which is some twelve feet long and weighs more than 400 pounds.

Although I had glided through Antarctic waters in a Zodiac before, I was as excited as the passengers. The ice-blue colors of the bergs are a sight that jolts the imagination. The glistening forms create large-scale Rorschach tests. You can make whatever you want of them, from fairy-tale castles to cathedrals to sculptures from the Museum of Modern Art in New York. The other three Zodiacs were fanned out a mile or so away in their own probings, as the *Explorer* rode the still waters quietly, perhaps two miles away. She looked like a toy ship from where we were, a bright red hull and spanking white superstructure. Her radar scanner was spinning in a lazy circle, and I knew the officers from the bridge were keeping a weather eye on all four Zodiacs through binoculars.

I began to notice that the other three Zodiacs were considerably nearer the *Lindblad Explorer* than we were. A slight breeze, barely discernible at first, had suddenly begun to sough. But now it was beginning to whistle in our ears, to the point where the floating ice pancakes were starting to close in against each other. I swung the outboard rudder around and began to weave the boat toward the *Explorer*. A jagged ribbon of water was ahead, and I gunned the outboard to take advantage of it. But in moments, the water between the ice cakes grew less, squeezed shut by the new wind. Now the channel was barely wide enough to accommodate the Zodiac. Up ahead, the water was narrowing down to a V. It was obvious that I had picked the wrong channel.

Across the ice, now almost a solid sheet, I could see the other three Zodiacs moving nearer the mother ship. They were in good hands. John Green was at the throttle of the Zodiac nearest me. He was a leprechaun of a fellow with a bushy beard and a hearty, raunchy sense of humor. He served as a specialist in Antarctic survival and had been a former station chief with the British Antarctic Survey. I was glad he was willing to work with us on our cruise.

Farther away, the second Zodiac was being handled by Captain Edwin MacDonald. Retired now, he had been deputy commander of the U.S. Navy's Operation Deep-freeze, and at the moment I looked across the ice toward him, he was weaving through the floes with his dozen or so passengers.

Francisco Erize, an Argentine veteran who had been with our Antarctic tours since 1966, was gunning his Zodiac load of passengers toward the *Explorer,* but seemed to be having some difficulty with the jamming ice floes. His lean and aristocratic face was buried in his parka hood. I was watching all three boats to take my cue for action, as my thin channel of water came to an abrupt dead end.

The others were facing the same problem. John Green had already hauled his Zodiac out of the water, and it was being pushed by him and his passengers like a sled across the floes. The other two Zodiacs were following suit, as the passengers in their bright red parkas scrambled over the ice, pushing toward the mother ship.

In our position, I did not have enough water to maneuver in, nor enough solid ice to use the boat as a sled. It wasn't long before I reached the dead end of the false channel. I slid the boat up against a natural wharf formed by the edge of a substantial ice floe. At least we now could do what the others had done: push the boat cautiously toward the *Lindblad Explorer* and treat ourselves to a welcome mug of hot tea.

The passengers scrambled up on the floe with little effort, as I hauled the Zodiac up on the surface. At almost that moment, an enormous leopard seal jetted himself out of the water to within a few feet of me, his mouth an open cavern. His murderous teeth were showing plainly. My passengers, now a safe distance away, were not alarmed; they knew nothing about the unsavory habits of the sea leopard.

I looked over and noticed seventy-year-old Dorothy McKenna as she stood by our Zodiac; she was a study in contentment: calm, relaxed, smiling at the antics of the animal. One of our best clients, she had come to the Antarctic with us seven times. Next to her was Edward Skowrup, a business executive I had met through Charles Tillinghast, the former chairman of TWA. Skowrup was thoroughly enjoying the scene, with not a sign of fear. To the other passengers as well, the sea leopard was just another warm and loving Weddell seal, which would willingly roll over on his back and let anyone pat his stomach.

I tried to give no sign to them that the picture was anything different. Keeping one eye on the sea leopard, I answered their relaxed banter by asking them if they had ever wintered on an ice floe. My words had nothing to do with my thoughts. Backing up away from the animal, I kept a sharp eye on him as I fumbled for an oar from the Zodiac. I grasped it in my hand, just as the animal waddled toward me. My one objective was to bat him back into the water with the oar. What was disturbing was that the water behind him no longer existed; the ice pack had closed in still tighter.

I'm not sure the next move was wise. I drew the oar back like a cricket bat, and smacked him hard in the face and head with the flat side of the oar. His answer was a terrifying roar. Then he retreated a few feet, stopped, and advanced again. By now the others realized that the action was serious. Like a feeble Saint George against the dragon, I continued the bizarre duel.

I looked back over my shoulder and saw that the *Explorer* was attempting to push through the ice toward us. But she was still at least a mile away, with the other Zodiacs and their passengers safely hauled aboard. The ice looked tightly packed now, enough for us to skate our Zodiac across, if I could only get rid of the leopard seal. The packed ice was good in one way: we could get back to the ship. But it was bad because the *Explorer* would be at great risk if she tried to bulldoze her way to us through the thickened ice.

I had little time to speculate, as the enraged animal was coming toward me again. It would do no good to turn and run, for it would be impossible to fend off the beast as we tried to push the Zodiac. All I wanted was some open water to push him into, but there was none.

The flat of the oar was doing no good at all. I decided quickly on another technique. I poised the oar like a spear and jammed it down the creature's throat. It hurt me to do this, but it hurt the animal more. Unworldly sounds came from his throat. He backed away, gasping for air. Suddenly I realized that the oar was going away with him. I quickly wrenched it back out again, but the animal did not retreat. All 400 pounds of him came toward me again. The best I could do was to ward him off.

Another quick glance behind me showed that the *Explorer* was pushing toward us, but was still a long distance away. Behind the sea leopard, I could now see an open spot of water. With the oar handle poking his stomach, I tried to push him back toward it, inches at a time. Ironically, I thought of all the work I had done for the World Wildlife Fund, trying to preserve animal species all over the world. Now, for safety's sake, I was turning into a forced hypocrite.

Both the open water hole and the mother ship were getting closer. I was worried enough about the ship in pack ice, with the big icebergs close by. I was also getting exhausted. But one final lunge sent the leopard seal into the open water, where he disappeared as quickly as he had shown up. By now, the *Explorer* was almost at hand. We scrambled up the gangway moments later. Instead of tea, I had a stiff drink. But at that time, I had no idea what else was in store for us within the short span of a single day.

It is roughly sixty nautical miles from Hope Bay, at the northern tip of the Antarctic, to Admiralty Bay in the belly of King George Island to the northeast. I was sorry we would have to miss our visit to the Hope Bay Argentine station. Nearby, huge flat icebergs, some up to twenty miles long, break off from the Filchner Shelf and move like ghosts toward the South Atlantic and extinction. In former visits, we had been royally welcomed by the Argentine army and scientists. At both Chilean and Argentine bases in the general vicinity, I have found the staff members of every rank to be supreme gentlemen and congenial hosts. We had also missed the chance to penetrate into the challenging Weddell Sea, and to search on shore for fossil specimens of small ferns, mosses, grasses, and equisetums—horsetails—going back 140 million years to the Jurassic period, which prove without doubt that this spit of the Antarctic was once tropical or semitropical land.

During Juan Perón's regime in Argentina, when the British territory of the Falkland Islands first became a political issue, the Argentines actually shot over the heads of the British as they tried to land a party of scientists at Hope Bay in February 1951. It was a minor skirmish that soon quieted down to an uneasy peace. No one could have guessed that it would be an ominous forerunner to the 1982 conflict. When the International Antarctic Treaty came into force in 1961, the twelve major nations involved in research there created at least a temporary peaceable kingdom.

Not so benign are the winds that spring up in Hope Bay, or Esperanza, as it is also called. In the winter months they can mount up to 200 knots. In the summer they can also be hard to grapple with, often reaching at least half that force. In fact, as we steamed toward Admiralty Bay, the gentle winds of the morning were turning tyrannical. In spite of our roll-dampers, the ship was pitching and rolling in the unrelenting waves, and now some ominous clouds were crawling across the sky.

When we were able to reach the shelter of Admiralty Bay, I was hopeful we could anchor off the Polish Artowski Antarctic station, invite the scientists there for lunch, then cruise to see the four-ton elephant seals and penguins that lie along the rocky shores. Along with the Adélie and Gentoo penguins, the Chinstrap penguins are abundant here. The chin marking of these elegant birds makes them strut as if they were the Coldstream Guards at Buckingham Palace, and at the same time, comically reminds one of the scraggly line when Snoopy smiles at Charlie Brown.

All the penguins become skittish at the mere suggestion of a leopard seal, even a rock that's shaped like one. They dive in and scramble out of the frigid waters again in order to prevent themselves from becoming lunch meat. In 1915, when twenty-two of Ernest Shackleton's men were stranded on Elephant Island, the Chinstrap penguin was their almost exclusive diet for 127 days.

There was also at Admiralty Bay an ancient site of a deserted whale station, now gratefully gone. Here whales were once flensed of their blubber and the skeletons were left to rot on the shores. Not far away on the island is the Soviet Bellingshausen scientific station, where we had often been welcomed, since most international enmities are dissolved on this continent.

The beauty of Admiralty Bay is shadowed by an inescapable sense of loneliness, especially in an Antarctic storm. And as we approached the bay, there was no question that a storm was at hand. The bow of the *Explorer* was plunging down as green water surged over the foredeck. Little relief was in sight as we entered the mouth of the bay. The Antarctic summer sun, holding light for most of the twenty-four hours of the day, was blotted out by the storm clouds. Inside the bay, we had to cope with the winds that swept down from the mountains and glaciers.

I moved to the bridge to talk with the captain. It was obvious that we would have to anchor, but the question was where. The depths in Admiralty Bay range from 40 to 400 fathoms. Any storm anchorage must be firm. However, I learned at this time that we had the use of only one of our anchors. The windlass of the starboard anchor had broken, and we could not drop the anchor since we would be unable to haul it up again. Two anchors would be essential in a storm that now had turned into a full-blown blizzard.

Antarctic anchorages are not the best. The hard rock bottoms fail to give the anchors a bite, and the thick anchor chain has to lie along the bottom to share in the holding. Sometimes the floor of the bay will have enough of a layer of lava and even guano—the soft and almost infinite excrement of the penguin rookeries that has slid into the sea—to help hold the anchor in place. But even this is uncertain.

The captain decided on a safe maritime maneuver often used in cases like this. We proceeded to move in a figure-eight pattern inside the bay, as far away from the strait as possible. By steering a figure-eight we had to maintain a fair speed to bring stability, although the turns increased the roll of the ship. We had done this some five years before, in 1967, in the lagoon at Deception Island—a huge sunken crater open to the sea through a pass known as Neptune's Bellows, very accurately named. That same year, a volcanic eruption had wiped out a former Norwegian whaling station and a British Antarctic Survey station, leaving their remains buried under a gray blanket of volcanic ash. All had escaped, but as we spiraled around the bay in the 1967 storm, we could see that the mountains were smothered as deep as seven yards by black ashes. To the passengers, the event had been a great adventure.

Now, in 1972, they were in the same spirits. I went below to the lounge, with its soft lights and muted recorded music, where the passengers were enjoying a drink before dinner. They were still chattering about the activities of the day on the Hope Bay ice floes. The lurching of the ship seemed only to liven the pre-dinner conversation. The storm outside, still raging, punctuated the comfort of the ship. In a sense it created the same feeling as a log fire in the Maine woods while the snow beats against the frosted windows.

I decided to retire to my cabin early, tired from my duel with the sea leopard. Some of the staff officers were having a birthday party, but I couldn't get myself into the mood for the festivities. The cabin itself was inviting enough, although I could feel the struggle of the ship against the winds that whistled louder now outside the sealed cabin. I could sense the impact as the storm hit the side of the ship on certain compass headings, where the hull and topsides acted as a sail. I wondered if the rest of the ninety-two passengers felt as tired as I did. There was still some light in the southern midnight sun, but the whipping snow cut the visibility almost to zero.

In bed, I could feel more than ever the heavy swells and waves lifting the ship, then the heeling as the winds caught the ship broadside. I wondered what Bransfield Strait was like if it was this deep in Admiralty Bay. Whatever the winds did, they accentuated the loneliness of our position, far from any shipping lanes and more than 600 miles from Cape Horn to the north of us across the Drake Passage.

If it is possible to be in love with a ship, I guess that is the way I felt about the *Explorer*. I knew she could take it, regardless of how rough the going. Her bottom is round and her draft is shallow. This was done intentionally, so that she could edge her way into all the out-of-the-way places around the world, where other passenger ships couldn't because of their deep drafts. Since 1967, she had weathered trips from the Arctic Circle, along both coasts of South America, across the Pacific, down through Indonesia, around Australia and New Zealand, up through the Indian Ocean and the African coasts—and, of course, the Antarctic. This was the most stirring and challenging place of all. There were risks, of course, but they were glorious ones, and the passengers who frequently repeated their trips with the *Explorer* all seemed to enjoy the same challenge.

Whatever the circumstances, however, I was not prepared for what happened next. At three in the morning I heard the sound—a sudden grating crunch that shook the ship from belly to bridge. The moment I woke up I knew what had happened. We had crashed into some of the saw-toothed rocks that rim the bay. One of the enormous swells must have carried us there and dropped us down on them, like a cargo from a crane.

I closed my eyes again, and for many seconds, I'm sure, I was paralyzed. It was not from fear but from an almost physical pain of having been wounded. With the *Explorer* wounded, I was wounded. I felt as if someone had plunged a meat cleaver into my back. The ship was groaning. With each groan, I could hear the rocks boring into the outside of the hull. The noise, combined with the shuddering and heaving that would not stop, was overpowering. It seemed that the sea and the shoal were shaking the ship the way a terrier shakes a rat.

I think I was on the bridge in less than a minute. Bjarne Aas, the captain, arrived at almost the same moment. He is Norwegian, small in stature, and moody. He seemed jittery and indecisive as we assessed the situation from the bridge. The bow was partly on a gray beach at the bottom of the mountains, while at midships we were humped up over the rocks and listing about twenty degrees. From aft, the ground swell and the waves were lifting the stern and dropping it back again. The ship was half hanging on the shoal, like a semibeached whale.

Another look at the captain showed that he was now in a state of genuine shock. To a captain, his ship is his life. I feel the same way, but he has the technical command and responsibility. Immediate action had to be taken. We didn't know how badly holed the hull was and whether we would sink if we slid off the rocks. It was well to assume that we would. Instinctively, the captain threw the engines into reverse, a common procedure for any sort of grounding. The huge propeller whined and cavitated with the swell, but the ship did not move. We were still listing, and there was the real danger that we might capsize. If we did, it was inevitable that we would lose some lives.

It was hard to tell how far up on the beach the bow was, but it seemed logical that the farther up we could get it, the less the sharp rocks below would saw into the bottom. The captain threw the engine into full speed ahead. We crawled up on the beach a little further and gained slightly more stability. But as we did, I could hear the propeller grinding down on the rocks. I could picture the huge bronze screw pulverized down to a useless stub, while the sixteen-inch shaft spun helplessly without it. But we now were more stable, with part of the ship on the beach and part in the water.

When it was clear that the ship was not going to come clear of the beach, I turned my attention from the bridge to the radio room. Radio officer Edward Simonsen, a thin, balding man in his forties who knew his craft and sophisticated equipment well, was on duty. I had seen him make radio contact with almost anybody at any time the occasion required it. He was already sending out the SOS in both voice and Morse code.

The first ship to answer was the Russian supply vessel the M. S. *Navarin.* She was in the process of crossing the Drake Passage, and advised us that she was changing course and heading toward us. But she was twenty hours away, even under full steam, and it was clear that she would be of no help if we should founder and capsize.

The next ship to answer was the Argentine tug *Zapiola,* which reported a position much closer than the Russian vessel. The problem in communicating with the ship was that none aboard understood English. Even in the lonely Antarctic, others responded: the American icebreaker *South Wind;* the British icebreaker the H.M.S. *Endurance;* and two Chilean vessels, the seagoing tug *Yelcho* and the scientific supply ship *Piloto Pardo.* Both reported they were changing course and heading toward us.

I was relieved to hear from the *Piloto Pardo.* She was navigating in the Gerlache Straits, heading south away from us, but was now heading north in a heavy swell and would reach us at eleven that morning. The radio officers spoke fluent English and had made contact with us almost every night. Just the evening before, the officers had been dinner guests aboard the *Lindblad Explorer,* and they were only seventy miles away. The *Piloto Pardo* reported that the weather would improve dramatically in the next twenty-four hours. Even if we had to abandon ship and go into the lifeboats, we could survive in better weather with help close by.

From former trips, I knew many of the officers and men from nearly all of these ships. We had had them aboard the *Explorer* at various times for lunch or dinner. We had toasted them all, whether Chilean, Argentine, British, or Russian, and had joined with them in the sort of camaraderie found only in the waters of the Antarctic. I could sense their friendship and concern in the truncated radio messages that told us help was on the way.

But there would still be many hours before the nearest ship could arrive. The twenty-degree list was not critical, but it could change at any moment. This was our greatest fear. The decision had to be made quickly as to whether we should abandon ship. Prudence suggested that we should. The captain had already made a futile and, I have to say, irrational attempt to pull the *Explorer* off the rocks with a lifeboat and a slim line. It was a move of desperation, reflecting the impact of the shock the captain was facing. I could understand it, but I also knew that the responsibility to abandon ship was his alone.

It was far from an easy decision. Outside, the storm had changed to a mixture of snow and stinging sleet, whipped by the wind and slanting rather than falling. The half-light was murky. The waves were still pounding, except that they were considerably less in the lee of the ship, still half in the water and half out. But if the lifeboats stayed in the lee, there was the danger of the ship capsizing on top of them. I felt that abandoning ship was obligatory, at least until we could check the stability of the hull on the rocks and the beach. We had a full complement of ninety-two passengers aboard, and a crew of seventy-one. Many of the passengers were senior citizens, to say nothing of two sisters from Los Angeles, Thelma and Rosemary Brown, both in their eighties. Except for the latter, all the passengers were used to clambering down the gangway into the Zodiacs almost daily in both calm and fairly severe weather. "Abandoning ship" under these conditions was a routine ritual by now. Dressed warmly, they could survive until the *Piloto Pardo* reached us from seventy miles away. After explaining this to the captain, he finally agreed to abandon ship.

Almost fifteen minutes had gone by since the ship had gone up on the rocks. I was surprised that none of the ninety-two passengers had come topside. Later, I learned that many had heard the sound and felt the impact. But they had taken it for granted that we had run into a sturdy ice pack in a mounting storm.

The captain and I decided that we would not use the intercom system that was piped into each cabin. Nor would we sound the ship's whistle. Instead, I got together our cruise leaders to divide up the job of quietly and personally waking the passengers in each cabin. Along with John Green, Captain MacDonald, and Francisco Erize, there was Keith Shackleton, the naturalist and artist, and Esperanza Rivaud, my assistant cruise director, whose quiet and calm would serve well in organizing the passengers and whose knowledge of Spanish would be invaluable when the rescue ships arrived. Both she and Keith had been with our Antarctic cruises since 1966. We went through the boat, main, A-deck, and B-deck corridors and asked the passengers to dress warmly in their parkas, thermal underwear, and warm boots. Then they were to move without rushing to the emergency stations. No baggage whatever was to be taken.

They did not panic and were remarkably calm. The job was completed in minutes. They paraded up the stairways in life jackets, with plenty of whimsical joking on the way, a gallows humor that fitted the event and reduced the element of fear. The two frail sisters in their eighties joined the others and seemed just as hardy.

We launched two lifeboats and all the sturdy Zodiacs, with ample room for everyone. There was enough light to make the launching safely, although the snow and sleet were biting in the wind. We distributed blankets and tarpaulins, along with chocolate bars, apples, and cheese. The crew also lowered several cases of liquor, which I immediately ordered dumped into the sea. Drinking hard liquor is most dangerous in the cold, as liquor opens the pores and provides only a false sense of energy.

In the lee of the ship, I looked up at her battered side. But I could not see the bottom where she was resting on the rocks. Although the list seemed to have almost corrected itself, it was safer to take the boats out from under the lee. This meant rougher water for the lifeboats and Zodiacs, but remaining under the tilting ship was a chance not worth taking.

The snow and sleet were so heavy now in the thirty-degree temperature that slush began forming in the bottom of the boats. Passengers huddled under the tarpaulins and blankets. Outside the lee of the ship, the Zodiacs and lifeboats pitched and tossed in the breakers. With help still hours away, I tried to think of alternatives. Wet suit divers from the crew were already below the surface, trying to find out exactly how big the holes were in the hull, and more important, whether the double hull had been penetrated through the inner skin. If not, it would probably be safer to re-embark the passengers to prevent possible hypothermia, in which even above-freezing temperatures can be lethal.

I also knew of an abandoned British station around the point of the small peninsula where the *Explorer* had become rockbound. There would be emergency blankets and some shelter there. Pondering the idea, I found my Zodiac suddenly pulled out into the larger breakers, with green water breaking over us. At the same moment, the outboard motor died. Impossible to control, the Zodiac swung farther and farther into the huge breakers, carried by the current. I tried everything to get the motor started again, but with no luck. Suddenly I discovered the problem. I was holding the end of the disconnected fuel line in my hand at the same time I was squeezing the rubber bulb that was designed to squirt the fuel into the engine. I fumbled for the connection and finally was able to lock the hose into it again. Within seconds the motor started. Meanwhile, I yelled to crew members in a Zodiac to try to test the waters around the other side of the peninsula to see if it was safe to bring the boats there.

The crew members placed the passengers from their boat into several others, and the two crew volunteers took off. Rounding the corner of the peninsula, the hapless boat was battered and then capsized by the waves. The crew members were able somehow to right it, and retreated with the recognition that we could never safely land any passengers at the British station, even if we could reach it.

With low tide, the list of the ship had improved. We drew the boats into the lee of the *Explorer* and waited for the report of the wet suit scuba divers. It was encouraging. Although there was an enormous hole in the outer hull, the inner shell was holding up well. Inside the ship, the report was that there was only oil seepage. If by any chance the ship was tossed off its rock base, she would not sink. The passengers were ordered back on board into the dry warmth of the ship. They were still incredibly cheerful.

Once aboard, we were able to feed the passengers cheese and crackers and hot chocolate. I had the bar opened for beer and soft drinks, but again no liquor. I explained that the immediate danger was over, and that the *Piloto Pardo* should be arriving near our anchorage within hours. Now that the *Explorer* was riding at low tide and hard aground, the most ominous danger of capsizing was gone.

We instructed the passengers to go to their cabins to pack their luggage, and then bring it to deck level where it could be transferred to the Chilean rescue vessel in dead storage in the hold. Each passenger could take one small survival kit, but nothing else. The Chilean naval vessel would be hard put to handle the rescued passengers, let alone the luggage. There would be over 160 passengers, crew, and staff from the *Explorer*. The rescue ship would be overloaded, but a godsend. By the time the *Piloto Pardo* arrived early the following afternoon, the weather was sparkling, the water was calm, and Admiralty Bay had returned to its ravishing beauty. The transfer of passengers began almost immediately; it was a slow, methodical process to squeeze some 160 of us in the lifeboats and Zodiacs onto a ship designed to hold only eighty Chilean navy men. The bay was crawling with an endless chain of miniature ferries. The Chilean crew, working with efficiency and courtesy, was magnificent. It would take the rest of the day to complete the job. It would take a second day to off-load all our food, provisions, blankets, and beverages to share with the Chilean officers and crew.

Just the sight of the Chilean officers and crew aboard the *Piloto Pardo* was of great comfort. Their clean, crisp uniforms created a marked contrast to our disheveled parkas and wet boots. On the deck, the commander in chief of the Chilean Antarctic Flotilla, Commodore Ladislao d'Hainaut, a distinguished gentleman with a full beard and charming demeanor, came forward to greet me. We had sat together at dinner on the *Lindblad Explorer* just two evenings before. Although our greeting was cordial, it was apparent that he and his fellow officers were not at all impressed with the performance of our officers and crew. I can't say I blamed them; I was feeling the same way.

With the passengers safe, I now turned to the fate of the *Explorer.* Further examination showed gaping holes in the outer hull, one of them big enough to drive a truck through. But the inner hull still remained intact. I was convinced that if we ever got her off the rock, she could float again safely. But she looked miserable sitting at a slight angle on the beach. You speak of ships as if they were people, and all I could say to myself was that she looked terribly sick. She was barely two years old—the fulfillment of a longtime dream. My Norwegian partners and I had poured love and affection into her design.

I did not think immediately of potential financial disaster, but the shadow was there in the back of my mind. I owned a substantial part of the $2.5-million, 2500-ton *Explorer*—the backbone of Lindblad Travel's year-round expeditions. The ship was almost fully booked for the rest of the year. There was obviously the possibility of a total loss of the ship that insurance could never fully cover. Hundreds of cancellations would also have to be made. Some of the passengers for the next Antarctic trip were already in South America, en route to the departure port of Ushuaia, Argentina's southernmost city, at the tip of South America. The matter of life and death of the people in the shipwreck had been the biggest nightmare. This situation no longer existed. The life or death of the *Explorer* was next. My resolve to salvage the beautiful ship grew stronger every minute.

While the cumbersome process of shifting provisions went on, several other ships arrived in the bay and stood by. The British icebreaker *Endurance* dropped anchor near us, along with the American supply ship *South Wind*. The Russian ship *Navarin* had offered full assistance en route, but she was not needed now and went on to her scheduled stop at the Bellingshausen station at the tip of King George Island. Most welcome was the sight of the Antarctic tugs, the *Yelcho* of Chile and the *Zapiola* of Argentina. Here was hope that the two tough tugs might be able to yank the *Explorer* from the grip of the rocks so that she could be towed to a South American dry dock and checked for possible salvage.

The *Piloto Pardo,* along with her scientific laboratories, carried two choppers. The commodore generously offered me the use of one of the helicopters to observe the salvage operation as the two tugs put out their giant hawsers in the attempt to drag the *Explorer* out to open water. I quickly accepted. In moments, I was in the air, hovering directly over the *Explorer* and watching the scrappy little tugs, one from Chile and one from Argentina, prepare to steam with full power in the attempt. Here was another Antarctic irony. On the South American continent, Chile and Argentina are more often than not at each other's throats about their Antarctic claims and disputed waters and islands east of Darwin's famous Beagle Channel. Yet here in the Antarctic, they worked peacefully together.

I looked down from the chopper directly over the hulk of the *Explorer*. Suddenly the tugs lurched ahead in concert, churning up the waters behind their propellers. I tensed as the *Explorer* began to shudder. I felt as if I were personally being stretched on a medieval rack. The *Explorer* did not seem to budge. I felt that if she would only free herself from the grip of the rocks, she would be safe. But she did not move an inch backward toward the sea.

It was one of the most horrible moments of my life. Convinced now that the ship would never come off the beach and rocks, I wanted to lean down from the chopper and haul the ship off myself. I could not picture that beautifully sculptured hull lying forever on that desolate beach. Yet if two tough, burly Antarctic tugs couldn't do it, what could?

I have always found that when I run into a potential disaster, I will be upset and crushed for only a short period. The adrenaline cuts in quickly, like an emergency power station. I simply would not let myself give in to despair. My first thought was a ridiculous one: I could turn the *Explorer* into the first hotel in the Antarctic. Touring groups could come there and spend a week in glorious isolation in one of the rarest spots in the world. But, of course, this is not what I wanted. The Antarctic, rugged as it is, is too fragile to allow anything but carefully planned tours of seriously interested people who want to learn more in depth about it. That is why the *Explorer* carried no band or floor shows.

In place of this were nightly lectures by such naturalists as Roger Tory Peterson and Chilean polar experts, along with Antarctic specialists such as Captain Edwin MacDonald, USN (ret.), and others. They lectured on marine biology, meteorology, ornithology, and Antarctic history. Conservation was the key, and the *Explorer* carried on her own scientific research to contribute toward it, with direct reports to the National Science Foundation, the British Royal Society, and other institutions, plus bird counts, the collection and identification of plankton samples, and the recording of the numbers and species of whales and dolphins over wide areas where very few other ships sail.

With the *Explorer* stranded on the beach, my mind continued to race against what could surely be financial disaster. Was there *any* way to get the vessel off the rocks now that two tugs had failed? If so, could she be safely towed to a place where she could be examined and repaired? Buenos Aires? Santiago? All the way to Norway? Could she make it in tow across the rough and choppy Drake Passage, or even the North Atlantic? How much time would it take to repair her, if indeed she could be repaired? I estimated at least a year. How could such mammoth expenses be financed? How much expense would be involved in refunding the disappointed travelers booked on the cruises planned for the coming year? How much cost would be involved in air fares and extra hotel bills for those waiting for the next Antarctic cruise that would never be taken?

They were ugly questions, but trying to answer them actually eased the pain. A problem is like a bitter lozenge: if you work on it, it's bound to dissolve. Back on the *Piloto Pardo,* I was able to get on the radio and talk to salvage experts in Norway, Europe, and South America to gather every scrap of advice possible. The Antarctic summer was coming to an end. The great ice packs would be closing, and speed was essential.

Speed was also essential for the *Piloto Pardo.* Jammed with an overload of passengers, she first had to bring vital supplies to several Chilean stations, and to relieve scientists and other personnel there before they would be locked in for the long black winter. There was another immediate rescue mission at a small Chilean base near Anvers Island, over 200 miles to the south, where scientists were within a hair's breadth of running out of provisions. There was an additional stop at the Chilean station Aqhirra Cerda on Deception Island, also to the south. This would mean five extra days for the overpacked *Piloto Pardo* before she could begin her final leg across the Drake Passage to the nearest Chilean port, Punta Arenas.

The spirit aboard the *Piloto Pardo* was miraculous. Much of it was due to the Chilean naval crew, which was unbelievably attentive and affable. Mattresses were spread along the corridors, even on tables. We had to sleep in shifts, and to get to any part of the ship meant stepping over half-asleep bodies—all of them grateful, however, to be alive and well. Luggage from the *Explorer* had been salvaged, but was in dead storage in the hold. There would be no change of clothing for anyone during the rescue trip. Conventional modesty went by the board. There was some attempt at separate washroom facilities, but emergencies made this ineffective. One young couple from Europe were quite active sexually, in a vertical position against the wall, sometimes before a half-appreciative audience.

The gallows humor continued; both crew and passengers shared it.

There was almost a total lack of complaints. Rosemary Brown, one of the octogenarian sisters, continued to be quite ill during the whole trip and had been unable to go on any of our excursions to shore. A Chilean navy man brought her a penguin bound for the Santiago zoo. Holding it in her arms she said, "Finally I got to see a penguin. And I did one better than all of you—I got to hold one!"

After eight days of sardine-living, the ship passed Cape Horn and approached the mainland. Small planes circled above, with photographers poking their lenses out of open doors. At Punta Arenas, on the Strait of Magellan, there was a big reception with bands playing and journalists swarming.

I got in touch with Lilo and Alexander Nesviginsky, our representatives in Buenos Aires, and arranged for a chartered Boeing 707 to fly our passengers from Punta Arenas to the Argentine capital. I flew there with the plane to begin the grim job of trying to save the stranded *Lindblad Explorer*. By now, the news was spread across the front pages of newspapers throughout the world. The Lindblad office in New York was being swamped with calls from anxious friends and relatives, and Kevin McDonnell, our general manager, organized teams to reassure the callers that all were safe.

From the Chilean Antarctic station at the southern end of King George Island, not far from the scene of the wreck, I received a radio message that the *Lindblad Explorer* was still fast on the rocks a week after the accident, but was in no danger of sinking or capsizing. Captain Aas, three officers, and a cook were standing by at the Chilean station, waiting for a rescue vessel with enough beef to haul the *Explorer* from the rocks. I learned of the giant German tug *Arktis,* some 17,000 tons and 36,000 horsepower, now berthed in South Africa. She was said to be one of the most powerful tugs in the world, and I arranged for her to be dispatched to Admiralty Bay at once.

It was anybody's guess as to whether the tug could get our ship off the Antarctic shoal. The thought of the vain attempt of the two small tugs and their straining hawsers still remained a nightmare for me. Would the efforts of the German tug simply be a replay of the whole futile attempt? Ever since I had started my efforts to open the most remote and interesting parts of the world to adventurous travelers over twenty years before, I had not given in to setbacks, which had been many. I found some solace in thinking about my early efforts to create something new for travelers with a sense of genuine wonderment about the world, as well as a sense of responsibility for it. As the German tug was steaming over the Atlantic Ridge, toward the Southern Ocean and the Antarctic, I could find many past experiences to bolster my morale while I waited for news of the fate of the *Explorer*.

II

INDIA

The Beginnings

THE names have haunted me since I opened my first history book: Kashmir, the Punjab, the Taj Mahal, the Hindu Kush, Darjeeling. There was magic in all of them, even in the gray severity of my Stockholm schoolroom. India loomed in my mind as a fantasy of maharajas, turbans, palaces, and elephants festooned with jewels.

It would be a long time before I would be able to bring my dreams into focus. As I grew up in the calm prosperity of Sweden in the 1920s, I found that school was more a window to adventure than a chore. I was a serious reader by the time I was seven. I didn't read books; I devoured them. I found myself spending nearly all my allowance on flashlight batteries to read under the covers long after I was supposed to be asleep. Except for their worry about my eyesight, my parents were only mildly upset. My father had an insatiable love for nature, for art, for the wonders of the world.

Erik Lindblad was a complex man. Born in 1901, he was the son of a police commissioner in Stockholm who committed suicide when my father was still a small child. My grandmother remarried another police official who eventually retired and bought a farm some eighty miles from Stockholm, where I developed a love for nature and animals that has never faded.

My mother, Greta, the daughter of a master cabinetmaker, managed to bring up five children without too many battle scars in light of my father's frustrations with not being able to work in the creative arts. Instead, his career was that of an expert on wine for the Swedish Liquor Monopoly. He did, however, spend as much time as possible in the arts. He painted, sculpted in wood and iron, and played a battery of musical instruments, including the zither, balalaika, and guitar.

His other passion was cars. In the 1920s and 1930s very few people in Sweden had cars, but we always managed to have one, which I'm sure put a heavy strain on the budget. The first car I remember was a Chrysler convertible, with a rumble seat in the trunk, bought in 1932 when I was five. Some of my first memories are connected with it. The second car was an elegant Packard limousine that my father bought from the American ambassador to Sweden. It was a formidable vehicle with a window between the front and back seats, and a tube telephone to connect both sections.

My father would often pack our family into this black behemoth, and we would drive all through Sweden and our neighboring countries of Norway, Estonia, and Finland. Even during World War II, we still motored inside Sweden. There was no gasoline, of course. We then had a German DKW, which was powered by a strange two-wheeled trailer that burned charcoal and wood chips. It was little more than an ordinary wood stove on wheels.

I never had to work hard at school. My extracurricular reading mentally transformed our home in the suburbs into all the exotic places of the world. On the printed page, the great explorers became my best friends. I didn't merely read about Amundsen, Shackleton, and Scott in the Antarctic. I felt I was *there* with them. The Swedish world explorers Sven Hedin and Nils Nordenskjöld were my special favorites. Wherever any of the giant explorers went, I went, whether it was to Central Asia, the polar icecaps, the Great Rift Valley, or the Himalayas.

Of course, the American Wild West was irresistible. I first learned about it through the German writer Karl May, who carried the cowboys and Indians into my living room. In addition, books like *The Last of the Mohicans* and Mark Twain's lively adventures changed Stockholm into an early American settlement or a Mississippi riverboat.

I was twelve when World War II broke out. Students were expected to help on farms to contribute to food production. I frequently went to my grandparents' farm to do chores, bring in the harvest, and pick strawberries—with plenty of time to fish through the ice or go elk hunting with my father. I soon discovered that hunting was not for me. I love animals too much.

Just a few weeks after the war ended in 1945, I was ready to continue my studies in Zurich in business administration and economics. During vacations I joined other students traveling throughout Europe—in France, Italy, Yugoslavia, Czechoslovakia, and Hungary—where my urge to travel was incubated.

I met my future wife, Sonja Buschinker, at the university in the spring of 1947. She was a Swiss girl, although her mother had originally come from Vienna and her father from Russia. She was very beautiful, with large dark eyes and sensitive features. She was studying commercial English, which didn't quite seem to fit her. We married just before I received my degree in 1948, when I accepted a job offer from a steel company in Sweden. To tide us over until my regular job would begin in the coming fall, I found summer employment with the Stockholm office of the travel firm Thomas Cook & Son.

From the start, I arranged tours for the company, a most enjoyable job. Before the summer was over, I had decided that the steel business was not for me. But I felt confined working in Europe. I was convinced I could find wider horizons in the United States, although I'm not sure why I thought so.

In the interim, I transferred to Zurich, and our son Sven-Olof was born. The decision to uproot the family and come to America was difficult under the circumstances. In September 1951, after weighing the pros and cons, we finally decided that Sonja and Sven, who was now a year old, would remain in our comfortable Zurich home until I had established myself in the United States. Neither of us knew how long this would take, but we were confident this was the right step.

Luckily, Sonja was offered a job with Swissair as secretary to one of the executives in the Zurich headquarters and I landed a job at $53 a week with American Express before noon on the day I arrived in New York. It was far from a gold mine. It wasn't possible for Sonja and Sven to join me until 1953, when we moved to an apartment in Queens. Swissair arranged for Sonja to transfer to their New York office.

I worked with American Express only briefly. A chance came up to join another large travel agency of Dutch proprietorship, Lissone-Lindeman, in their New York headquarters. Although it was not as well known as American Express or Thomas Cook, it had become one of the largest travel agencies in the United States. It was principally a wholesaler creating tours that were offered through retail travel agents throughout the country and other parts of the world.

In a short period of time, several facts about the travel industry became evident to me. The tours of the 1950s were concentrating on only a tired handful of countries, or Grand Tours of Europe. Europe was swarming with tourists who were being crowded into a few beautiful and historic spots. Tourist overkill was subjecting small and vulnerable areas to thoughtless destruction: hotels, cheap trinket shops, and parking lots were taking over the scene. Tour operators were not exercising their inventiveness.

In the meantime, the more beautiful and fascinating places of the world—the Middle East, the African wilds, the islands of the Pacific, India, Japan—were largely being ignored. My earliest dreams had been of these places; I was burning with the desire to go to them. Travelers, I thought, must be feeling the same way.

In 1953, my second year with Lissone-Lindeman, I began to notice a trickle of requests from more adventurous travelers. They wanted to reach out to more exciting places, and they could afford to do so. My company was a little afraid of the idea. No real research had been done to see if travel to exotic but undeveloped places was viable. Distances would be much longer than with the conventional trips to Europe. In the early 1950s, the lumbering DC-4 was still being used on the European run, although the DC-6 would soon take its place. Even to fly to Europe took anywhere from seventeen to twenty hours, with an awkward stop at Gander Bay or Goose Bay or even Iceland for refueling. The Pacific was formidable by air. But when Lissone-Lindeman offered to send me around the world in late 1953 to explore the possibilities of this long-distance travel, I was thrilled. My assignment was to establish closer contacts with a network of travel representatives in the countries of the Orient and the Pacific to represent us abroad.

It was still uncertain that travel beyond Europe could be made profitable. Much depended on the foreign travel agents, who would have to provide hotels and sightseeing arrangements that would be suitable for travelers who could afford this kind of trip. These travelers would be more discriminating than the average traveler, and more demanding. My job was to visit the agents, hotels, and potential sites of interest and evaluate them in terms of this new breed of traveler. I also had to find out exactly how much these services would cost. This sort of travel research required careful judgment and assessment. I had my work cut out for me in learning every detail about the places we were going to sell and then reporting back to Lissone-Lindeman with the results.

I concentrated first on what was called in the trade FIT, standing for Foreign Independent Travel. An FIT was a prepaid, all-inclusive tour for a small number of people, in contrast to large groups. The FIT was made up of two to four persons traveling together. Hotels, arrangements at airports and railway stations, and sightseeing by chauffeur-driven cars with guides were all prearranged. It was an expensive way to travel, but the demand for it was already showing by the time I took off for my first round-the-world travel survey in 1953.

One of my first contacts was with the Oberoi hotel chain in New Delhi. Raj Bahadur Oberoi, the founder and owner of the chain, had already created the finest luxury hotels in Delhi, Calcutta, Simla, Lahore, Peshawar, and Rawalpindi. They matched the best hotels in the United States and Europe in services, appointments, and comfort, with an added touch of charm that reflected Oberoi's personality. Working with the Oberoi organization was a young Indian named Gautam Khanna, son-in-law of Raj Bahadur Oberoi. He was in the process of setting up a new travel agency in India called Mercury Travels, a subsidiary of the Oberoi company. He shared my views that travel should consist of more than gaping; it should be enriched by knowledge and understanding. We became fast friends immediately, and have remained close ever since.

I returned from New York to India in 1954, and from then on I spent considerable time in the subcontinent every year, handling FIT travel groups and continuing extensive travel surveys. My superiors at Lissone-Lindeman were pleased, as they now realized that travel beyond Europe could be profitable. The Round-the-World department I set up within the company was an immediate success, and the number of travelers wanting to visit India became more than we could handle. This created an urgency to dig more deeply into the country and to research, set up, and arrange for more tours.

My immediate objective was to learn everything I could about this country with a land frontier of nearly 10,000 miles and a coastline of over 3000 miles, and to keep enough of the FIT tours coming to finance the research expense. The land stretched out before me like the richest Oriental carpet in the world, from Sri Lanka and the tip of Cape Comorin in the south, where the Bay of Bengal meets the Indian Ocean, to the frosty peaks of the Karakoram in Kashmir to the north. In these areas, I would develop new tours for both Lissone-Lindeman in New York and Gautam Khanna's India company, Mercury Travels. In a sense, I was on loan to Mercury, and we all would benefit from the discoveries made.

In working with Gautam Khanna in India, my focus was on extending travel away from the larger cities. I had to teach travelers that there was more to India than Delhi, Calcutta, and Bombay, and that although the Taj Mahal at Agra was magnificent, the temples, forts, and palaces in Rajasthan and South India were equally fabulous. I set out on each visit with a long list of lesser-known places to assess from both the practical cost and the esthetic point of view. Most of the time, I drove alone.

My surveys covered a span of three years, from 1954 to 1957. At the same time, I was coordinating the mechanical details, through Gautam

Khanna and Mercury Travels, of all the necessary arrangements, from air schedules to hotels to local guides, for the Lissone-Lindeman clients.

The early tours, though still limited, were working out well in spite of many bureaucratic problems. In the first few years, Lissone-Lindeman was fast becoming known not only as the best-equipped travel organization for around-the-world travel, but also as the authority on travel in India. I was becoming so absorbed with the subcontinent that I had less and less time to return home to Sonja and Sven, which was a considerable strain for all of us. India haunted me. As my stays in India became longer, I speculated on whether I should bring my family and settle there. I had to postpone that decision until Gautam Khanna and I had covered the whole subcontinent.

We wanted to bring the great historical sites to life so that momentous events of the past could be illuminated through deeper understanding. There were also the game and bird sanctuaries, where knowledge and understanding of the species would add luster.

For instance, when I went to survey the cave temples at Ellora and Ajanta in central India at Aurangabad in 1954, I felt I was catapulted back through 2000 years, when Buddhist monks began to carve the temples out of solid monolithic rock to live in as they worshipped Lord Buddha's search for enlightenment. These exquisite monuments were not built but were chipped away in the most delicate form of architecture, an architecture by excavation rather than construction. They took from the second century B.C. to the eighth century A.D. to complete. Then they lay dormant and unknown for seven centuries, smothered by jungle growth.

At Ajanta, there are thirty of these treasures, cut into a towering horseshoe cliff. Even the ravages of time have not obscured the pictures of daily routine, with dress and customs revealed in great detail.

In contrast to the monuments of Ajanta, the Ellora structures jut out from the face of the cliff, all thirty-four of them, to give the impression they were actually built rather than stripped out of the virgin cliff. The monoliths stand in a quarry of their own making. Hindu and Jain caves are intermingled, with the Hindu goddess Saraswati blending with the figures of Buddha.

The Kaziranga Wild Life Sanctuary in Assam in northeast India is another must for tourists interested in wildlife. Here the famous *Rhinoceros unicornis* carries his overlapping armor plate and single horn as a living link to prehistory. With a surly, unpredictable temperament, he mingles with wild water buffalo, wild boar, jackals, tigers, and deer, which are all fighting extinction.

The India of Kipling's time, in the last years of British supremacy, was no less evocative than that of the ancient temples. In designing my ideas for the traveler, I made sure that the British hill stations in the south would be included, and also areas in the north where the Northern Frontier steam railway still chugs uphill to reach an altitude of 7000 feet in fifty winding miles on its way to Darjeeling from Siliguri in the plains. Here is the sight, sound, and smell of pure nostalgia as the train passes the mountain tea plantations of Somerset Maugham's stories.

In Darjeeling, coal fires burn in the morning Himalayan chill, as the mist lies thick in the valley and the peak of Kanchenjunga towers in the distance, over 28,000 feet in altitude. In Darjeeling I first met Tenzing Norgay, the Sherpa who conquered Mount Everest with Sir Edmund Hillary in 1953. He had just moved to Darjeeling with his family after the conquest, to the disquietude of his native Nepal and to the pleasure of India, which came to regard him as a national institution. I met him in 1954 by the simple expedient of knocking on the door of his house and introducing myself. He is a modest, unassuming man who handled the surge of publicity about his feat with calm Sherpa dignity, even in the presence of British royalty and world statesmen.

I made my first trek to Gangtok in Sikkim with Tenzing. This eventually led to a continuing close association over the years. He has lost none of his charm or vigor. Through him, I was introduced to the vast potential of travel in the Himalayas, which at that time was in its infancy.

In the north of India, the celebration called Dussehra goes on for ten days every year. Although Dussehra is rich in tradition in depicting the classic *Ramayana* drama of the battle between good and evil, it is not for weak stomachs. The sacrifice of thousands of animals to the ancient Hindu gods still takes place as a religious ceremony. On my first survey, I watched a Gurkha regiment separate the heads of several hundred hapless goats, buffalo, and chickens with deadly kukri knives in a swift single stroke. Only the most skilled will try the larger animals, because by tradition, if anyone misses in the attempt and a second stroke of the kukri is needed, no one will speak to the offender for a full year. A slicing motion is used, with pressure put on the blade when it reaches the bone. The custom continues even now, with dance and drama accompanying the ritual sacrifice. In neighboring Nepal, a goat is sacrificed over the landing gear of Royal Air Nepal's Boeing 727s to ensure safety in the year to come.

The weaving together of places like these, the Ellora and Ajanta caves, the wildlife sanctuaries—along with the historical highlights of Delhi, Sanchi, Khajuraho, the hill stations, and many other sites into practical itineraries—worked out well. By 1956, the tours had slowly expanded from groups of two to four travelers to larger groups of forty or more. We were able to conduct tours from Delhi to Jaipur, Udaipur, Aurangabad, Bombay, Agra, Khajuraho, and Banaras, and to Kathmandu in Nepal by land and air on what we called Glimpses of India and Nepal. Other itineraries were expanded to include Sri Lanka, the Maldive Islands, the Vale of Kashmir, and Sikkim, with tours ranging from six to thirty-two days. Later I went on to apply the same in-depth research approach to Indonesia, Thailand, Malaya, the Philippines, Hong Kong, Japan, and Africa. The pioneering paid off, and Lissone-Lindeman came to dominate this important segment of the travel business both in India and the Orient.

In the meantime, in late 1957, the Oberoi hotel organization asked me to take on a permanent position with them and Mercury Travels to further build and expand the market for tourism in India. It was an attractive offer that I couldn't turn down. To take the job on a permanent basis, Sonja and Sven would have to pull up stakes in Connecticut and join me, a step that Sonja was not too enthusiastic about. We agreed to try it, however, and within a few months after I took the new position, we moved into small quarters at the Maiden's Hotel in Old Delhi, a hostelry that had great charm for me, but was lacking in most essentials that a woman needed for living in a strange city with a young child.

There were some failures and many successes. But by 1958, Lissone-Lindeman had become the leader in extending travel beyond the conventional traditions of the 1950s, and I personally had become known to many retail travel agents in the United States because of my pioneering work with them and the Oberoi organization. All this was constantly brought out in the trade press of the travel industry, which made me begin to think about opening my own company in the United States. The volume of business I had developed for India had reached nearly $1.5 million. I was having great fun and rich experiences in India, but I was convinced that my ideas for a fresh approach to travel were right and could succeed far beyond India, throughout the rest of the world. What was becoming evident to the travel industry was a new thirst for adventure and understanding about the world, as opposed to passive visitation.

Living in Old Delhi at the Maiden's Hotel was not easy for Sonja, confined by child-rearing and not really having a home of her own. Humorous minor problems added to the other inconveniences. For instance, we couldn't open the window of our bedroom without a swarm of chattering monkeys coming in uninvited and making off with our clothing. They draped it, out of reach, over the branches of trees outside the window. We were unable to recover some pieces.

By the summer of 1958, Sonja found it hard to accept that we would continue to live in India. The choice was for me to remain and continue my work, or return with them. Although I would miss India and my cordial relations with Gautam Khanna and the Oberoi organization, the tempting idea of opening my own business in New York was still growing in my mind. I had no working capital and barely enough to rent a New York office for a month. But I did have confidence, and my extensive contacts with the retail travel agents throughout the United States would give me a good foundation on which to build. By the time we left India in July 1958, Lindblad Travel was already formed in my mind.

III

PIGS, ART, AND ANTIQUITY
Setting the Stage

IT is one thing to declare independence and another to put it into effect. On September 20, 1958, the day I opened the Lindblad Travel office in New York, I knew I had to produce immediately. I had practically no working capital, but I knew I had real assets. First was the conviction that there must be many people who felt the same way I did about educational and adventurous travel. Second, I never shied away from taking calculated risks. Third, travel agents throughout the United States knew they could count on me to provide unusual travel experiences. Because of all this, I was able to begin setting up projects from the first day. A travel agent is, in effect, like an artist facing a blank canvas. He must be able to paint the picture to the satisfaction of the buyer.

I was lucky to find a partner who was extremely knowledgeable about South America, a relatively unexplored tourist attraction. She was Jeanne Westphal, who later became a U.S. commissioner for tourism under President Carter. Her expertise enabled me to concentrate on creating and selling the programs while she handled the business details.

Our office at One East Fifty-third Street was small. We had one assistant, Gerardo Cadavid, to handle our air reservations and air tickets, a critical and often thankless job. In 1954, Sonja and I had moved to Wilton in exurban Connecticut, an area that reminded me of some of the more delightful parts of Europe. She continued working for Swissair, gaining valuable experience for the later time when she was to join Lindblad Travel.

Fortunately, the travel business doesn't need much capital. I generated my initial capital by selling tours beginning on the first day. Later, when it became necessary to invest heavily in ships, vehicles, and airplanes, I added several partners. They included James G. Rogers, one of the original founders of the Benton & Bowles advertising agency and now a partner in the investment firm of Fox, Wells & Rogers; George Washington Hill, Jr., son of the legendary figure of the American Tobacco Company who sent "Lucky Strike green to war"; Alan Sidnam, then president of the Ogilvy & Mather agency; and Brown Bolte, also an advertising man. They not only invested but, being creative men, also contributed many ideas.

To make ideas work in this business, you have to be a juggler. You don't have the luxury of concentrating on one job at a time. My interests in wildlife, archaeology, marine life, history, art, and the unique cultural differences in societies were intense. From the beginning, I started to line up organizations that would respond to these interests on the highest level: museums, universities, zoological societies, and the "Friends of . . ." groups in arts and sciences.

Lindblad Travel was lucky to be selected to handle large groups from the U.S. Junior Chamber of Commerce for a series of tours in South America, in connection with the chamber's annual conference that in 1959 took place in Rio de Janeiro. The tours set up in 1959 and 1960 were financially successful, with nearly 300 in each group. But they still fell short of the pioneering sort of educational projects I wanted to develop.

In 1960, I was lucky enough to run into Fritz Legler and his wife, Elizabeth, in Connecticut. Fritz was about to retire from the successful advertising agency Warwick & Legler and move to Florida. Neither was too enthusiastic about the idea. Fritz was an active, creative man, and Elizabeth had the same vitality and enthusiasm. To avoid an unwanted retirement, they both joined Lindblad Travel to work on new tour ideas.

Elizabeth Legler was a prominent member of the Garden Clubs of America, and I began working with her on a world tour for this organization that would focus on the botanical and horticultural wonders of the world. In April 1960 we planned an around-the-world tour that shaped up beyond my expectations. It contained the two elements that I used as foundations for building Lindblad Travel: the bringing together of people with common interests and the use of the most qualified experts available to enrich the tour. Through Elizabeth Legler, I was able to get Tom Everett, head of horticulture at the New York Botanical Gardens. He is an outstanding authority and was perfect for the job. Originally from England, he had been at the Botanical Gardens since the 1920s and is a spellbinding lecturer.

The Garden Tours Around the World covered fifty-six days, at a cost of $3800 per person, a trip that could not be duplicated at that price with today's inflation. We repeated it often in the years that followed. Others tried to copy it, but were unsuccessful. The sixty guests made up a distinguished group who shared an enthusiastic interest in horticulture. Among them were Jim and Peggy North: Jim is the president of the Birdseye division of General Foods, and Peggy is a leading expert in gardening. There was Cecil Croxon, head of a large electronics firm in London, who enrolled merely because he had heard of the tour by chance. When he joined the tour in Honolulu and found that he was going to spend nearly two months with what he called a "bunch of garden fanciers," he laughed out loud. He remained a friend but never turned gardener, although he proclaimed his experience later as the "best tour of his life."

From the successful Garden Club tour in 1960, the seeds for future projects scattered to fertile territory. Shortly afterward Mrs. Irenee Pabst and Mrs. Eloise Spaeth came to me as representatives of the Archives of American Art. They told me that Mrs. George Du Pont and other friends of theirs had gone on the Garden Tours Around the World, and were impressed with the way the trip had been handled. They wondered if I would be interested in organizing a fund-raising tour the following year to Egypt and Greece. I was delighted to take it on, since the Archives of American Art typified the sort of clients I wanted to appeal to, clients who had a specialized interest and intellectual curiosity.

Eloise Spaeth had a capacity for organization that made the preparations for the tour a pleasure. She was both feisty and beautiful, impeccably dressed and groomed, and combined wit and enterprise to move the project along. The cost of the twenty-seven-day tour would be $2200, of which $500 represented a contribution to the work of the Archives of American Art. It was the first of many fund-raising tours I was to conduct over the coming years. Getting together the hundred people required for the tour was a job that took patience and persuasion. Eloise, with her charm and personality, was adept at that, along with William Woffenden, director of the Archives.

My preoccupation with preparing this and several other complex tours in 1961 was absorbing so much of my attention, I hardly had time to review our progress in those early years. We were steadily increasing our volume of business, and the cash flow was growing with it. From the first week, our sales had gone up at a gratifying rate, and scores of our clients were writing glowing letters of approval.

But there had been one problem: the total figures for the first year had shown that we had suffered a $56,000 loss in the face of the rapidly expanding business. It wasn't lack of business. It was simply that we had been underquoting all our prices. For every $10 we were taking in, we were putting out $12 in cost—cost of facilities and transportation, especially for travel research and scouting new areas, on which my whole concept of unusual travel tours depended.

I was determined not to cut corners, and the only answer was to charge higher rates even though our tours were near the top of the price spectrum. Our average tours were running anywhere from $800 to $2200 for land travel, not including air fare. Again this was high for the times, but low in comparison to the cost in the 1980s. I have never been afraid of charging higher prices, as long as I have been convinced that what I have to offer is worth it. I was stubborn enough to stay with the concept.

The success of the Archives of American Art journey in October 1961 was of tremendous importance to the future of the company, especially in light of our first year's financial loss. The only promotion that counts in the travel industry is word-of-mouth recommendation, which creates repeat business. In light of this, I made sure that all travel and accommodation arrangements were double-confirmed so that the tour would go on without a hitch.

From Cairo, we flew south to Aswan, down the fertile ribbon of the Nile in a chartered Comet jet. At Aswan we reached the first Nile rapids, called the First Cataract. Six of these cataracts mark a drop of over 900 feet between Khartoum in Sudan and Aswan. When we arrived at Aswan, I was thankful that we had rooms confirmed at the New Cataract Hotel, because the temperature was a boiling 114° F in the shade, and the New Cataract had air-conditioned rooms, a rarity in the early sixties in that area.

While the baggage was being unloaded into the cool lobby of the hotel, I went to the assistant manager to check our room assignments. He greeted me cordially, but embarrassment showed in his face.

"Mr. Lindblad," he said, "I'm afraid we've got a problem."

"I'm sure it's nothing we can't solve," I told him.

"The problem is this, sir," he said very solemnly. "There is a British group here with over a hundred people who refuse to vacate their rooms until tomorrow. The only thing we can do is put you up in the old Cataract, which is not air-conditioned."

I could feel the blood draining from my head, and my knees felt weak.

"Not only that, sir," the manager went on, "but the hydrofoil boats are not operating because the water in the Nile is too low. I'm afraid it might be impossible to get to the Abu Simbel temples."

It may be hard to believe, but the fact remains that my knees buckled, and I literally fainted.

I'm not sure how long I was out. When I came to I asked him to repeat what he had said. The words were just the same—not only were our accommodations unavailable, but the major attraction on the trip would have to be canceled.

Half recovered, I got our group together in the lobby and told them that the rooms would not be available until after lunch. Meanwhile, there would be a brief bus tour. There was plenty to see nearby: the tropical gardens of Kitchener Island and the world's best collection of Nubian antiquities on Elephantine Island, in addition to brilliant flowers everywhere from bougainvillea to poinsettias ten feet tall.

In spite of jet lag and the heat, the group took everything in stride, and the buses took off. Then I went to the manager. He explained that the British group was supposed to have gone up the Nile to Abu Simbel, but wanted to wait for another day to see if the boats could operate. They had insisted on staying because of this and had refused to check out. At the moment, they were out on a local tour. He said he was powerless to make them leave, even though he had asked them to do so.

I showed him the written confirmation of our reservations and told him that my entire reputation was at stake. He repeated that if he were able to, he would remove the baggage of the British contingent, and that although they had violated their agreement, he didn't see how it could be done.

I said, "I'll tell you what we can do. Do you have a list of the British room numbers?"

He gave me a copy reluctantly. Then I went and got several members of my staff. We went room by room through the hotel, packed the British luggage, and brought it down to the lobby. Then we carried the luggage of our group up to the rooms. As we did so, the manager told us that he had wanted to do what we were doing, but hadn't been able to make the decision.

The first problem was solved, at least until the British contingent returned. When the first lady from England came up to the desk to ask for her key, the clerk pointed to me as the villain of the piece and indicated that they had stayed beyond their reservation time. The lady came over to me, her face livid. She pointed her finger and said, "You should not have done that, sir. That was very naughty of you!"

But that's about as violent a reaction as I got. The others were remarkably calm. They chose to sleep in the air-conditioned lobby rather than shift to the old Cataract Hotel.

But the main problem was still not solved. I had guaranteed a hundred members of the Archives of American Art that they would see and learn about Abu Simbel and its temples. The four sitting statues of Ramses II were carved over 1200 years before Christ, almost freestanding out of solid rock, each sixty-five feet in height. They were threatened at this time by flooding from the artificial lake created by the Aswan High Dam, and international efforts were being made to save the statues and temples by carving them out of the mountainside to lift them 200 feet above the new high watermark. The whole chartered flight to Aswan had centered on our visit to Abu Simbel.

Near the southern end of newborn Lake Nasser is Wadi Halfa, a sleepy Sudan town in the Nubian Desert. For years, several old paddle steamers, the romantic kind I had always loved, had sat at the dock. But Wadi Halfa is 200 miles south of Aswan. I also had no idea about the condition of the boats, or whether we could possibly charter another plane.

The steamers were a vestigial remnant of the sort of boats that the famous travel organization Wagon-Lits operated on the Nile before World War II. The cabins were large, and there were even some elegant suites. The new Lake Nasser was not yet charted, especially on the sector below Abu Simbel. For this reason, the service between Aswan and Wadi Halfa was suspended. I was told, however, that the rising waters had not reached Abu Simbel itself and that we would be able to navigate over that portion.

Telephone communications even to Cairo were almost impossible at that time. I went through a tangled series of calls to Khartoum, Cairo, and London, where friends of mine at BOAC were able to get through by phone to Wadi Halfa to confirm that a boat would be available. I was also able to find a British-built Comet jet from Egypt Air which easily held our hundred passengers. The boat charter cost $6000, while the Comet jet cost $15,000—both unexpected expenses. We left Aswan by air at 3:30 A.M. to arrive at sunrise. What concerned me was that I had no chance to check on the condition of the boat. I wondered if after all this frenzy the whole project might go down the drain.

My fears were groundless. At the dock was a gorgeous turn-of-the-century vessel, clean and perfectly appointed. Without delay, we made the four-hour cruise to Abu Simbel and saw for one of the last times the Ramses II temples and statues at their original site (they have since been lifted that 200 feet in a remarkable engineering accomplishment).

The trip back to Wadi Halfa took six hours, under brilliant starlight, and was one of the most beautiful moments in my life. A potential disaster had turned into a gratifying experience.

The aftermath of the tour was more than I expected. Word got around swiftly that Lindblad tours were unusual, if not downright exotic. This word-of-mouth recommendation was critical at this stage of our development. The problems at Aswan could have had a devastating effect on our future. Instead, they turned into an asset.

While I was conducting the Arts and Garden tours, Fritz Legler was putting in full days at our New York office to develop a broad spectrum of contacts. Among them was an idea that appeared strangely unrelated to the travel business. It involved, of all things, the breeding and raising of hogs.

Although my love for the farm has never diminished, I hadn't connected the idea of farming with international travel. But when Fritz Legler introduced me to Carol Streeter of the *Farm Journal* in 1962, an idea began to grow.

Carol Streeter told me that the European farmer, though not generally ahead of the efficient American farmer, still had many beneficial ideas to offer. The European packing houses in Denmark, Britain, Ireland, and other countries paid a premium price for the lean meat. Streeter and the *Farm Journal* editors were persuaded that many American farmers would like to learn how this better meat was being produced. Streeter suggested that I could design special tours for them.

The idea was unconventional but challenging. With the aid of the *Farm Journal*, I blocked out a series of tours to be called The Hog Breeder's Tour of Europe and took off for Europe to work out logistics. Since I would be bringing over some fifty farmers to traipse through a procession of European farms, I had to do some effective persuading. In addition, I had to get many agricultural research institutions to cooperate.

Our first tour began in September 1962, lasted seventeen days, and cost $998 plus air fare from New York. The price included travel arrangements and lectures by specialists. In and around the research institutes we learned everything from the percentage of fish meal in the feed to what minerals should be injected to increase weight.

I have never traveled with a more congenial group. Most had college degrees and enjoyed discussing anything from literature and antiquities to the treatment of piglets during their first minutes of life. I soon began to fancy myself a hog expert. However, I was quickly brought to reality when I mistook a boar for a sow. I hadn't realized that the male of the species is endowed with almost as large mammary equipment as the female.

The project was so successful we expanded the itinerary to include Ireland and Holland, and then further by adding other livestock breeders and renaming the tours Europe for Hog Breeders, Dairy and Cattle Farmers. The success also reinforced that important principle in travel: people with a common interest, whether it's wildlife, birds, archaeology, marine life, or hogs, generate more enthusiasm and congeniality than mixed groups of varied interests.

I'm convinced it was this concept that brought a rapid increase in our business. On the Journeys into Antiquities tours alone, we were scheduling nearly fifty departures a year, with roughly thirty clients on each tour, averaging $2000 per person at 1960s prices. Museum, zoological, scientific, and other groups of common interest swelled the volume. From our first year in 1958, our gross grew rapidly, and by 1962, it had quadrupled.

In 1960, Sonja was able to leave Swissair and join Lindblad Travel, and her sound sense of business management brought a stability to the office that my frequent outside journeys made it impossible for me to provide. In addition, an auditor named Kevin McDonnell, who had come in to review the books of the first year, turned out to be a major stabilizing force. With rusty hair, enormous vitality, and sharp perception, he was far from the proverbial prototype of an accountant. He joined the company as a permanent fixture and has become one of my closest friends.

With a staff of five working in our small New York office, we had been able to turn the financial picture around by the end of the second year. I conducted many tours myself, and Fernando Maldonado came over from his job as sales manager of Aerolineas Argentinas to become an outstanding tour leader and executive of Lindblad Travel.

We gradually increased our tour leader staff with the addition of more experts in specialized territories, supplementing them with the trained staff guides to handle the programs and details. Cyrus Gordon, the outstanding authority on eastern Mediterranean culture from Brandeis University, agreed to work with us, enabling our tours there to provide a sound education as well as a fascinating journey. J. Alden Mason of the University of Pennsylvania Museum, considered the leading expert on Central and South American archaeology, also joined us. A man well in his eighties, he was fiery and enthusiastic about his archaeological digs.

One of our favorite tour leaders was Doris de Ruthie. She had a tremendous interest in and knowledge of archaeology, along with a strong sensitivity for the places we visited.

Doris led some thirty tours over the years with us and was a capable survey researcher. On one reconnaissance trip to Burma in 1977, she decided to take a picture at the Rangoon Airport. She aimed her camera, and within moments, a Burmese soldier shot her dead. The incident was the worst tragedy in Lindblad Travel's history.

Selling ideas was not really an effort for me. I found that you didn't have to be aggressive if your ideas were good, your way of expressing them was articulate, and your research and survey were sound. It was like selling Bibles—no one slams a door in your face. On the other hand, if your idea is contrived or there is chicanery involved, you will never succeed. As a wholesaler for 5000 or more retail travel agents across the country, I depended on them and could not let them down. The retail agents have neither the time nor the expertise to create specialized tours themselves, and we shared commissions with them. Creating original tours is a long and expensive job, with considerable risk. I have found that only 10 percent of the areas we scout turn out to be worthwhile, and many of these need special planning to develop them imaginatively. Ninety percent of the cost of travel survey has to be wasted.

One change in public attitude becoming evident was the rapidly expanding interest in the developing countries. When I was working on the Garden and Archives of American Art tours in 1961, I juggled my time so that I could survey in depth the continent of Africa. India contained the greatest cultural treasures of the world, but Africa was unsurpassed in natural wonder.

At the beginning of the sixties, only two hotels in Nairobi could be used for tourists, the New Stanley and the Norfolk. There were a handful of lodges in the bush. In Masai Mara, there were no lodges. Keekorok had some self-service bandas, or huts. The Northern Frontier District was without any, while Tsavo had some small, family-style hostels. In Aberdares, there was Treetops—the forerunner of what was to follow in the next decade.

Most of the countries of Africa were just gaining independence and had not yet stabilized. Visa clearance, customs, transportation, and accommodations were uncertain. Even to scout the alluring sub-Saharan countries would not only be tremendously expensive, but also time consuming. Although our volume of business was continuing to grow, I had to weigh carefully the risks of expanding too fast. But Africa was a challenge I couldn't resist. I set off in January of 1961 to begin the long job of establishing the most comprehensive program we could devise for this giant and fascinating continent.

IV

AFRICA
Wings and Safaris

To do the job right in Africa, I needed help. I was lucky to get it so quickly. BOAC had appointed a new sales manager in the United States, a friend of mine by the name of Peter Baker. He and I had met each other back in 1948 in Sweden when I was working for Thomas Cook and he was representing British European Airways. He was enthusiastic about the idea of developing new concepts in Africa for tourism and arranged for me to get BOAC cooperation. This would help defray part of the expenses for my reconnaissance trip.

By 1961, I had created a reserve of several hundred clients who were eager to explore and probe new areas in travel, and were willing to pay part of the freight. They actually preferred the excitement of discovery and the uncertainty. One was the irrepressible Huldah Lorimer, from both the Hog Breeder's Tour of Europe and the Garden Tours Around the World. Another was a banker from Oklahoma, Bud Hale, with the same inclination for pioneering tours. Representing BOAC would be George Edwards, sales representative. George was black, originally from Grenada, with a great sense of humor and a capacity to get along with almost anyone. We planned to survey Kenya and Tanzania in East Africa, then swing across the continent to the west coast of Africa.

As soon as I could charter a plane, we took off from Nairobi to survey the territory of the Masai tribe, near Ngorongoro and the great Serengeti Plain. Our vest-pocket tour group represented a small cross section of America: I from the Northeast, Huldah Lorimer from the South, Bud Hale from the Midwest, and George Edwards from Grenada. We four had a single-engine Lockheed, plus what turned out to be East Africa's most seasoned pilot.

The sense of freedom in flying across the plains and around the great mountains was overwhelming. It entered my mind that a wing safari would be a fresh way to see Africa, if a practical method could be worked out. I would put that in the back of my mind for later. Meanwhile, we embarked by Land-Rover the next day to drive down through Kenya and over the border into Tanzania to the village of Arusha for an overnight stay.

Not far from Arusha lies some of the richest territory in the world for game: Lake Manyara, where the tree-climbing lion sprawls indolently in branches to sleep off a meal; where leopards, buffalo, and barking troops of baboons largely ignore one another. Here, the Ngorongoro Crater stretches twelve miles across at an elevation of 7500 feet to support herds of hartebeest, waterbuck, zebra, and eland—which in turn support their predators, the lion, leopard, wild dog, and hyena. Above them flies a spectacular mélange of birdlife: ibis, geese, spoonbills, flamingos, and nearly 300 other species including such unlikely names as Kittlitz's sand plover, European shoveler, and rattling cisticola. From the top of the crater, the wildebeest herds seem to move in black ribbons, but when you descend you are able to get an intimate view of their long, lugubrious faces.

At Arusha we had time to reflect on the fragment of choice territory we had seen coming down from Nairobi. Arusha is a pleasant atmospheric colonial town of some 30,000, once the classic base for the big hunting safaris of the past, led by the traditional white hunters. Fortunately, hunting is now outlawed in both Kenya and Tanzania; only the poachers remain.

In 1961 the enforcement of game rules was just beginning, after ten years of indiscriminate extermination. One reason was the growing practice of making room for the domestic herds of the Masai tribes. Strangely enough, the domestic herds wreak greater havoc on the grass-lands than the largest wild animals. Domestic animals graze in tightly packed herds, trampling the grass and chewing it down to the roots.

After checking in at our hotel in Arusha, George Edwards and I pre-pared to go to the assigned room that we were to share. Tanzania had just achieved independence and the cultural customs of the past still clung. The African clerk at the desk stared at us for some moments. I couldn't quite figure out what was going on in his mind until he spoke. He seemed embarrassed.

"Excuse me, sirs. But are you two gentlemen sharing the same room?"

I replied yes.

"I'm afraid that will be impossible, sir," the clerk said.

George, with a pleasant smile on his dark face, said, "Why is that, brother?" He emphasized the word brother.

"You see," the clerk said apologetically, "he is white and you are black. That arrangement is not customary here."

George assumed a deeply serious expression. "You don't under-stand," he told the clerk, "don't let Mr. Lindblad's white skin fool you. He is one of *us!*"

The news of our incident traveled fast. Two days later at the Crater Lodge at Ngorongoro, a government official drove up in a state Land-Rover to meet the black American travel agent. When George intro-duced him to me, the official looked me up and down and said, "But you're not black."

Again George came to the rescue. "You've got to understand this, sir," he said. "Mr. Lindblad is an *honorary* black. They are very rare."

Most important was George's effect on our small party of travelers. I could sense at the beginning some had been uneasy about traveling with a black person. Years of American prejudice could not be wiped out overnight.

I think the turning point came when an educated Masai tried to bait George about his being an integral part of our party. George turned to him and delivered a dissertation on the greatness of the United States, including its faults and foibles and century-long discrimination against blacks. George's speech could have gone down in history books as an articulate statement of the problem.

From that moment on, our five-person group was totally integrated. Whatever doubts there had been changed to complete acceptance. Later, when Huldah Lorimer's daughter was married in Georgia, George Edwards was an invited guest at the wedding. Later George became an effective vice-president of Pepsi-Cola and has remained a good friend of all of us who went through our first exploration of Africa.

From the game parks of Kenya and Tanzania, we flew westward across the continent to Léopoldville in the Congo, since renamed Kinshasa and Zaire, respectively. At this time, however, the devastating war in Katanga was continuing. We quickly learned that the rooms had been commandeered by government officials. It was dark, and the streets were not safe for whites. As we stood out in the street, an angry crowd began forming, shouting the slogans of the time.

George Edwards lost none of his sense of humor. He turned to us and said, ''Friends, if they start attacking us, don't count on me. I'll be running toward them.''

We were lucky, however. A Swedish air force officer happened to be walking by, and I addressed him in Swedish to see if he could suggest any other hotel. I suppose he was delighted to hear the voice of a once–fellow countryman. He immediately arranged for us to sleep in the officer quarters of the Swedish base there.

This was Africa at that time: fascinating, volatile, colorful, changing, unpredictable. It was already becoming another love of mine, even before we had completed our first survey. Not the least interesting part of that trip was our visit in Gabon to a man I had always revered, Dr. Albert Schweitzer. His hospital at Lambaréné was a modern legend and still remains so. This Nobel Peace Prize winner had been called everything from saintly to testy. As a scientist, philosopher, missionary, theologian, and doctor, he had built his hospital almost bare-handed, and had served the tribesmen in the region for many selfless years. Declared one of the finest organists in the world, he eschewed musical fame to content himself with lonely concerts on a splendid pump organ at his jungle home.

En route to Lambaréné, I ran into a black doctor from the United States who was on his way to see Dr. Schweitzer in the hope of joining him in his medical work. Very excited about the prospect, the black doctor was willing to donate his time as a urologist, a specialty badly needed in the area because of the prevalence of venereal disease—up to 80 percent of the cases there. He asked me to persuade Dr. Schweitzer to let him stay and work there. I told him I would do my best, and he joined us in flying to an airstrip from which we embarked in dugout canoes for Lambaréné.

In spite of his reputation for sainthood throughout the world, Dr. Schweitzer had been accused by some journalists of being anti-black, because he did not treat the local people as equals. I was puzzled about this and wanted to learn why such an accusation had been made. Since I was able to speak the same Swiss-German dialect as Dr. Schweitzer, he was very much at ease and spoke to me at length about the accusation.

"I am very hurt about what these journalists say," he told me. "I love my people here dearly, but it must be admitted that there is a difference between me and the people I am treating. I am a product of European civilization; they are a product of an African tribal system. I am a father figure. We are not equal except in the eyes of God. If I treated them as equals, I would *fail*. They come from the jungle and have faith in me to get them well. I treat them with love and faith and medicine. As a result, we are successful."

Dr. Schweitzer had been criticized for not soliciting enough money to build a new and modern installation. There was no question that his hospital was far from imposing. When I visited the surgical facilities there, I saw an arm lying on the floor, apparently the result of a heavy workload that day. But when Dr. Schweitzer spoke again, these things seemed unimportant.

"You see," he told me, "the Austrian fathers nearby have a very clean hospital. They even have air conditioning. But the irony is that they have a higher rate of postoperative infection. The people arrive here from their villages where we have no air conditioning or modern food. I try to create their own environment. They are very worried and scared when they come here. I insist they bring their families to cook their meals and care for them. They live with the same natural bacteria they have in their own huts. Not the new strains that thrive in oversanitary surroundings. We must not trade an old environment for a new one.''

His thoughts made sense to me. The results he obtained were evidence that he was right. So many modern ''improvements'' imposed on Africa have proved illusory. Dr. Schweitzer was very concerned with the way the U.S. Peace Corps was building housing in the region.

''Do you know President Kennedy?'' he asked me, not realizing that I hardly had a pipeline to the White House. ''If you do, please, you must ask him to change the way the Peace Corps is building houses here. They are square. There is no cross ventilation. Where there are windows, the sun shines through them and brings heat in the day and suffocation at night.''

He took me to his hospital buildings. ''Look and you will see how they are built long and low, with the windows running along the length and underneath the overhanging roofs. On each end, the roof overhangs the doorway. The sun comes up over the ends of the long buildings and goes down over the other end. Please tell President Kennedy that.''

I was captivated by this man, with his combination of naiveté, knowledgeability, compassion, and stubbornness, and by the paradox of his gentleness and strength.

I had almost forgotten to put in my promised word for the doctor who had asked to help. I emphasized that he was a urologist, knowing how that skill would be especially helpful under the conditions there. As I spoke, I pointed him out to Dr. Schweitzer across the compound. Schweitzer studied him for a moment, and then shook his head in an emphatic ''no.''

I was disappointed because I knew how intensely the volunteer wanted to work in Lambaréné. I planned to broach the subject again. My suspicion was that Dr. Schweitzer had seen that the doctor was black and had turned him down because of that.

The next day, I had a chance to talk with Dr. Schweitzer again. He was very proud of the carpentry he had done himself. As he pointed out examples of his own carpentry, he happened to bring up the enormous percentage of venereal disease cases he had to deal with.

"Dr. Schweitzer," I said, "in view of this, I can't quite understand why you turned down the offer of the young American urologist. He seems just what you need."

Dr. Schweitzer stopped in his tracks. Then he threw his head back and laughed. "Urologist? I thought you said *neurologist!* Of course I can use him. Let's talk to him right away."

I was glad that I had been wrong about Dr. Schweitzer's prejudice. We left in an uplifted mood: we had had the chance to meet one of the most unusual geniuses of the era before his death. I returned to Lambaréné one more time before he died.

From Gabon our small exploratory group continued up the west coast of Africa to Cameroon, a country of surpassing beauty and rugged highlands. We flew into Douala, the main coastal city, where we faced the slowness of African customs and immigration.

The Douala customs official was inordinately painstaking, to the point where George Edwards was getting restless. From past experience with George, I knew something unpredictable was about to happen. It seemed that Huldah Lorimer was carrying with her a black patent leather box that contained a dress wig, with a mold underneath to keep the wig's shape. As the official continued to open every piece of our luggage, he at last reached the patent leather box.

At this point George spoke up. "Sir, if you don't mind my saying so, I don't think you want to see what's inside this box. If you open it, you'll be sorry."

The official insisted that he had to inspect it.

"In that case," George said, "I think I'd better open it for you."

He opened the lid very slowly. As he did the top and back of the wig appeared in view, looking for all the world like a disembodied head. At least that is what the official appeared to take it for. It may be hard to believe, but the customs official literally sank to the floor in a dead faint. When he recovered he was not amused. He opened and went through every piece of luggage again.

All through our exploratory trip, I was making notes on what would be best for discerning tourists that would be culturally enriching and at the same time reachable in terms of travel time and distance. It was obvious that East Africa was the most concentrated area of striking potential, while in West Africa the distances between potential areas of interest were so great that it would seem to make them impractical. There was also the climate. It was not by accident that some of the coastal areas of West Africa have been called the armpit of the continent. Compared to the fresh, clear highlands of Kenya and Tanzania, the steamy regions of West Africa are hard to take. The average annual temperature of East Africa runs between 68 and 72° F, as comfortable as the best of New England in the summer, in contrast to West Africa's sweltering range that hovers at 100° F.

All these things had to be weighed as we continued our safari into Nigeria, Senegal, the Ivory Coast, Mali, Togo, Dahomey, and Upper Volta. This region had been under French influence for years in the sprawling conglomerate that had been known as French West Africa. The British dominated the east and had made little attempt to assimilate the native population, using indentured East Indians as civil servants. In the east, the British had settled in and called it home.

The French were different. They trained the Africans to run everything. Only the big decisions remained in French hands. Those educated in France often became superb masters of the French language. All the French colonies were considered departments of the mother country and had elected representatives in Paris. Former President Léopold Senghor of Senegal was actually asked to write the present constitution of France for the Fifth Republic in 1958 because of his extraordinary knowledge of the French language. At the time, he was a deputy from Senegal in the French legislature.

We were traveling in the early sixties on the greatest wave of independence ever to strike a single continent. The phenomenon was almost synchronous, with country after country forming in the wake of the old unsavory days of colonization. I couldn't help thinking that if they ever erected a monument to independence in West Africa it should be dedicated to the mosquito. Its prevalence in the area was enough to dishearten the most robust colonist who sought to make a home there.

We arrived in Nigeria, a former British colony, before the terrible catastrophe of the Biafran war of 1967–70, but the rivalries that eventually caused it were already brewing. It was a war that never should have been fought. The Hausa tribes of the north were dominating the political scene, but the Ibos of the southeast were infiltrating government offices everywhere, as they were considered more intelligent, shrewd, and enterprising. When Nigerian oil was becoming productive in the Bight of Biafra, the Ibos bordering the shores claimed it as their own, leaving the bulk of Nigeria stripped of its benefits.

There was no such territory as Biafra. It was created by the Ibo military, who solicited a skillful European public relations firm to distribute pictures of starving "Biafrans" and to set up charity drives throughout the west. There *were* starving children, but they were everywhere in the country. Just before Biafran independence was proclaimed, thousands of Ibos in the north were ordered by the Ibo general Odumegwu Ojukwu to silently leave their posts under the cover of darkness to retreat to their home territory.

That first African exploratory trip in 1961 was interesting and rewarding. I learned much about what we should and should not do. I came to several conclusions. One was that the former French West Africa countries would be difficult for tourism because of the climate and the language barrier. Another was that the American traveler basically wants to go to Africa to see two things: wild animals and a totally different culture from his own. West Africa was moving swiftly into big cities with great progress, but offered few really spectacular opportunities to view within a practical time span great herds of animals or cultural contrasts. It did have many assets, and the accommodations were becoming increasingly attractive. The Hôtel d'Ivoire, for instance, on the Ivory Coast, is a match for some of the best hotels in Paris, London, or New York. Yet that was not among the important criteria.

The choice seemed to narrow down to the sub-Sahara that once had been the key jumping-off and receiving station for countries in East Africa and the countries below it, in addition of course to ancient Egypt and possibly Ethiopia, which I had not yet had the chance to explore on the 1961 survey.

During 1962 I had to handle many fund-raising tours for museums and institutions, and the time available for scouting trips was limited. It wasn't until 1963 that I was able to take off for a second scouting trip to Africa. With our company being so new, the budget continued to be tight. I wanted to consolidate the features of East Africa in the shortest possible time. Even there, the distances were great and land travel was slow and difficult, especially where the game and scenery were at their best.

When I got to Nairobi again, it was obvious I could never cover what I wanted to by road. This time, Peter Baker of BOAC assigned W.R.O. James, more often called Jimmy, another friend of mine, to lend a helping hand. We found a Nairobi charter company named Wilken Air and obtained a small plane for a swift survey of the choice places. Excellent landing strips were available in most of the places. What would take two or three days of dust and heat by road would take us only forty-five minutes by plane. Few of these places had been opened extensively to safaris in 1963.

Tony Irwin, then public relations director with Wilken Air, obviously shared my enthusiasm. Wing safaris would enable entire groups to see the Africa they wanted to see in the most swift and practical way. The cost per mile by air was often less than by road.

Jimmy James, Tony Irwin, and I made a whirlwind reconnaissance trip in a twin-engine Piper Comanche. The airstrips in the choicest game locations were small, but safe and viable. We were able to soar across the Great Rift Valley, the forests of the Aberdares, and past Mount Kenya and Mount Kilimanjaro in speed and comfort. By flying between the game reserves, we were able to spend more time at each location, with close-up encounters near the game lodges that were growing in number and comfort. The small planes had all the advantages of a car, and the airstrips made it possible to park the plane near a lodge or tent site just as easily. There was also an unequaled sense of freedom, enabling us to sweep to the emerald waters of Lake Rudolph in the northern frontier provinces of Kenya, then down to the Serengeti Plain in Tanzania with little time and effort.

After our air reconnaissance, I went to our East African agents, the United Touring Company. I told Fred Salzer, the managing director at the time, "Fred, this is the way I want to do it. I want to bring a continuous series of groups here and establish regular wing safaris, using Wilken Air as the carrier."

Salzer looked at me as if I were not fully balanced and said, "Absolutely impossible. You're going to have airplanes stuck in the mud all over Africa. There is no way it is going to work."

I insisted that it would work. But I couldn't budge him. He finally turned to me and said, "Look, if you want to do something as absolutely crazy as that, I don't want any part of it."

I glanced over at Tony Irwin, who looked very supportive because I think he guessed what was on my mind. Then and there, I decided to form a new company with Tony as managing director. We would buy into Wilken Air and create our own air transportation. It would involve enormous risk and investment, and if Fred Salzer was right the whole idea would crumble. But I didn't let myself think about that. My entire career was being built on risks, and this was no exception.

In 1963, Wilken Air had available five-passenger twin-engine Piper Aztecs. By using two of these craft, we were able to handle a total of ten persons for each departure, with each group staying two nights at lodges such as the Paraa Lodge at Murchison Falls, the Fort Ikoma Lodge in the Serengeti, Lamu Island off the coast of Kenya in the Indian Ocean, and others. The idea worked right from the start. The safaris were not tied down by frequent breakdowns on the rough roads, and we were able to fly over the areas that had no roads at all. And no planes were stuck in the mud.

One problem was that there was such heavy utilization of the planes we were unable to keep up with the demand, and we had to buy more planes at considerable investment. The cost of the first twenty-one-day Wing Safaris came to $1600 per person at that time, plus air fare, compared to $900 for the land safari. But the results were worth it. A ninety-five-year-old could soar in comfort to the choice spots of the game reserves as ably as a young executive, and even the disabled could enjoy a safari. Our pilots were expert and enabled us to enjoy maximum excitement with minimum danger. The safety record has been unblemished since the start. The road safaris with more limited scope were not ignored, of course. Within a short period of time we were able to schedule our safaris originating in the United States every second day.

Our pioneering efforts in 1963 with the Wing Safaris included all three East African countries—Kenya, Tanzania, Uganda—then trouble free. With effortless freedom, the tours would move from Nairobi to the Amboseli game park in forty minutes, with the Piper Aztec making a low pass at the strip to clear it of animals. Within minutes after landing, the game could be spotted and photographed: Grant's gazelles, wildebeest, giraffes, elephants, rhino, and a wide variety of brilliant-colored birds. From there, the group would be whisked to Tsavo National Park, the largest in the world, where the stay at a tented camp brought a sense of intimacy with the dry and open country, its baboons, waterbuck, impala, and elephants and an occasional pride of lions.

The Wing Safari was more interesting and different than land safaris, because it included much more than game viewing. We could be in a game reserve in the morning, and in the briefest of time be on the East African coast fishing in the Indian Ocean. On the next day, we could be at the luxury of the Mount Kenya Safari Club. From there we would move over the rugged lands of northern Kenya to Lake Rudolph for another contrast. In pioneering the Wing Safari, I felt a strong sense of accomplishment because of its uniqueness in the travel world.

The itineraries varied as we discovered new places or new facilities opened up. Many could be reached by either land or air travel. The average time for each safari was two weeks. Nearly all included Treetops and the Ngorongoro Crater. Later, when Idi Amin took over Uganda in 1971, and when President Nyerere closed the Tanzania border to Kenya, we were forced to discontinue our safaris in these countries, although we are now able to continue separate safaris (not using the Kenya border) to Tanzania. We also later extended the Wing Safari idea to Ethiopia, Brazil, and other countries where road travel is difficult.

Over the years, Lindblad clients constantly report favorite incidents that linger long after the events, some of them involving unusual trivia. Mrs. Fritz Wiessner of Stowe, Vermont, recently wrote to remind me that she can't get out of her mind the last Wing Safari to Uganda before Amin took over. En route to Lamu on the coast, there was a stopover at a tented camp well equipped with blue tents that served for rest rooms called "blue loos"—one for men and one for women. Taking a flashlight, she stumbled out in the darkness to grope for the ladies' "loo."

Not far from her, she noticed a dark moving figure and apologetically asked, "Do you know which tent is the ladies' rest room?" At that moment, the moon came out from behind the clouds, and she found herself face to face with a large waterbuck. Startled, the only thing she could think of saying was, "Oh, excuse me. It's a dark night, and I couldn't see who you were."

Mrs. Louis Twyeffort, of Sutton Place in New York, also found the Tsavo Tented Camp slightly different from the Manhattan traffic that surrounded her at home. She ran into a situation that was the reverse of Mrs. Wiessner's. A year-old rhino called Rudie utilized the front of her tent to answer nature's call, but she quickly forgave him for his indiscretion. By the end of the day, however, Rudie and a rhino brother had gone on a rampage at a nearby camp and had become a definite threat to life and limb. Both had to be removed to the remote reaches of the region.

Even at the lodges, startling things can happen. Ruth Rittmeister, an executive from Honolulu, was enjoying a Lindblad Wing Safari at the bar of the Mara Serena Lodge. For a moment, she thought that she might have downed one drink too many when she saw a British traveler, dressed in a classic safari jacket and pith helmet, with a couple of cameras slung over his shoulder. With his clipped British accent, he ordered a stiff drink and said, "There is a huge elephant at the door!"

Ms. Rittmeister was now sure she was on the set of a B movie, until she went to the doorway and saw that it was completely jammed with a bull elephant that would move neither in nor out. Finally, the lodge staff and manager were able to coax the elephant away. The traffic at the bar increased considerably that evening.

I returned to Africa as much as possible from 1961 on. What I found was that a safari is the most satisfying vacation anyone could take. Beyond the obvious, one of the reasons that people find contentment is that the safari removes the most important reason for stress: that of decision making. The decisions are all made for you. You get up at six in the morning and are ready for superb game viewing. You wear the simplest clothes. Your meals are prearranged and your entertainment at night is sitting around the campfire. On a tour of Europe, you still have to decide what to wear, where to eat, which hotel to stay at, which airline to fly, and what to see. The greater the choice, the more the strain.

The extraordinary amount of repeat business in the safari tours confirmed their appeal. Over the years, we have booked more than 26,000 African safari clients, with over 60 percent returning for another tour. As with the farm tours, they were life-seeing instead of sight-seeing. Waking up in a tent at Amboseli, you look out to see Mount Kilimanjaro swept clean of its clouds, while nearby you may see a herd of elephants. A few steps away, you might see the lion you heard through the night at its kill. In the distance, you may see the Masai with their herds, silhouetted in the morning sun.

The classical safari, of course, is best in the tent camp. Here the smell of the dust and the intimacy of the campfire enrich the scene. The tent camps have been most frequently run by the true man of the African bush. I remember one camp in Amboseli run by a British gentleman named Scott. In the early tradition of the bush, he liked to put on a dinner jacket for the evening meal, and sit before the campfire sipping champagne and serving chilled caviar from Russia or Iran as he spun fantastic yarns of his experiences with lions, leopards, and elephants while their footprints were often still visible.

That sort of man—the civilized man who loves the smell of Africa so intensely he wants to be nowhere else—is slowly dying out. In building our own tent camps, I sought out this type with the help of Tony Irwin and was lucky enough to find several to enhance these stations with character and affection.

Some of the best staff members of Lindblad Travel were black Africans, including John Odera, who joined us in 1965 as a safari leader and went on to become director of our East African company, Lindblad Travel (EA) Ltd. John would keep our clients spellbound talking about the interactions of various tribes and the local gossip. Another witty and productive African staff member was Ben Ouko, whose charm and wisdom illuminated the safaris he conducted for us. He was so adept at handling groups that I had him made cruise director in 1981 for our cruise on the Yangtze River in China. He was a favorite of the passengers as well as of the Chinese.

Americans were shocked to pick up the morning papers on January 5, 1980, to read that Joy Adamson, author of *Born Free,* was killed by an ''animal'' near her remote camp in the Northern Frontier District of Kenya. The irony was apparent: had she been killed by a lion after her long and affectionate experiences with Elsa, the lion who became world famous through her book? When the facts emerged all the signs pointed to murder, and a herdsman, a former Kenyan employee, was taken into custody after three stab wounds were discovered in her side and no signs whatever of her being mauled by an animal.

In spite of the warmth of her writing, Joy Adamson was not particularly liked by her associates. She was constantly dismissing her employees and was very demanding of them. Kathy Porter, a former secretary and later a Lindblad tour director, told a friend, ''She got so lost in her animals, she lost compassion for *Homo sapiens.* I never had the nerve to say this to her face.''

But she was generous in her support of the World Wildlife Fund, turning over most of her royalties to that organization, and she traveled around the world lecturing on animal conservation. When the film of *Born Free* was being made in the early 1960s, she arranged to have the film company return to her custody the tamed lions used in the film so that she could free them. The Kenya Game Department was horrified, however, to learn that they would be released in a game park inhabited by local tribesmen. Since the lions were tamed, they would innocently approach a village as the villagers either ran from them or shot them, not knowing the lions meant to be friendly. The idea was dropped.

I met Joy and her husband, George, several times. George was as affable as she was severe and stern. They finally went their separate ways. Part of the problem was that she became so obsessed with the memory of Elsa that she was sure the lion was watching out for her safety after the animal died. She credited the spirit of Elsa with saving her life in a near-fatal car crash as she and George drove from her camp to Nairobi, and was convinced that she could communicate with her animals telepathically, but never with humans.

Yet there was a strange paradox in her outlook. She would at times wear a leopard skin coat, and at one point in the filming of her book was going to permit two pet hyraxes to be killed by an injection to make the film more realistic.

The pet animals had been lent by Tony Irwin, and I was having Christmas dinner with him at his home in Nairobi when the news of this idea came in by telephone. Tony was so upset by the call that he jumped into his Land-Rover and drove six hours to the film location to save them. I have never seen Tony so distraught. But in spite of her faults, Joy Adamson was a major contributor to wildlife awareness and conservation.

Lake Baringo, north of Nairobi, is a remote area that Tony Irwin and I found ideal for a tent camp that could be easily reached on a Wing Safari. It is one of the Rift Valley's lakes, with the largest nesting colony in Kenya of goliath herons, as well as Verreaux's eagle. Here we found a charming gentleman by the name of David Roberts, who with his wife and children made a living catching birds and reptiles for zoos throughout the world. One day the lake rose to the point where his house became an island, flooded to the second floor.

He and his family were living in tents when Tony and I flew up in 1963 to discuss creating a tent camp that he would manage for us. The arrangements shaped up quickly, and we were ready to celebrate the occasion with a festive pink gin. But David told us that if we wanted gin, we would have to swim out to his house for it.

As we were plunging in to swim for the stranded house, David called out to us to watch out for crocodiles. I knew there were many crocodiles in the lake, but I was certain so many fish were available that they would hardly be in the mood for a human meal. Our intention was to swim through the half-submerged kitchen door to reach the second floor where the gin rested. The problem was that the kitchen was knee-deep in crocodiles. We finally swam to a back window, pulled the gin out of a cabinet, and swam back with the bottles high over our heads.

We set up a successful camp for our Wing Safari, and helped David expand his little zoo with a supply of zebras and elands. We had problems with one eland who repeatedly poked his horns through our Land-Rovers, and the zebras had an incurable habit of nipping you until you turned your pockets inside out.

At the same time we were developing our tent camps, we had the greatest respect for the attractive game lodges that offered the utmost in luxury. We worked in cooperation with many of these, either by helping them start out or by arranging our tours with them in a mutually profitable way.

Some of the most beautiful safari lodges in the world were built in Kenya during the late sixties and early seventies. The government of Tanzania owned and operated the lodges at Lake Manyara, Ngorongoro Crater, and Seronera, but they were never well run.

In Kenya, the government built several first-class lodges. It also joined with private enterprises such as British Airways, Pan Am, and Lufthansa to build lodges at Tsavo. TWA and Hilton built the magnificent Taita Hills Lodge there. Its annex, the Salt Lick Lodge, provided an artificial pool under the lodge where the guests could watch elephants, waterbuck, zebras, impala, and other wild animals come to drink. Sometimes as many as several hundred elephants would arrive there on a single night; the buffalo could reach even greater numbers.

The Mount Kenya Safari Club was especially attractive. Built some years before by an Indiana millionaire named Ray Ryan, along with such notables as William Holden and Robert Ruark, it is situated on the lower slopes of Mount Kenya and surrounded by flowers and alpine meadowlands. It has a swimming pool, tennis courts, riding facilities, and gourmet meals. This and lodges like the Ark, Treetops, and Samuburu are ideal safari stopping points. Or they can be woven into the tented camp safaris. All of the better ones have great respect for the surroundings and maintain the integrity of the environment.

In 1963, Mount Kenya Safari Club's Ray Ryan had joined with John Williams, founder of Wilken Air, to buy a remote fishing camp at Loiangalani on the shores of Kenya's Lake Rudolph, now called Lake Turkana. The camp was ideal for our Wing Safaris, and I arranged a management contract with them. It was on a sparkling emerald lake, where Nile perch grow to over 200 pounds, and where the pastoral Turkanas nurture their camels and cattle on sparse grazing lands. Loiangalani is also the home of the El Molo tribe, the smallest in Africa, totaling less than 200 and on the verge of extinction. The northern end of the 150-mile lake tips into Ethiopia.

The camp had been built originally by a Briton named Harry Selby, of the world-famous Kenya safari company Kerr, Downey & Selby. Only a handful of huts had been used as a fishing camp for people taking extensive and expensive hunting safaris. It was ripe for restoring, and we found a delightful hot spring there that we utilized for a swimming pool.

On our first Wing Safari there in 1963, Ruth and Norman Tishman, who headed up the large Tishman real estate operation in New York, were part of the group. They thoroughly enjoyed the scene up until the last night. The Tishmans went to bed filled with many exaggerated stories. Halfway through the night, Ruth Tishman woke up feeling something heavy on her stomach. She reached down and felt something that was unquestionably fur. There was no question in her mind that it was a leopard.

To lie awake without moving was agony. But she did so, until daylight. On her stomach was a large house cat, peacefully asleep. In spite of that, she let out a scream that woke the whole camp.

By 1964, the fishing camp had become the most attractive oasis in the raw northern Kenya landscape, mainly through the efforts of Tony Irwin. He transported fishing boats all the way from Mombasa, and stocked the camp with delicious food and delicacies, as well as supervising the remodeling. The fishing was superb. One eighty-seven-year-old lady named Ruth Green from New York caught an enormous perch that matched her age in pounds, and she claimed that it was the greatest thing that had ever happened in her long life.

Not all our travelers liked the extreme remoteness, so far away from everything, but to me this was the essence of adventure travel, a trademark of ours that was to become the keystone of our operation. Such an idea was new in the mid-sixties; adventure travel has since burgeoned. We even built an airstrip near the camp at Loiangalani where at night the pilots had to pile stones around the wheels to prevent the planes from flipping in the strong night winds. In other spots, we did the same to prevent the hyenas from eating the tires.

It began to look as if the initial success of the Lake Rudolph venture would be more than worth the investment. We were lucky to have Guy Poole and his wife as managers. Guy, a native of the Seychelles, was in love with Lake Rudolph. I have so often found that those who work best at running our operations throughout the world have a genuine love for the place where they are stationed. No efficient managerial talent can replace that. Guy was such a man, and when he joined our organization, I looked forward to many years of working with him there.

We were able to fly in plane after plane in a long series of safaris, with almost unanimous praise from the passengers. We were aware, however, that some hostile Somalian tribesmen would occasionally infiltrate the rugged territory surrounding us. Because of this, Guy Poole kept in close touch with the police, reporting daily by radio to the Kenya security forces.

On March 5, 1969, after a Wing Safari had taken off to return to Nairobi, Guy Poole was helping the Italian truck driver who brought in supplies every week unload his truck. The camp was almost deserted. Guy's wife and children were making one of their infrequent trips to Nairobi. Aside from Guy and the truck driver, there was only a Catholic priest who had dropped by for an informal visit. Nearby were a few local Turkanas who worked at the camp.

It is not quite certain what happened next. Only a piecemeal account by the African staff revealed what occurred. A group of Somalian terrorists called Shiftu descended on the camp. They tied the priest and Guy to two chairs and simulated a trial. Both were accused of being informers for the Kenya security forces. The terrorists set up an execution squad and shot both Guy and the priest. They then proceeded to destroy the camp and the vehicles there except the supply truck. This they commandeered and ordered the Italian driver to take them toward the Somalia border. Soon the truck ran out of gas, and another gruesome event took place. They apparently became intrigued by the many tattoos on the driver's body and brutally skinned him alive.

The following day, the police became suspicious because Guy Poole failed to report to them by radio. The Kenya Police Air Wing flew over the camp to discover that it had been gutted. When they landed they found the two bodies and dispatched a unit in pursuit of the truck's tracks. They captured the invaders who still had the telltale skin of the driver with them.

Tony Irwin and I were participating in a fishing tournament off the Kenya coast when the news came in by radio. We flew to Lake Rudolph at once, where we faced a scene that left us speechless. The police had already flown out the bodies, but the sight of the gutted camp was almost as devastating as the loss of our friends. Guy's wife and children had been able to escape only because they were in Nairobi at the time, and I felt their sadness deeply.

Shortly before this incident, Sir Malin Sorsbie, founder of East African Airways and a great wildlife conservationist, had bought the fishing camp from Ray Ryan, and he graciously took care of Guy's widow and children. It has since been a Catholic mission post and now is an Italian resort camp. Even though we later developed another camp on Ferguson Gulf on the lake, I have never felt the same about the area.

In 1965 we had found that we had to add more equipment to Wilken Air to keep up with the demand. At the same time, Tony Irwin found that with his own small plane he could cover the East African territory much more efficiently. We both learned to fly it, with the idea of exploring a Wing Safari operation in Ethiopia, where there were many undeveloped areas that would be historically fascinating.

Tony knew Ethiopia well. He was something of a soldier of fortune. During World War II he had served behind the Japanese lines in Burma, where his father, General Noel Irwin, had been commander in chief of the first part of the Allied campaign there. After the war, Tony was lent to Emperor Haile Selassie to serve the First Ethiopian Army. Then he went on to join his father in Kenya. Later, the emperor asked him to return to Ethiopia to, of all things, set up a jockey club in Addis Ababa, including a racecourse. Tony went back to take on the assignment. As Haile Selassie was preparing to leave for a state visit to Brazil in 1961, Tony learned that a coup d'etat was in the making while the emperor was away.

Tony went to Selassie and told him about the conspiracy, but the emperor refused to believe him. Selassie informed another general, who happened to be part of the brewing takeover, of what Tony had told him. Then Selassie left for Brazil. Somehow the British ambassador in Addis Ababa learned what was in store for Tony and told him, "Get in your Land-Rover and drive with all the speed you can muster to Kenya."

Tony took off immediately, with the conspirator's troops in hot pursuit. He barely made it to the border. The plot to kill the emperor later failed, but the emperor's bodyguard massacred many usurpers in the royal palace and left the bodies just where they fell. After the emperor returned to see the mayhem, he never reentered that palace again.

At the invitation of Ethiopian Airlines, Tony and I began our reconnaissance trip in the fall of 1965. We had Tony's small Cherokee 165 and decided to fly ourselves there for the survey. The fact that Tony had only ninety hours of flying time and I had practically none didn't stop us. Tony would be the pilot and I would be the navigator, flying over the rugged peaks of the Ethiopian highlands to Addis, which sits at an altitude of nearly 8000 feet.

I laid out what I thought was a competent air route, but the mountains looked as if they were reaching up to grab us, and the lakes I had counted on to fix our position were mainly dried up. I'm not sure how we finally made Addis, but we landed there in late evening. At Addis we laid out plans to visit Gondar, Lalibela, and Bahar Dar high in the mountains to the north. Here lay the historic route to ancient sites, rich in subterranean churches and temples carved out of the mountains as in India.

Before we moved ahead with our scouting trip, Tony took me to meet Haile Selassie. The emperor was still grateful for Tony's warning. I think it was for this reason that we were given a free hand to explore the historic route.

We took off for Bahar Dar, following the Nile, running northward to Lake Tana. Here on some of the islands we found fascinating medieval monasteries with lovely Coptic paintings. Then we moved on to Gondar, where the palaces of Emperor Fasilidas were built in the 1600s in unclassifiable architectural grandeur.

Next was Lalibela, where the most striking of the religious edifices were built as far back as A.D. 1200. Again I had trouble with my navigation. We simply could not spot the village, which was situated so high up in the mountains that to reach it from the base by foot takes several days. There was still no visual clue of its whereabouts when we noticed that we were getting low on gasoline. There was no turning back now, and we didn't dare think about a crash landing in those ominous mountains.

Suddenly, we saw a reflection, like a mirror. It must have been one of the tin roofs in the village. With that as a beacon, we were now able to find a road and follow it down to the airstrip in the valley. I don't believe we had a gallon of fuel left.

Through Tony's connections, we were able to stay with Princess Ruth, who has since been jailed with all the royal family, after the emperor's overthrow. The priests and monks in their long robes move about with staves, while the young shepherds look like Greek gods with an ebony sheen to their striking aquiline faces.

Undaunted by our close call, we took off and headed back toward Addis Ababa. But our direction finder failed to work, and we could only fly in the general direction of Addis. We had to push the plane to its limit to gain altitude to see over the mountain that blocked our view. We finally spotted the city in the distance and were able to come in safely. In retrospect, we were very foolish and very lucky, but we had a marvelous time and were able to open up the now famous historical route through Ethiopia. The tours were interrupted when the emperor was deposed, but they have since been resumed as extensions to our other African tours, averaging $900 for eight days. We avoid Eritrea and the Somali border, however.

My search for the most exotic and interesting places in Africa was endless. Because of the international strife in Zaire, travel there was almost out of the question until the later 1960s. Yet the symbolic image of Africa had long been that of the jungle and the Congo, even though that impression was erroneous.

Just to the east of the Congo's source is Rwanda, home of the giant Watusis (often called Tusis). Gorillas are found in the high forests of this mountain country. Rwanda has been called the Switzerland of Africa, with its mountain lakes and green valleys.

When the terrible days of the 1960–65 strife in the Belgian Congo had cooled, I felt it was time to reopen these areas to travel. Some of the bloodiest battles had been fought in the northeast near Stanleyville, where the Katanga mercenaries matched the atrocities of the Simba terrorist called Gbeneye in the winter of 1964. He stirred his rebels into frenzy, dressing them in monkey skins, supplementing firearms with poison arrows, filling them with dope, and having them march to the beat of the drums of the ju-ju man. The mercenaries were no less savage with their raping and massacring. Gbeneye fought back by seizing hundreds of whites and ordering his men to kill on sight throughout the region. Seven years after my first exploratory trip to West Africa the ravishing beauty of eastern Zaire (then called the Congo) and neighboring Rwanda was again becoming accessible.

With my close friend George Holton, the former photographer for Time-Life, I began another reconnaissance journey in the fall of 1968 to see what we could do about opening up the region. George had a great sensitivity to people and animals, and we were to work together for sixteen years until his untimely death of a heart attack in China in 1979. We had only a month's time, and discovered that it would be safer to rent a Land-Rover and drive rather than take our chances with uncertain flights.

Driving along the roads in Rwanda, you see thousands of villagers walking on their way to the markets in a heavy pedestrian traffic jam. Near Lake Kivu is the volcanic mountain Verunga. On its slopes lives the largest-known concentration of wild mountain gorillas. We crossed Lake Kivu on a lake steamer, heading for the Zaire town of Bukavu near which King Leopold had set up the Irsac Scientific Research Station to study the behavior patterns of gorillas and chimpanzees in the Kahuzie Gorilla Reserve. The scientists helped us find Pygmy guides to search for the gorillas.

It was impossible to walk through the jungle; we had to bend and crawl and half stand as we groped toward the site where the gorillas might be. I kept thinking to myself, how are we going to get out of this if we lose our Pygmy guides?

George Holton suddenly crawled through an enormous anthill. Within moments we were all covered with a carpet of ants and turned into wild screaming men, slapping at the insects and tearing off our clothes as we did so.

It took over half an hour to scrape the army ants from our bodies, but they kept reappearing in crevices of our bodies for days to come. We hardly had put our clothes back on when I heard an eerie roar and a heavy drumming that could only be a male gorilla beating his chest. It sounded as if he were only a few feet away, but since sound travels so far in the rain forests, he must have been a hundred yards from us. We crawled on toward the sound and soon emerged face to face with a large family of mountain gorillas. It was one of the most incredible sights of all my travels. The sting of the ant bites faded with the view. There must have been eight of them, young, old, and gray-back old. We stared at them and they stared at us. Then suddenly, a large male beat his chest, threw his head back, and screamed again. This was a typical gorilla threat display, but it did not foreshadow an imminent attack. Fascinated and deeply moved by this sight, we stayed for several hours before we returned to our base.

We decided to drive on to Stanleyville (now Kisangani), since we were assured that the road was now open, and we could eventually make our way down the Congo River to Léopoldville (now Kinshasa).

We were also told of a Catholic mission en route where we would be able to spend the night. Starting early in the morning, we hoped to arrive there before nightfall.

We set off with our African driver down the road toward Stanleyville. The road was rough and our progress slow. When darkness came there was no sign of the mission. Suddenly we came on a crude sign, barely readable in the darkness, pointing up a side road to the mission. We turned onto the road, and before long it became an overgrown tunnel of twisted vines leading to a narrow bridge that in the headlights looked rotted and in disrepair.

I got out and examined it. It was made of logs that seemed as if they would crumble under the weight of our Land-Rover. I tested it with my weight, and it appeared somewhat stronger under closer examination. We decided to risk crossing the bridge in our Land-Rover and inched across it. We succeeded, but the road still remained little more than a tunnel of thick undergrowth.

It was eight o'clock in the evening before we slowly edged into a clearing. Just ahead of us what seemed to be an enormous white church loomed in the darkness. There was no sign of life.

Our driver and I got out of the car. We could hear nothing but the night noises of the forest. With a flashlight in hand, we opened the door of the church. The inside was nothing but crumbled and charred ruins. Only the walls and the spire remained. The roof was entirely open to the sky, and the stars shone above us, creating an eerie glow. What had once been a floor was now nothing but grass. You felt that the entire shell was floating above the ground.

We came back out in the darkness and groped our way toward the car. Suddenly, the flashlight beam swept across something in front of us. It took a moment for me to take in what it was. A wide circle of hundreds of Congolese people had silently come into the clearing without our being aware of them. They were closing in on us silently in an ever-narrowing circle. Soon they were only inches away. At this moment, I felt our driver reach for my left hand. I realized that he was slipping a gold ring onto my finger. A Ugandan who spoke English, he whispered to me, ''I am going to tell them that you are a Catholic bishop, and that you have come here on an inspection trip. They are very dangerous. You will have to let them kneel before you and kiss the ring. It is the only way we might be safe.''

Then he turned to the barely visible crowd and addressed them in their tribal language. He spoke with quiet authority, and I waited tensely to see what would happen. Suddenly, one of the crowd kneeled down and kissed the ring, then another and another. I was trembling so much I could barely hide my fear. But they continued to kneel and kiss, and then disappeared into the forest.

When I got back in the Land-Rover, my shaking increased. I don't believe I have ever been so frightened. We made our way out of the tortuous side road and back onto the road toward Stanleyville. It seemed to go on endlessly until we came in sight of a settlement on the main road. It was nearly midnight. Here we found another mission station. This one was inhabited, run by a Congolese priest educated by American missionaries. He greeted us warmly. The mission was a welcome sight after the shock of our recent experience. Speaking with an American accent, the priest revealed what had happened to his station during the insurrection.

Gbeneye's Simba warriors had captured the mission. Day after day, they had lined up all the whites, women and children included. They had placed them against the wall, five or six at a time. Then they loaded, aimed, and fired—but the bullets were blanks, a cruel method of mental torture. Eventually, real bullets were used, a few at a time. For over twenty days this continued, until all the white missionaries and their families were shot and killed. In addition, our priest was placed against the wall day after day and fired at with blank cartridges. He survived only because he was an African.

In spite of this, he extended all the hospitality he could. There was only a partially destroyed room for us to sleep in, but we were grateful for it. Exhausted and emotionally drained, we retreated into sleep, and even the rats running across our beds failed to bother us.

The next day we went on to Stanleyville in sadness, down the Congo in a riverboat that brought us to Léopoldville, and then we continued by air to America. It was hard to shake off our experiences; the regions we had explored would not become possible to undertake until several years later, when time had healed many of the wounds this ravishing part of Africa had endured.

This trip was, of course, seven years after my preliminary probes into Africa in 1961. Back in the early 1960s, I was still going through all the growing pains that would eventually lead to Lindblad Travel's branching out all over the planet. There would be many successes and many disappointments to follow. The problem was not knowing which would be which, a problem that sometimes brought me to the edge of disaster when I least expected it.

V

*M*ONGOLIA
The Gobi and Kublai Khan

BY 1964, I found that the special group of clients willing to take a chance with me on exploratory tours was growing from a hundred to several hundred. They were people with a tremendous curiosity about the planet and a deep respect for it. By paying regular fees, they helped me defray the enormous cost of researching and surveying new locations. This expense was a heavy burden on a young company.

Our gross billings were now moving over the million mark. I was still developing tours that I myself would enjoy, on the basis that at least a few hundred other people would share my tastes. I did not believe in skimping, because I was selling luxury travel and insisted on giving people their money's worth. My success depended on picking the most interesting places possible, and convincing reluctant government officials that we should be allowed to go there. Some places sounded good but weren't. Other places seemed unappealing but were fascinating. It took constant digging.

In probing for these offbeat, adventurous places, I found myself asking the question: where are the most *unlikely* places that an intelligent American traveler would like to go?

One of those times came in 1964. I had a talk with a close friend of mine, Dr. Roy Sexton. Roy was a prominent Washington physician who had been medical director of a Smithsonian expedition to the Belgian Congo in 1955, in addition to thirty other missions to Asia, the South Pacific, and Africa. He combined his specialty in internal medicine with a penchant for travel, and was willing to join with me in several expeditions as a counselor and consultant. In his enthusiasm for travel, he was constantly egging me on.

One day at the Explorers Club, he said to me, "I've just been talking with Justice Douglas." Roy was the justice's personal physician, so I waited with interest for what he was going to say. "He has just returned from a trip to Outer Mongolia."

I'm sure Roy wasn't surprised at my response: "When can we go there?" I asked.

"Well," he said, "the justice doesn't think there would be too much difficulty in bringing in a tour group. In fact, he recommended it highly."

That was all the stimulus I needed. I made preliminary inquiries about entrance visas, accommodations, and transportation. There didn't seem to be too many stumbling blocks. I was thrilled with the idea, and so were some two dozen clients who were waiting for the next crazy idea I could come up with.

I had been excited about Outer Mongolia from the time I had read about Marco Polo as a child. His odyssey was one of the chief propellants that made me dream of being an explorer. Squeezed between the Soviet Republic on the north and China on the south and east, the nomad Mongols had been galvanized by Jenghiz Khan into an enormous pack of marauding warriors who almost took over the known world back in the thirteenth century. To the purportedly civilized world then, they were known as barbarian Tartars.

The discipline and organization laid down by Jenghiz Khan, especially for travel and communication, would be a nonelectronic marvel even today. With post stations twenty-five or thirty miles apart, some 200 horses were always held in readiness at each post for the sacred messengers of the Great Khan. Nothing was to deter them, even a nobleman, in the swift movement of the message on to the next post. The size of the operation dwarfed the later pony express system in America. The Mongolian messengers slept in their saddles and were bandaged from head to foot to survive the rough ride at top speed. As the message moved from post to post, a new horse was always ready at the sound of the bells the messengers wore around their belts. The result was that messages and documents were relayed at the rate of up to 250 miles a day.

Kublai Khan, two generations and thirty years away from his progenitor, might be considered more civilized than Jenghiz, but he was not without his own lust for conquest. He was a bold and uncompromising leader. Unawed by the mountain ranges of the Himalayas and the hundred-mile-long chain of Kunlun mountains, he moved a 100,000-man army along the borders of Tibet, through high mountain passes to the region of Yunnan, where the Chinese king of Nan-Chow was forced to surrender his capital city, Tali.

Although Jenghiz Khan was considered the greater warrior, I was always more fascinated with Kublai Khan. I could understand why Samuel Taylor Coleridge waxed so eloquent about him in his poem. It was strange how this nomadic man operated out of the remote desert town of Karakorum, and then shifted the center of gravity of the world's greatest empire of the time to Peking. Here he lived in exotic luxury, fostering art and culture along with his often brutal conquests. He invited scholars, artists, poets, and engineers from all over the world to create what later became the Ming dynasty in China. At the same time he was capable of ordering the death of 20,000 hapless tribesmen whose paths accidentally crossed the cortege carrying the body of a deceased lesser khan to his burial place in the Altai Mountains.

I decided that our first experimental trip to Outer Mongolia would be called Explorer's Tour of Central Asia since it was a venturesome foray into unknown territory. It also was part of my inclination for expanding the concept of adventure travel, which I was convinced would become a heavy part of future tourism. Before the tour began, I talked at length with Justice Douglas, who felt it would open up new horizons for people to learn firsthand about this powerful center of world history. The justice was the sort of man I admired most—brilliant, scholarly, physically active, and as devoted as I to the preservation of nature and wild-life.

I also searched for the best possible lecturer to accompany our tour, someone who knew Mongolia and other central Asian regions and could make them come to life. I found him in Owen Lattimore, who had traveled in and written extensively about Manchuria (under the Social Science Research Council), Peiping (under the Harvard-Yenching Institute), and Mongolia (under the Institute of Pacific Relations). He was a brilliant and learned man, who had undergone a vicious tidal wave of unwarranted slander in the McCarthy era, which he wrote about so movingly in his book *Ordeal by Slander*.

There were routine problems. Mongolia had gone through violent convolutions. Since the days of the great khans, it had reverted to a nomadic state. Agriculture is looked on with disdain. The populace roams on horseback with their herds from summer to winter pastures. They are still proud, however, and seem to dream that some day a new Jenghiz Khan will come along to be their leader as a Son of Heaven. The wide steppes in which they roam stretch across Outer Mongolia for a distance equal to that from New York to South Dakota. From generation to generation, the campfire stories have been handed down of how Jenghiz Khan had been proclaimed a ruler of the world by a shaman whose powers were never questioned.

As we prepared to go to Outer Mongolia in 1964, the country was becoming remarkably stabilized under a strange coexistence agreement between China and the Soviet Union. The country remains independent of both, but politically leans heavily toward the Soviets, through whom it receives most of its assistance. However, Inner Mongolia, just to the south, is an integral part of China.

Stabilized as Mongolia was, its embryonic travel organization was steeped in suspicion of Americans and swamped with bureaucratic delays. Letters were never answered. All my arrangements were made through a clumsy chain of cables. What accommodations there were were prescribed by the officials, and we would have to be at their mercy. Regardless of accommodations, I figured that the land cost would come to roughly $50 a day per person.

Among the applicants for the trip was a Mrs. Featherstone, an eighty-year-old lady from Pennsylvania. When she applied I had tried to steer her on to one of the milder Africa tours because of her age. But she would hear none of it. Her one ambition in life, she wrote me, was to follow the footsteps of Jenghiz Khan. I warned her that this Explorer's trip was a long one, sixty-four days in fact, with rugged country and uncertain accommodations. She would not give in. I insisted that she have a thorough physical examination and send me a signed physician's report that she was in perfect health; otherwise I could not permit her to go along. Not long after, her doctor's certificate came in confirming that all was well with Mrs. Featherstone and that she had no health problems.

The first person off the plane at Tokyo was an elderly lady in a wheelchair, and I knew it had to be Mrs. Featherstone. She was carrying a small bag with a Lindblad Travel tag on it. As soon as the confusion of the arrival of the two dozen other travelers was cleared, I spoke to her privately.

"Mrs. Featherstone," I said, "have you had an accident since we talked on the phone?"

"Oh, no," she said. "No, I always have to use a wheelchair. My hips are fused, you see."

My mind flashed ahead to the trip that was coming up: sleeping out in the Gobi Desert in those black felt tents called yurts; riding on Bactrian camels across the Gobi; primitive hotels; long motor rides across the steppes; constant changes from boat to plane to bus, none with the amenities of Western travel.

I was livid. "Mrs. Featherstone," I said, "I have a letter here signed by you, saying that you have nothing wrong with you. Your doctor's certificate also says there is nothing wrong."

"That's right," she said. "There's absolutely *nothing* wrong with my heart or liver. Just the hips."

"But dear Mrs. Featherstone," I pleaded, "you can't walk, and we have to go to so many different places. It will be impossible, much as we'd like to take you."

She was a sprightly little woman of great dignity. She was also stubborn. ''Mr. Lindblad,'' she said, ''I'll be perfectly all right if somebody helps me here and there.''

For her own good, I had to be equally stubborn. ''I'm sorry, Mrs. Featherstone. But I am going to have to send you back to America.''

Then she started to cry. She said that for thirty-three years—I don't know why she picked that exact number—she had wanted to follow in the footsteps of Jenghiz Khan. Now I was denying her that pleasure, probably one of the last she would have in her life. I was now so hopping mad that her tears had little effect on me. But then she cried again, and I softened.

The problem was that I had to carry her everywhere the wheelchair was unable to go. In spite of the difficulties, her spirit was continually soaring. Meanwhile, I felt I was in acute danger of getting a hernia. Waiting for a bus, I leaned her back against a tree where she went into rapture about the beauty of Hokkaido, our first side trip. I found it hard to share her enthusiasm. I finally went out and found her the lightest folding wheelchair I could, and managed to get her aboard the ship en route to Siberia, and on to the Mongolian capital, Ulan Bator.

I had been so busy with Mrs. Featherstone that I hardly had time to prepare for our arrival in Mongolia. We arrived by way of Irkutsk in Siberia to find a formidable barrier of government officials. Since we were the first group to arrive under the new, more relaxed open-door policy, none of the Mongolian officials seemed to know how to greet us. They were very suspicious and hurried us into two small rooms, one for men and one for women. Here they made each of us undress and announced that all our cameras would have to be confiscated.

This was a major blow. Our entire tour had been built as a camera safari, and we also had a professional filmmaker with us planning a major documentary. I pleaded for the cameras to be released, but the officials stood their ground. I gave in temporarily as we went by antiquated buses to the main hotel in Ulan Bator, with Mrs. Featherstone cheerily accompanying us in her new folding wheelchair. It was much easier to get her on and off the bus, and my fears of a hernia lessened.

The new hotel had been built by the Czechs. The ventilation could have been better; the rich and sour fumes of Far Eastern cooking penetrated every room. I got in touch with several higher government officials and invited them to join me in some choice Russian vodka I had brought with me. I was determined to get our camera equipment freed, and not averse to using the vodka as a tool.

We started a congenial conference through interpreters in midevening, and the vodka sank lower in the bottles. By four in the morning, the Mongolian officials were roaring drunk. The problem was that I was, too. But I finally drove home my point about the cameras. To my great surprise, they not only agreed but commandeered some Russian jeeps, rounded up a sleepy group of airport officials, and we made for the airport just before sunrise. Here the cameras were released with great ceremony, and from then on, we were all brothers.

In spite of their inborn suspicion, the Mongol people are warm and friendly once the barrier is broken. Although they are closely bound to the Soviets, their sense of freedom is strong, and they lean toward the West in feeling if not in politics. They have been under Communist dominion since the 1920s, but their strong attachment to nomadic life helps them maintain a proud individualism characteristic of the West. Geographically, the steppes of Mongolia are windswept and desolate, yet the herdsmen have now been able to produce the highest per capita rate of livestock in the world, a ratio of 25 million head of livestock to one million of population. Compared to other Communist countries, Mongolia actually has the highest standard of living in eastern Asia, if judged by how much money is left after the essentials are taken care of.

This modest surplus may be because their nomadic aspirations are lower, leaving them more money for discretionary use. They don't dream of automobiles, but they do go for motorbikes. Their meat consumption is high because their stock breeding is efficient and skillful. In spite of the arid Gobi, they are able to raise camels, sheep, goats, and especially horses in enormous quantities. The latter are rugged animals and require skilled horsemanship. I tried one out on a wooden saddle and had to walk like a bowlegged cowboy for several days as a result. This was in cossack country in the west of Mongolia where horsemanship reaches its peak as an art.

Owen Lattimore's graphic and erudite reconstruction of ancient and recent events brought action and life to the barren landscape. A feature of the visit was our trip to the Gobi Desert, where we would be sleeping in the native yurts, eating by the nomad campfires, and absorbing the atmosphere of the ancient camel caravans.

Our conveyance to the Gobi was a rattling Ilyushin 14, the Russian approximation of a Convair, that sat very high off the ground. We had no trouble getting Mrs. Featherstone up the metal ramp and into the plane. Now that we would be flying directly to the routes taken by Jenghiz Khan's and Kublai Khan's armies, her enthusiasm was soaring. There were no seats and no safety belts. Everyone, excluding Mrs. Featherstone, had to sit on the floor. For her, it was just another great adventure as she sat in her wheelchair, brakes locked.

The Gobi below excited me as much as it did Mrs. Featherstone, with her obsessional attachment to Jenghiz Khan. Soon we were beginning our descent, and I looked in vain for an airstrip. We dropped lower, and there was still none in sight. By the time we were almost touching down, it became obvious why. We were landing on a flat stretch of grass that was neither an airstrip nor a road.

The Mongolian pilot emerged from the flight deck, opened the door, and unceremoniously threw out a rope ladder that barely reached the ground. This sort of thing added zest to our journey, and I was pleased until I rediscovered Mrs. Featherstone. Her eyes were sparkling, her spirit undimmed. The others were swinging down the rope ladder like Tarzans, as one by one they landed on the turf.

I had no idea that there would not be any sort of portable ramp. I looked at Mrs. Featherstone's beaming, expectant face, all prepared for her encounter with the ghosts of the Great Khans. I didn't have the heart to tell her it was apparent that she would have to stay on the plane while we brought her food and drink and made her as comfortable as possible. Then I found that the plane had to leave almost immediately.

I looked out the cargo door at the ground below, with the flimsy rope ladder. Fortunately, the pilot had another length of rope, and I lowered the wheelchair first. Then, with meticulous care, I was able to place the rope under Mrs. Featherstone's arms and gently lower her to ground to a waiting cluster of the other passengers. All the way down, she was laughing as if this were an everyday occurrence.

Her enthusiasm failed to dim when we camped overnight in the yurts of the nomads, where she seemed to fit in as if she had lived in them in a former life. That first night we sat around the campfire in the chill desert air, talking of the past scenes of history and drinking the distinctive Mongolian beverage called koumiss, which we alternated with tea and cheese. In the background were oxen and Bactrian camels with their double humps and sleepy eyes. Herds of horses were everywhere, of course.

Drinking koumiss is not to be taken lightly. Consisting of fermented mare's milk, slightly effervescent, and carrying a wallop, it has been the Mongolian drink of choice for centuries, and Marco Polo waxed eloquent about it during his journeys with Kublai Khan. The mares are not always enthusiastic about giving up their milk for this purpose and often have to be tricked into it. This is done by having their colts stationed nearby while the milking process goes on. If a mare begins to resent the intrusion on her privacy, a colt is brought over to do some legitimate nursing, and in a few moments is taken away, allowing the milking to continue.

The mare's milk is then poured into a big skin or bottle and churned vigorously to separate the butter from the koumiss, as the latter boils up and begins to ferment. Kublai Khan had some 10,000 mares on hand for this purpose, but each one had to be spotlessly white or it would not be milked for the khan's private stock.

We shared a considerable amount of koumiss that night around the fire in that strange and lonely atmosphere, which evoked the graphic imagery of trade caravans, archers, swordsmen, and kingly convoys. We were also given an extra treat, a contrast to the primitive world we were in. We were able to watch in the far distance a 1964 Russian missile launch, a spectacular sight. Afterward, Roy Sexton, Owen Lattimore, I, and a handful of others were feeling very mellow, and began talking about what new adventurous tours we could dream up. It seemed that I had gathered a group that thirsted for exotic new places as much as they did for the koumiss.

The only map I had on hand was a sketchy Pan Am route map, but it stretched all the way across the world. Feeling no inhibitions, I studied it in a roseate haze. It was hard to think of new places in the wake of burgeoning jet travel. The map showed plainly the interlaced routes of the Pan Am flights. Few regions were untouched.

I looked down at the bottom of the map, unmarked by airline routes. Then I noticed that Antarctica wasn't even on the map. My enchantment with Antarctica had been so great since childhood that I wondered why I had never thought of it before. I was aware that the idea of setting up tours to that frozen continent would be tangled with complications. Going there might even be impossible. But inspired by the koumiss, I boldly announced to everyone, "Our next exploratory tour will be to a place that isn't even on the map."

Roy Sexton immediately agreed. Along with me, he felt that the more opportunities for travelers to learn firsthand about science, the more meaningful the tours would be. Antarctica offered rich opportunities for this, as well as for adventure. For the others in the group, the idea was compelling. They were veteran travel buffs who wanted to be among the first to break ground in new territory. This included Mrs. Featherstone. I would have to give a lot of practical thought to her indomitable spirit, because I was becoming bone-tired from the sheer logistics of getting her around.

The greatest challenge came the next day, when we were scheduled to take a sightseeing trip on the two-humped camel. I was willing to stay back with her while the others went, but she would hear none of it. She insisted that she could go herself. There was only one way to grant her wish. We draped her over and between the humps, stomach down, legs dangling on one side, arms and head down the other. As the caravan took off, I could hear her calling out, "This is absolutely fabulous, Mr. Lindblad. Just the way they did in the old caravans of Kublai Khan!"

It was easy to slide her onto the camel or onto the bunks in the yurt tent. But when the plane returned two days later to take us back to Ulan Bator, it was another story. It was the same Ilyushin, high off the ground, with nothing but the rope ladder again. There were no wooden steps around, no wood to improvise a rigid ladder. Sizing up the situation, I found that there was no other choice but to tie Mrs. Featherstone to my back while the others held the bottom of the rope ladder taut. As usual, Mrs. Featherstone was bubbling with laughter as I started my precarious way up the wobbly rungs. The trouble was that her laughter was contagious. The others below were breaking up along with her, and the base of the ladder slipped from their grasp. In a fraction of a second, I was literally pasted to the underside of the plane, as Mrs. Featherstone called out, "Don't drop me, Mr. Lindblad. Please don't drop me!"

I think I learned at that moment that the elderly and the handicapped have a much greater capacity for enduring travel to primitive areas than we believe. What's more, they seem to appreciate it more than others who are lucky enough to have sound bodies.

We did several other side trips into the desert, including a visit to the dusty remnants of Jenghiz Khan's forsaken city of Karakorum, far across the wolf-infested steppe from Ulan Bator. Except for crumbling mounds of stones and an exquisite giant stone turtle, little is left of the palaces, pleasure domes, and temples, a sharp reminder of the fragility of once mighty civilizations.

On one side trip to Arvaiker, the plane that took us to Karakorum failed to come back to pick us up at this desolate spot. A brisk snowstorm was brewing, and there were no overnight accommodations. Our government guide informed us that the only option we had was to drive back to Ulan Bator, and pointed to some buses and cars that looked as if they could never make the first bend in the road. He reminded me that we ought to leave immediately to avoid the snowstorm. When I asked him how long it would take, he estimated some thirty-six hours.

I could not visualize Mrs. Featherstone or any of the others being able to survive such a trip on hard, unforgiving seats without heat in the vehicles. The temperature was down to the thirties, and the roads were merely tracks in the sand and turf. There were also mountains to cross. I went out to the airstrip with our local official, in the hope that the plane might come in. Of course there was no sign of it. There were, however, two ancient Russian-built single-engine biplanes. Two Mongolian pilots were resting under the wings of one of the planes.

I asked our guide why we couldn't take these planes back, even though their fabric fuselages looked alarmingly fragile. He said no, that would be impossible. However, one of the pilots spoke English, and said that the planes were in good shape and ready to fly and that they were free to take us.

But the official was adamant. He said that we would definitely have to drive back. But I went aboard and found there was room for twelve passengers in each plane on long board seats. I had ample cash with me to cover the fare, and finally persuaded the official to let us fly back. He insisted that he would drive back himself. Later, he admitted the reason: he was afraid the planes would never make it.

At least the aircraft were built close to the ground, and it was easy to get Mrs. Featherstone aboard. We took off in the two planes, well ahead of the snowstorm. But the pilots had a bit of a problem gaining altitude to get over the mountain range that stood between us and Ulan Bator. It took us more than half an hour of circling to climb high enough to clear the peaks.

Before we left Mongolia, we had enough time to visit the very interesting Museum of Natural History at the capital city, where there is a display of rare dinosaur bones discovered at the beginning of the century, in addition to even rarer dinosaur eggs. The Mongolians take pride in their natural treasures as much as they do their traditions. Modern industry is beginning to creep in, and their prosperity in relation to other areas of central Asia is marked. Both education and health services are improving, and consumer goods are surprisingly available.

In spite of the prevailing friendliness of the people, we still ran into stiff bureaucracy on leaving the airport. Small souvenirs such as driftwood or even pebbles from the Gobi Desert were confiscated. But we left in good spirits for the rest of our sixty-four-day tour through central Asia, and on to the Middle East. Throughout the entire trip, Mrs. Featherstone remained one of the hardiest of the lot.

As we flew on, however, the idea of the Antarctic, generated around the nomadic campfire, burned in my mind. I knew that the idea of a tourist trip there was outrageous. There would be enormous obstacles to meet and I had no precise idea as to how I would go about it. Actually, I had been half joking when I brought up the subject, but by now I had painted myself into a corner. By the time I got back to the United States, the wheels were moving fast inside my head, even though I was very uncertain what direction they would take.

VI

ANTARCTICA II
The Bottom of the World

AFTER our 1964 plunge into Mongolia, our tours there continued sporadically, in spite of visas having to be cleared through Moscow and tangled red tape everywhere. Other travel agents began undertaking similar tours, but did not find them congenial. The magazine *Travel Agent* ran a story in the mid-sixties headlined: ONLY STAUNCHEST SO-JOURNERS STILL TRY MONGOLIA WILDS. I didn't feel that the journey was that severe, recalling Mrs. Featherstone's hardiness. I found that when people are prepared for rugged travel, they don't miss the conventional amenities and hot water isn't all that important. Our first tour was obviously too long. We cut that back to half the time, and included Tashkent, Samarkand, and Moscow as checkpoints on the old caravan routes where vestiges of the khans still remain.

Meanwhile, the African safaris and other tours set up during our early days continued to operate beyond our expectations. During all this, I never stopped scanning the world for new ideas. After my spontaneous announcement of the Antarctic idea in Mongolia, the word spread fast that we were going ahead with the tour. I couldn't have dodged it if I had wanted to.

The problem was that every expert and official I talked to said the

Antarctic operation was impossible. People would die, they said; bringing women there would be out of the question; the numerous Antarctic scientific stations would resent any intrusion; strong international rivalries would prove difficult; no standard vessel could cope with the stormy Drake Passage, to say nothing of the pack ice and Antarctic storms (the impact of which I would regrettably encounter later).

Antarctica is a land of statistics. All of them seem to be superlatives: the highest of all continents; 95 percent of all the world's stock of permanent ice; the highest wind speeds and the lowest temperatures. It was a legitimate question to ask why anyone would want to go to such an inhospitable place. A scientist would naturally be interested in fieldwork there. A painter could become rapturous at the free-form sculpture of the icebergs. But for the average tourist, there was still a question mark.

The endless unsnarling of official red tape led me eventually to Argentina. Roy Sexton had talked to people at the National Science Foundation who recommended the Argentina Antarctic Institution as a logical source of guidance. Not only was Argentina one of the two closest jumping-off points, but it was claiming the largest wedge of Antarctic territory, despite British and Chilean claims to the same territories. Roy felt the Argentine officials would be receptive to the idea because they would have a chance to display their flag in the Antarctic to outsiders for the first time.

I have to admit I was slightly nervous when I was ushered into the office of Admiral Varela at the country's naval headquarters in Buenos Aires. In 1964 he was the chief of staff of all Argentine forces. His decision would be final as to whether our proposed expedition would be possible. I had no idea what kind of reception I would get. Typically, he was a classic gentleman, a perfect portrait of Argentine courtesy. He greeted me cordially, with great ceremony, took me around his office, showed me pictures of Antarctica, brought out charts and maps, and seemed to be as excited about the idea as I was.

Antarctica was his favorite love. He had been there eleven times. The long absences of each trip had had an unusual effect on his family life. He confessed that he had eleven children because he was so vigorous each time he returned home. When he invited some of his staff from the naval transport section into the office to talk with me, I knew his cooperation was assured.

My main concern was whether I could charter a vessel sturdy enough for the ice packs and roomy enough to carry about fifty travelers. I needed this many to reach a break-even point for the risky operation. To my surprise, Admiral Varela offered to charter to us a navy transport, built in France, that could handle fifty-six people in reasonable comfort. The M.S. *Lapataia* was a ship that had been used to carry scientists and staff personnel to the Antarctic before, and would be ideal for our purpose. The admiral also threw in an icebreaker, the *San Martin,* and the *Irrigoyen,* a small Antarctic tug to accompany us.

After inspecting the *Lapataia,* I was more than pleased. It was no luxury liner, nor was it meant to be. Passengers would be warned about this, and I knew that the sort of traveler who would undertake this voyage would know what to expect and join the cruise as a learning experience rather than a luxury junket. Travelers would be warned that we would be crossing the world's roughest waters in the Drake Passage. We would have to stock the ship with a reasonable number of amenities, and furnish warm and efficient parkas, balaclavas, and other cold weather gear to keep the passengers safe and comfortable.

The operation would require a commitment of some $100,000 before I had confirmed a single passenger. My enthusiasm was so great I didn't hesitate. I decided on the spot and went back to the States to bring the project to life.

To my delight, I had no trouble in booking fifty-six stalwart passengers within a short time. I then set about planning the trip so that it would be an intellectual as well as an adventuresome experience. Roy Sexton was of great help in this. Together, we arranged to set up parts of the ship as a scientific laboratory so that we could supplement the many studies being conducted at the scientific bases in Antarctica, as well as frame an itinerary that would acquaint the passengers with the important international work being done at the various bases there.

Roy was particularly interested in plankton. This microscopic plant and animal life abounds in the ocean and is scooped up by whales and fish, which sustain themselves on the proteins, carbohydrates, and fats contained in these large masses. Because of this, scientists have stated that there is more food per acre in the Antarctic seas than anywhere else in the world.

There are over 150,000 billion tons in the oceans. We also hoped to contribute to the studies of krill, the tiny shrimplike animal also abundant in Antarctic waters. Recently, a single school of krill was discovered there that formed the largest school of sea animals ever found. Like plankton, krill is protein-rich and can be mashed and treated to form animal meal or spreads for crackers, or mixed with other foods to supplement the world's food supply. The single school discovered represented 14 percent of the total fish and shellfish harvest for a year.

We also hoped to add to the store of knowledge of climate, geology, and wildlife in our limited way. To do so, I planned to search for scientists to accompany us who would not only bring learning to the passengers, but who also could add to their own studies. For our first trip, I was able to persuade Captain Finn Ronne, a prime explorer of the Antarctic, to be educational director of the tour. He had named a huge slice of the continent Edith Ronne Land, after his wife. An international convention later decided that one name was enough and made him drop the ''Edith.'' Our itinerary would take us to the scenic wonders of Half Moon Bay, Esperanza, Deception Island, the Bay of Whales, Le Maire Strait, and Anvers Island. We would visit four Argentine bases, and one American and two British stations. En route to the ship, we would also be greeted by President Arturo Illía, view parts of Patagonia, and embark for our cruise at Ushuaia, Argentina, the picturesque village that is the southern-most town in the world.

I went down to Buenos Aires one day ahead of the group to meet Roy Sexton. He would be serving as ship's doctor as well as a scientist. I went aboard the ship to meet the navy commander, Captain Bolino. He was a distinguished looking gentleman with a pleasant face, but at the moment it was clouded.

''Mr. Lindblad,'' he said, ''my crew is extremely upset.''

I didn't expect this sort of greeting, so I asked him why.

''Because of the coffins, sir, and the embalming fluid,'' he said.

I had no idea what he was talking about. But before I could speak, he went on.

"We have stored the three coffins in the hold," he said. "But the crew may even refuse to sail with them. Perhaps you can tell why they were ordered aboard?"

"Captain," I said, "we never ordered any such thing. There has to be a mistake."

Then he showed me a cleanly typed letter from my secretary. It stated that the coffins and embalming fluid were to be taken with us on the trip, and the letter was signed by her. I knew she was one of the more conscientious people in the world, but this was utterly baffling. I rushed back to the hotel and called New York. My secretary said that Roy Sexton had asked for this macabre equipment, and she had faithfully carried out the order. I seriously wondered if Roy had not gone around the bend, and I went immediately to his room.

"Lord," he said, "did she really *order* those?"

"It looks as if she did," I said.

Roy looked sheepish. "Here's what must have happened," he said. "She kept calling me every day: 'Are you *sure* we haven't forgotten something?' "

"What's that got to do with coffins?" I asked.

"Well, it was getting me down," Roy said. "Finally, when she called back twice in one day, I told her, 'Oh God, yes! We did forget three coffins and twenty gallons of embalming fluid.' "

I rushed back to the prow, and one by one the coffins were lifted out of the hold to the cheers of the crew. The embalming fluid, however, turned out by accident to be not such a bad idea. We used it later to make plastic cubes to preserve insect and krill specimens. In the process, we accidentally discovered and preserved an unknown wingless fly.

That same night the full contingent of passengers was arriving in Buenos Aires for the first leg of the trip. Recalling Mrs. Featherstone, I made sure that all of them had certificates from their doctors with them. The oldest passenger was Mrs. Bessie Sweeney, of Washington, D.C., who was eighty-six at the time. She was the mother of Ed Sweeney, president of the Explorers Club, and more robust and healthy than most people half her age. She became a favorite of the press, with over 3000 papers picking up the AP story of her visiting the Antarctic.

The plane did not arrive in Buenos Aires until after midnight, and it was one in the morning before I gathered the passengers in the lobby of the hotel to give them a quick briefing. After all were dispersed, one elderly lady remained behind in the lobby. She came up to me and said, ''Mr. Lindblad, do you know my name?''

I thought she was testing my memory, and I had not yet learned many of the names and faces of the group. ''I'm sorry I don't know it yet,'' I said. ''But give me a day or two and I will.''

She looked distressed and said, ''The most ridiculous thing has happened. I went to the desk to get my key, and I couldn't remember my room number or my own name!''

I led her over to a chair, and assured her that she was just overexcited and that she would recall her name very quickly after she got a little rest. She eventually did, and I breathed a little easier. This problem was no sooner solved when another lady came down into the lobby to say that she was sharing a room with a roommate who at this moment was upstairs at her desk, burning her passport, page by page. I rushed to the room, where I found the roommate in the process of trying to burn the last pages. Only the covers remained. She was complaining bitterly that her passport picture was ugly and she would have none of it. Taking her to the American embassy the next day, I warned her not to tell the truth about how the passport was destroyed or she would never receive another one. I remained nervous about her all through the trip. She survived well, however, but I resolved to tighten up the screening of future passengers.

A less harrowing problem became apparent when we were under way toward the Antarctic. An attractive young woman took me aside to ask me bluntly what she could do about sex on the trip. She confessed that she was a nymphomaniac and had already singled out my deputy, the assistant expedition leader, to join her in the fun, even though he didn't know about her idea yet. Her concern was how she could conduct the calisthenics, since she had a roommate. Eventually she conferred with her roommate, who was most understanding and absented herself, first in the mornings and later in the afternoons.

In spite of these anomalies, the trip began smoothly. We survived the Drake Passage with only a few broken dishes. This latitude is known as the Screaming Sixties, where even modern freighters can founder. En route, Finn Ronne began his lectures that were to provide full information about the places we were going to visit. At each stop we planned to go ashore in the navy's seven-ton landing craft.

No one was better equipped than Finn Ronne to depict the history of Antarctica. His father had been with Amundsen, and he himself had been with Byrd in Little America, sleeping in a bunk that his father had once occupied. He had reached the South Pole himself in 1961. In his sixties, he was the last true Antarctic explorer in the old tradition. Although he had been born in Norway and spoke with a thick Norwegian accent, he had become a naturalized American.

To my regret, he also had an incredible knack of upsetting people. I learned later that when he was command officer of the U.S. Ellsworth Station during the International Geophysical Year of 1957, he came very close to causing the first mutiny in U.S. Navy history. When he discovered that the men under him had put his picture up on the wall and had thrown darts at it, he buried himself in his room and rarely emerged from it. On his own expedition to Stonington Island, the relations with his pilot became so strained that the pilot had to move out and sleep at the British base, a hundred yards away from Finn Ronne's main base.

But like many Norwegians, he was eminently able. As a cartographer, he had named numerous peaks, bays, and lands in Antarctica, including the huge territory he named after his wife, an area as large as the eastern United States.

As his lectures began, he revealed an obsessional hatred for Admiral Byrd, belittling everything that Byrd had done. He made it plain that the only ones who had accomplished anything of value were the Norwegian explorers. He also drove for the throats of Scott and Shackleton.

In his first lecture, he began a vehement diatribe about how Byrd was not much more than an incredible publicity man with a salesman's ability to get funds from the government.

After the first lecture, I took Finn aside and said, "Don't you think the attacks you are making on Admiral Byrd and the other explorers could be done in a different way? Couldn't you soften all that?''

Finn Ronne grew livid and said, ''Look, I want to tell the truth and nothing but the truth!''

But the length and depth of Ronne's attacks were turning the passengers off and alienating them. I finally had to ask him to step down from his job. Friends who had accompanied him on the journey went along with my decision. Fortunately, I had several Argentine scientists and botanists on the ship, and they joined with scientific personnel at the various bases, who came aboard later, to provide a broad spectrum of information.

Although our itinerary was carefully planned, we were entirely dependent on the weather—ice, winds, and snow. We were reasonably snug on the *Lapataia,* with bar and lounge, and a spacious dining room where the best Argentine beef was served, along with morning tea, full breakfast, luncheon, and table d'hôte dinner. This was anything but a luxury cruise, however. Emphasis was placed on our scientific program, which included marine biology, the history of Antarctic exploration, meteorology, glaciology, and other disciplines.

In our laboratory, our scientists dissected and explained all types of marine specimens, while a meteorological workshop was set up. The seals, penguins, and whales were feature attractions, as was the birdlife, which includes the wandering albatross. This bird has a wingspan of up to fourteen feet and can soar for hours like a sailplane without moving its wings.

I wasn't sure what kind of reception we would get from the scientists at the various bases because they had never been interrupted by unofficial visitors. Our first stop was to be at Teniente Camera, an Argentine base at Half Moon Bay, part of the chain of islands hanging just north of the Antarctic Peninsula. But the biologists studying marine life there greeted us as if we were from another planet. They showed us in detail what they had been up to for the past two seasons, and guided us across the snow to our first penguin rookery, where amid the shrieks and stench of the birds, we came face to face with the comical

Chinstrap penguins called *Pygoscelis Antarctica.* They also steered us farther to a rookery of Weddell seals.

At nearby Potter Cove we went ashore in the landing craft near a huge glacier, where we found a mass of elephant seals with cavernous mouths and unbelievable halitosis. We were able to walk right in among nesting giant petrels, and pick up specimens of many lichens and the small Antarctic carnation. There were also the vertebra bones of whales as souvenirs for those who wanted to pay the excess baggage charge on the return air trip.

We went on through the route that we were to take so many times later, to a royal welcome by the Argentine army and scientists at Hope Bay, or Esperanza; and to Deception Island. We were thwarted by the fast ice pack in trying to reach the Antarctic Circle, and also blocked in trying to get ashore at the U.S. Palmer Station at the southern end of Anvers Island. Even the U.S. icebreaker *East Wind* could not get through the ice that kept us 300 yards away from the buildings. Here the scientists waved to us and we waved back to them in frustration.

In spite of our problems, the first tentative probe into Antarctica was a success. It received such worldwide publicity that by the time I got back to New York, we were flooded with inquiries about the next such venture. The demand was beyond my expectations. I immediately began planning cruises for the following years. As soon as they were announced, most were sold out far in advance, with long waiting lists. My idle boast around the Mongolian campfire had paid off.

I was now forced to face the problem of expanding the passenger capacity to take advantage of the new demand. Also, the *Lapataia* was flying the Argentine flag, which made it persona non grata in Chilean waters. Because of the fitful rivalry between the two countries, we had been unable to cruise through the delightful archipelago off the coast of Patagonia, as well as through the islands and straits in Tierra del Fuego, where enormous glaciers flow into the Beagle Channel. I was also thinking that the Chileans might even protest my taking tourists to Antarctica in an Argentine ship. While permission is not necessary to cruise in Antarctic waters, you are supposed to inform other signers of the International Antarctic Treaty where you intended to go.

I was not surprised when I got a phone call from the Chilean ambassador to the United States, Ambassador Tomic, shortly after one of our *Lapataia* cruises. He asked me if I would like to come to Washington to see him, and I quickly agreed. I was afraid he was going to make a formal protest, and I wanted to head it off.

Ambassador Tomic was an important man in the Chilean administration, a former senator and presidential candidate. He faced me across his desk and said, "I have a letter here from our president. He would very much like to talk to you."

My fear of a brewing protest seemed to be confirmed and I said, "I'd be honored. I assume it's about our visits to Antarctica?"

"Yes," the ambassador replied. "He has learned about your trip to the Chilean Antarctic."

I froze on his possessive reference to the continent as Chilean.

The ambassador went on, "He has also noted that you are using an Argentine vessel."

I could see the boom falling now. "Well, sir," I said, "it was the best ship we could find for the purpose."

Then he broke into a smile. "Don't worry about that part," he said. "What we want to know is, why can't you go to the Antarctic in one of our Chilean vessels, too?"

My relief was great. I had pictured the nightmare of an international protest, while two fully sold trips on the *Lapataia* were held up. I took off for Chile the next day.

I met with an intelligent and delightful man in the Ministry of Foreign Affairs in Santiago, a Francisco Jose Oyarzun. He was a career diplomat in charge of Antarctic affairs, although he had never been there. He introduced me to President Eduardo Frei. Later, Mario Rodriguez of the foreign office joined us as we talked about the idea. It was obvious that the Chileans were eager to persuade me to add a ship for the voyages. Then a thought struck me concerning an idea that had been boiling in the back of my mind for some time.

I had always been intrigued with the Chilean possession of Easter Island, with its remoteness and strange cultural history and the giant, inexplicable monuments that ranged along its shores. As a living mystery story, its pages had not yet been opened up for visitors to read. I wondered if I could gain the favor of the Chilean government to add this treasure to my project.

I was lucky enough to have them offer a Chilean ship for the Antarctic. Almost as if I were looking for something in exchange, I asked the Chilean officials if they would allow me to plan tours to Easter Island as part of the arrangement. To my surprise, they agreed. I found it hard to control my excitement. But this project would have to come later. My priority now was to organize and establish a full schedule of Antarctic expeditions, combining both the Chilean and Argentine ships.

Most important was strengthening the Antarctic voyages with the most competent leaders available. I was able to persuade Sir Peter Scott to join us on one expedition. Peter Scott was widely known as a painter, author, ornithologist, and conservationist. Later, I was also able to enlist Keith Shackleton, a relative of the great explorer, and Dr. Roger Tory Peterson, the father of modern ornithology. Captain Edwin MacDonald, U.S.N. (ret.), who had received the Antarctic Medal and many other awards for his explorations at both poles, was immediately available. On the cusp of 1966 and 1967, I was able to schedule three complete Antarctic tours. Two of them were on the *Lapataia* and one was on the Chilean vessel the *Navarino*.

Because of the fragile environment of Antarctica, the international treaty there calls for the protection of flora and fauna, and I made it plain to our passengers that these regulations would be strictly observed. Not a cigarette butt or a film box would be left behind in this area. The only thing I wanted to see left there were our footprints.

Even without visitors, there are ominous signs in Antarctica from the pollution that reaches down from the north. Penguins and seals have been found with traces of DDT, along with other chemicals. Salmonella bacilli have also been found in their systems in recent years. It is suspected that these bacteria have traveled down in the food chain from the Mediterranean to the region that is still the most clean and bacteria-free area in the world.

Japanese and Russian whalers are still threatening the continued existence of whales. It is estimated that one giant whale has been harpooned every twenty-two minutes over the last seven years, for a total of 160,000. Killer whales are lucky. Not being of commercial value, they are maintaining their population.

The work of the scientific stations on the continent remains a blur in the layman's mind. Yet the research there is of singular importance. The glaciologists are studying the thick glaciers and their flow toward the edges of the polar ice cap. The pattern of how they grow and how they shrink indicates changes in past and future climates of the earth.

Paleontologists searching for fossils have found dramatic evidence to support Alfred Wegener's continental drift theory, that the continents seem to have floated apart like pieces of toast in a bowl of milk. Fossils of leaves that had existed only in Africa and South America tend to show that Wegener's theory, called plate tectonics, is not only possible but probable.

Marine biologists are studying how the emperor penguin can stay alive at temperatures as low as −60° C. They are also probing why seals can stay under water a thousand feet deep for over half an hour with no harm from the pressure or lack of oxygen, and what kind of navigation system guides them back to their air holes from these depths at night.

With the three cruises scheduled for the end of 1966 and the beginning of 1967, our operation gained from increasing experience. But again the unpredictable was always in the wings. I had to accept that you can't take such an adventurous step without hazard.

Some experiences involved passengers. One woman came on board fully certified to be physically and mentally sound. She was found wandering around the corridors naked and continued to do so for several days. With the aid of the ship's doctor and nurse, I was able to get her to her stateroom, but she broke away. We caught her just in time to stop her from going over the rail. Back in her room she tried to attack the nurse, as the doctor sedated her. From then on, volunteer passengers guarded her door, and she had to be fed with a spoon. When we reached the Chilean navy base at Tierra del Fuego, she had to be confined in a mental hospital. Here she broke every window in her room. To get her back home, we had to charter a plane to fly her to Punta Arenas still under sedation. We cabled her family to come and take care of her.

They refused to do so, and we were forced to engage a Chilean doctor to keep her sedated and deliver her to her family back in the States.

On our second journey with the *Lapataia,* we joined up with several Argentine navy ships at Half Moon Island to celebrate what they called Argentine Antarctic Day. This was our first experience with rafting up with half a dozen ships in that part of the Antarctic, and even the Chilean and Russian ships joined in. From this day on, it became a tradition for us to entertain the crews of all ships we encountered in the Antarctic.

On the following day, the other ships had cleared Half Moon Bay, and we prepared to lower our seven-ton landing craft to visit the shoreline. Here was a vacant Argentine station hut and a chance to see the seals and penguins that clustered there. A young Argentine navy officer was in charge of the craft. I warned him that a heavy swell was rising that could ride the heavy craft up on the beach unless it was anchored both fore and aft. I did not want the passengers getting drenched, even though the temperature was slightly above freezing, because hypothermia can kill above the freezing mark.

I went in with the first group. The aft anchor of the landing craft held well in spite of the swell. We returned safe and dry. The second shift of twenty passengers and crew took off from the side of the *Lapataia.* I stayed aboard watching the landing vessel approach the shore. The swell had grown measurably. Then without warning a thick fog closed in, and the landing craft was lost from sight.

I tried to reach the officer on the landing craft with a walkie-talkie, but got no response. Meanwhile, the fog had gotten much thicker and the swells had risen to above the danger level. There was no way we could dispatch another boat, because not only were the swells great, but we could become hopelessly lost in the fog. We kept calling on the radio phone, but there was still no answer. Far past the time when the boat should have returned to the *Lapataia,* there was no word.

The captain and I stood vigil the entire night. By now we had to take it for granted that the craft had overturned, and that more than twenty passengers and crew were lost. I said to the captain that if that aft anchor had not been secured, the boat would be destroyed on the shore. With no word from the officer in charge, I had to assume the worst. But early in the morning, a weak signal came through. The story came out in fragments. They had not secured the aft anchor, and the swells had ridden them onto the beach, then sideways, and then broken over the craft and drenched everyone.

The navy officer in charge was knocked unconscious. But the group had been able to force their way, soaking wet, into the deserted station hut. They carried in the unconscious officer, and two of the women lay down beside him to bring enough body warmth to revive him. By eight the next morning, the fog lifted. We could see the landing craft far up on the beach. It was completely destroyed.

I went ashore in a lifeboat to find everyone alive and well—and shivering. I was more determined than ever to anticipate the problems, and to take precautions against them. But even that would not be enough, as I was to learn later.

Strangely enough, many of the passengers said they had enjoyed this ''unforeseen adventure.'' When the tour arrived back in Buenos Aires, an inevitable press conference took place. Mariella Sartorious, a fashion editor from Munich, gave her impression of the event: ''The Half Moon Island episode in queer surroundings and glowing friendship was far more exciting than the most glamorous fashion show in Paris.'' She planned to return to the Antarctic as soon as possible.

I was not too enthusiastic when the Argentines decided to commemorate this day with a plaque inscribed with all the names of the passengers and crew, calling it ''Un dia de rocordo,'' or ''A Day to Remember.'' The day is still celebrated there, but I am too bitter about the lack of that stern anchor to take any joy from it.

Mr. Sartorious, husband of Mariella, ran into a different problem on the same cruise. As a philatelist, he was interested in the colorful Antarctic postage stamps and canceled envelopes from ships and bases. During the February 1967 cruise, he prepared 150 envelopes with a seal from each Antarctic naval base. When the *Lapataia* arrived in port at Ushuaia, Mr. Sartorious asked me if I would take them to the small post office there for mailing. To make sure there would be no slipup, I arranged to sit at the postmaster's desk and personally stamp them.

However, none of the souvenir letters was received by Mr. Sartorious's friends. He wrote to postal authorities in New York, Buenos Aires, and Ushuaia, but no results were forthcoming. Finally, he took up the case with the International Postal Union in Geneva, which actually sent an inspector to Argentina the following July to search for the missing correspondence. After checking Buenos Aires, the inspector went on to Ushuaia, where he found a Lindblad bag under a table. It contained not only Mr. Sartorious's letters, but the letters of all the other passengers as well. The bag was discovered just as I had left it back on February 18.

The Swiss inspector dispatched the mail with a special note of explanation, and the negligent postmaster ended up being transferred to an even smaller post office in a Fuegian village.

By 1968, our voyages still had not been able to cross the Antarctic Circle. We also had not yet reached the more remote bases in the Ross Sea covered in part by the Ross Ice Shelf. The greatest Antarctic expeditions had been launched in this area. Here was the closest penetration a ship could make to the pole itself, only 800 miles away.

To reach the McMurdo base on the Ross Sea, the cruise had to begin in New Zealand, the nearest land. This would involve our undertaking a much longer cruise than the one from South America. We would have to sail from Christchurch past several scattered islands until we went over the Antarctic Circle and into the Ross Sea. In 1967 we were offered a Danish ship, the M.S. *Magga Dan,* which had been chartered to a New Zealand shipping company. The *Magga Dan* was in every respect an icebreaker. She had been used over the years for scientific expeditions and to supply polar bases. Since she had space for only twenty-five persons, the cost of the trip was $7000 per person. Apart from the captain and the chief engineer, the officers and crew were all New Zealanders.

I had no trouble filling the first voyage, so I was confident that the second, which would follow on our return to New Zealand, would also be fully booked. It was difficult to work out a schedule that would allow for getting stuck in the ice on the first cruise, and the passengers flying down from America to New Zealand arrived to find that the

Magga Dan was unable to get back in time. What counted was that this would be the first passenger ship ever to reach the Ross Sea and the first to cross beyond the Antarctic Circle. All our other attempts from South America had been thwarted when we tried to accomplish this, because of fast ice.

The New Zealand press did not take kindly to the idea. Some articles contended that the visit would interrupt important scientific work at the research stations and that the personnel there would consider us an intrusion. The American Operation Deep-freeze at McMurdo was under the command of the U.S. Navy, and although they could not officially object to our coming, they did make it plain that they would not go out of their way to help us.

Captain MacDonald was again with us as a specialist on polar navigation. His lectures on the long haul down across open water would help prepare the passengers for their arrival. Biologist Marie Darby, from the Canterbury Museum in Christchurch, New Zealand, would enlist passengers to participate in several research studies.

I made sure our menu would help offset the rough waters and spartan rigors. We loaded on 1400 precut steaks, 200 chickens, 600 pounds of frozen vegetables, 400 dozen eggs, and all the exotic fruits we could muster. We would carry reserves in case we ran into the risk of being caught in a pack ice jam. Although the *Magga Dan* was fully reinforced and an icebreaker, this still could happen.

Another of our cruises was starting out from Chile on the *Navarino* at the same time, with Kevin McDonnell in charge. Although they would be going to a different part of Antarctica, I wanted to keep in close touch by radio about the progress of their trip.

Just before we embarked on the voyage, I had a sleepless night when I learned that twenty-one boxes containing the vital special parkas and film supplies had not arrived. The lack of the parkas would be a serious danger; the lack of the film would be disastrous to the morale of everyone. By some miracle, the boxes arrived just in time to load them before we left Christchurch.

With its round bottom, the *Magga Dan* rolled incessantly. At night, I had to wedge myself into the bunk. In the lounge the next day, I was sitting with a full glass of beer, when a pitch sent me across the floor. I managed not to spill a drop until I came to a stop in front of a lady with an ample bosom, onto which the beer was deposited in toto.

We made several scheduled stops at the desolate Chatham and Bounty islands, where we were able to make some worthwhile bird and fur seal counts. We crossed the Antarctic Circle at 8:33 on the evening of January 17, with a proper champagne celebration, and at 9:33 I sighted the first Antarctic petrel, which meant that the pack ice would be less than a hundred miles away. By now, however, our headway against the rough seas was so slow that I began to feel we would have to stick to the South American departures. The track from New Zealand was turning out to be too long, too rough, and too expensive.

When we hit the pack ice, it was thrilling, but our progress became even slower. With the ice, we were able to spot a few seals, and then the dramatic sight of killer whales. But we were now hopelessly behind schedule and would have to condense our itinerary, change our port of return, and shuttle our next group to a more southern spot. Even the sight of a towering iceberg failed to lift my spirits. I wrote in my diary the night of January 19: "The passengers seem to be in a good mood, but I am sort of hit by a depression. The total responsibility one has on a trip like this. I have never before wished that a tour would not materialize, but I am worried about the second tour that follows this one. I really wish they would not go and that I could go back to New York. Looking out the porthole in front of me, I see the Ross Sea stretching for another 480 miles. We pitch badly, and the speed is not above 6 knots (we had counted on 12 to 14). The waves must be about 10 feet high. The *Magga Dan* is not unpleasant, but when she rolls, she is a terrible ship to be in."

There were no sunsets now. The sun skirted the horizon, only dipping below it for a fragment of the day. On the morning of the 21st, the white tower of Mount Erebus, a live volcano that marks the location of McMurdo, appeared directly ahead of us. To the right was Mount Terror and the vast front of the Ross Ice Shelf. You really feel this must be land, which is exactly what the early explorers thought. Our ship rose and broke through the sheet of solid ice ahead of us, and then advanced some twenty feet at a time. Hundreds of killer whales were surrounding us as we entered the small harbor of the McMurdo Sound station. We approached Hut Point moving at only half a knot. The dock loomed ahead, and the bow nuzzled against it. But suddenly we began pivoting to the right and left. After several attempts at maneuvering, the horrible truth became apparent. We were aground on some unknown rock, ice, or lava bed, and we did not know what it was.

The U.S. Coast Guard icebreaker *West Wind* was in the harbor. At four in the morning it tried to pull us off. The operation got absolutely nowhere. With the bow in contact with the dock, I was able to go ashore with Roy Sexton and Captain MacDonald to meet the commanding officer at the base, Captain H. A. Kelley. He gave us a very cool reception. He said he was going to assist us with limited services only because he had been ordered to, not because he wanted to.

McMurdo base is a small city in the wilderness. There are close to a hundred rather untidy buildings, blending Quonset huts, sheds, dormitories, and supply dumps. More than a hundred scientists and navy personnel spend the long black winter here in a two-story dormitorylike building that houses a canteen, bar, micro-supermarket, game room, and cinema, and canned TV reception. Mobility in the winter is dangerous; men can be lost a few yards from a building, with winds of over 150 miles an hour and temperatures dropping below −50° F. In the summer, when the staff of scientists swells to several hundred, conditions and daylight are more benign.

The function of the scientists, most from the National Science Foundation, is research. The function of the navy is to provide support services for them. The navy also held control over our fate. Captain Kelley hardly made us feel at home. I tried to figure out the reason and surmised that we were intruding on their rugged life-style that gave them a heroic image back home.

In spite of the ship's awkward position, we were able to get ashore to visit the scientists in their labs, and to climb to Observation Hill where the cross placed in memory of Robert Falcon Scott rested. All through this, I was worrying about how they were going to get our ship free. For the first time I entered a comment in my diary that was not at all typical: "The grounding is worrying me a lot. I don't know if I should cry! My nerves are getting somewhat tensed."

Efforts to free the *Magga Dan* from the grip of the reef went on. She would not budge. Meanwhile, by radio phone, the press was calling from nearly every area of the world: rumor had it that our ship was sinking, the passengers were in panic, and we were locked in the Antarctic with no way of getting out. This reaction tore at my nerves; we were all safe and dry, but damnably inconvenienced.

By noon on January 23, however, the *Magga Dan* was freed and brought to anchor. Because the ship needed engine repairs, we could not dock and had to go ashore in our lifeboats. I was greatly relieved, however, because we still might be able to meet our schedule back to New Zealand and also complete our tour on the Antarctic shore. Just as I was ready to celebrate our success, I received a radio telegram from Kevin McDonnell aboard the *Navarino,* en route to the Antarctic Peninsula from South America with another group of passengers. It read: DUE TO ME-CHANICAL TROUBLE OUR RUDDER DELAYED FIVE DAYS STOP INFORMED TO-DAY ADDITIONAL EIGHT DAYS DELAYED STOP CANCELLED TOUR TODAY MAKING ARRANGEMENTS FOR PASSENGERS TO RETURN HOME. MCDON-NELL.

No sooner had that cable arrived than I received another from the Lindblad New York office: IS MAGGA DAN GROUNDED URGENTLY RE-QUEST DETAILS SO CAN ANSWER INQUIRIES. Here was a major built-in problem: the domino theory. If one part of an intricate plan went wrong, the others following it could tumble. Not only were the logistics and travel arrangements thrown into a cocked hat, but the job of notifying all involved, including friends, relatives, and travel offices, often flooded our capacity to handle it. With two major setbacks at the same time, the problem was doubled. If we could not get back to New Zealand for our second trip, it would be tripled. Meantime, our cost in refunds and hotel and transportation guarantees would multiply by logarithms.

While the mechanics continued to work on the engine, I went on with the planned visit to the New Zealand base, where we were cordially received. Then, with the engine finally repaired, I planned a stop at the two historic huts still standing: Scott's hut at Cape Evans and Shackleton's hut at Cape Royds.

We could not enter Scott's hut, which he built in 1911, but peeking through the windows we saw how beautifully preserved it was. Tons of canned foods were still unopened, and unbelievably, still edible. There was everything from Kilverts' Pure Lard and Hartley's Red Plum to Moir's Roasted and Boiled Mutton. At Cape Royds, we visited Shackleton's hut, built in 1908 after he had tried to reach Hut Point in his ship *Nimrod.*

But we had no time to dally. There were only seven days to make the 2200 miles back to Port Bluff in New Zealand. At most, we could make only 220 miles a day, if we were lucky. By cancelling a stop at the Balleny Islands, I figured we could make New Zealand one day late, but in time to board the passengers for the next trip.

Our passengers seemed happy, but we began to have problems with the crew. The captain became morose and the stewards became mutinous. We had a drunken deck officer who also turned out to be a flasher. But we reached Port Bluff on time and prepared to turn the ship around for the next cruise almost immediately.

I had learned a lot, but the most important knowledge for me was that I could no longer depend on chartered ships. I not only needed a ship that could attack the Antarctic, but one that could do the same with the Arctic, the Amazon, the islands of Indonesia, the Indian Ocean, and anywhere else we could find unusual harbors whose secrets could be unveiled on an intimate basis for people who preferred learning with their travel.

At this point I began dreaming of the *Lindblad Explorer.* I could visualize exactly the kind of ship I needed—sturdy, tough, comfortable, and friendly. Almost immediately after the shaky voyage of the *Magga Dan,* I was on the phone to Scandinavian shipbuilders asking for bids to bring the idea to life. I wasn't quite sure how I could finance the project, but I was dead sure it would work. I knew that even the most careful preparations can sometimes fail at the most unexpected times. But my philosophy is that without these risks, nothing can be accomplished.

VII

$\mathcal{E}$ASTER $\mathcal{I}$SLAND
Labor of Love

ALL the time our hectic Antarctic adventures and misadventures were going on, we were expanding and juggling many new projects as our volume grew and our staff expanded. By mid-1967, we had grown from a staff of three to a staff of thirty-two. Rather than expand piecemeal, I found a building at 133 East Fifty-fifth Street, and the owners were kind enough to name it the Lindblad Travel Building. This would add to the overhead, but I felt that the more we ploughed back into the business, the healthier it would become. We had started with 500 square feet; we now had 4300.

Already I had transferred our successful African Wing Safari idea to Brazil to take travelers into the seldom-visited Mato Grosso and Amazon Basin. As part of the project, I found a sixty-three-foot riverboat to serve as a ''boatel'' on a remote Amazon tributary called the Araguaya River, or River of Death. It created great interest and provided relative comfort. Further, we set up trips to Norway and Sweden and to the little-visited parts of Lapland. To that we added tours to Colombia, Peru, and Ecuador, which were full of surprises for visitors who knew little about the real South America. Meanwhile, we did not neglect our established Journeys into Antiquities in Egypt, Jordan, Lebanon, and

Greece, as well as the American Archives and the around-the-world garden tours, plus a whole new approach to visiting the U.S.S.R.

All during the complicated logistics of these ventures, I found myself on the road most of the time, leaning on Sonja, Kevin McDonnell, and the staff to keep an anchor to windward. Intent on keeping the leadership we held in the travel industry, I never stopped looking for new ideas.

My ceaseless traveling, however, had a severe effect on my personal life. Sonja was doing invaluable work in keeping the enterprise stable in the face of my peripatetic but necessary convolutions all around the world. The result was that our marital relationship suffered. We grew farther apart emotionally, but we continued to retain our business relationship.

There are dozens of reasons that a marriage can deteriorate, and much of the time no one is at fault. Both Sonja and I were strong-minded. As a result we found ourselves in competition with each other. We remained married, in name only, but our separation became very real, both physically and emotionally. As we went our separate ways, we stayed friends and partners. For me, this was very lucky because I still depended heavily on Sonja.

After my Antarctic conference with the Chilean officials back in 1964, my most passionate desire was to bring into being the first established tours of Rapa Nui, more commonly known in much of the world as Easter Island. As one of the most exciting archaeological sites in the world—and the most isolated—its mysteries were so hidden that they defied the most expert studies. By 1967, my interest had grown even stronger. Easter Island's nearest populated neighbors are Pitcairn Island of *Bounty* fame, 1300 miles to the west, and Juan Fernández—Robinson Crusoe's island—1600 miles to the southeast. It is a flyspeck on the map, only eight miles wide and fourteen miles long, surrounded by one million square miles of Pacific Ocean, and more than 2300 miles from the coast of Chile. Tahiti is over 2600 miles to the west.

Easter Island is the only island in the south Pacific where any writing developed, but the strange and delicate hieroglyphics inscribed on "rongo-rongo" tablets have not been decoded and still remain a mystery. No one yet knows how the island ever became populated, with its vast distances from any landmass. Thor Heyerdahl's theory is that the Incas came from Peru to Easter Island by way of the Marquesas Islands, near Tahiti. Heyerdahl and his balsa raft *Kon Tiki* proved that the Marquesas, 2000 miles farther west of Easter Island, are reachable from Peru in a flimsy craft like this. The walls of the huge stone altars on Easter Island are constructed identically to the walls of temples in Peru. The enormous stones are fitted together so precisely, without mortar, that it is impossible to slide a knife blade into many of the cracks. Also, the grass growing in the craters is a papyrus known as totora that grows in Peru's Lake Titicaca.

The giant stone statues on Easter Island, up to sixty feet in height, with their mysteriously pursed lips, tilted noses, and blind eyes, are solemn testimony to an extraordinary culture.

The statues, or moais, were patiently and skillfully chipped out by stone chisels made of a black rock called obsidian. To transport them from the volcanic quarry called Rano Raraku and bring them into an upright position seems impossible in a Stone Age time. Thor Heyerdahl, however, with the cooperation of the island's mayor, showed how it *could* have been done by levering up the moai inch by inch, as small stones were placed under it. The pile of stones would grow until the giant could be tipped upright. With some of the moais as tall as six-story buildings, and with hundreds of statues and ahus, or stone altars, rimming the island, their presence there remains inexplicable.

Some historians are convinced that there have been three groups of settlers from Stone Age times. First, there were the pre-Inca settlers who crossed from South America on rafts like the *Kon Tiki*. Next, there were the true Polynesians from the Marquesas Islands, where the curious custom of earlobe stretching was prevalent. Wedges were inserted in the lobes and increased in size until the ears hung almost shoulder-length. What is most interesting is that the giant moais also have ears of this length. The so-called Long Ear settlers soon faced short-eared Polynesian arrivals, who were thought to have massacred the Long Ears and then toppled and smashed the statues that they regarded as demons. There is no answer to the observation made by the earliest explorers that the Long Ears they discovered there in the 1700s were actually white, with European features. There is no full evidence of the moais being religious figures, and many believe they represented departed ancestors rather than gods.

The Tahitians who arrived during the nineteenth century called the island Rapa Nui, after another Polynesian island called Rapa. The name has stuck as far as the Polynesians are concerned. When the first Dutch explorers dropped anchor off the shores in 1722, they discovered a cheerful trait that the islanders considered as "sharing." A delegation of the natives came aboard Captain Roggeveen's vessel, and within seconds, several of them snatched the hats and caps of the seamen from their heads and dove back in the water with the booty.

Half a century after the Dutch came, the Spaniards arrived for a brief stay in 1770 under orders from King Carlos III. They found little of interest on the lonely windswept island, but they renamed it San Carlos, and halfheartedly annexed it for the Spanish crown.

Four years later, Captain James Cook sailed in to replenish his stock of food and water. There was little of either. Like the Spaniards, the English were amazed at the giant statues that towered so high with their inscrutable sphinxlike faces and cylindrical ten-ton topknots of red stone balancing on their heads. "It was incomprehensible to me," Cook wrote, "how such great masses could be formed by a set of people among whom we saw no tools."

It wasn't until 1886 that some kind of inventory was made of the statues by a young American seaman who was paymaster on the U.S.S. *Mohican.* In the eleven days he was there, he catalogued 555 of the giants, but by this time they were lying helpless on the ground, some of them beheaded. All had been pushed down from their stone altars in such a way that many of the statues' backs had been broken by the strategic placement of a fulcrum rock.

In 1888 the Chilean government finally annexed the island, without protest from Spain or any other country. As Captain Cook had said: "No nation need contend for the honour of the discovery of this island.'' When it was annexed, no one had sorted out the confused history, which remains as puzzling as it is fascinating.

In my original negotiations with the Chilean authorities, I had not only been able to charter the *Navarino* for further Antarctic journeys, but to arrange to visit another isolated group of islands, Darwin's Galápagos. I would concentrate first on Easter Island by air, but the Galápagos development would follow quickly. These islands where Darwin had collected much of his finest data among the isolated species there were intriguing in a different way.

The problem with both locations was transportation and facilities for travelers. Ship travel alone was slow and inadequate. In 1967, Easter Island was a remote appendage of Chile with a mixed sort of Polynesian population of just over a thousand souls. For years, its only visitor was a supply boat of the Chilean navy that arrived once a year. The U.S. Air Force contingent, supporting a NASA tracking station there for the Gemini-Titan missions, was extremely isolated. Major supplies for the twenty-man unit were dropped by parachutes from C-13s out of Panama, a hundred packs at a time. The shoreline was unprotected and uninviting, with no harbors. Supplies had to be unloaded on barges tossing in precarious open seas. A primitive runway was being built in the face of extreme supply difficulties. Air navigation to Easter Island was ticklish. If you missed the mark, there was no alternative airport whatever in the 2300-mile trip from the Chilean mainland.

With no airstrip ready, no accommodations, and no personal survey possible, I was told that bringing tourists there would be just about impossible. But my resolve was as strong as the facilities were weak. I gathered around me everyone in Chile who knew anything about Easter Island. There was Gonzalo Figueroa, who as a young archaeologist from Santiago University had come with Thor Heyerdahl in the mid-1950s on his Aku-Aku expedition to the island. Dr. Figueroa was invaluable in helping me frame a meaningful approach to the project. As a Chilean, he was also able to establish close relations with the Chilean authorities, a critical need for the success of the project.

There was Roberto Parrague, a general in the Chilean air force. His interest was long-range navigation. In 1950 he was the first man ever to try to land a plane on Easter Island. He brought in his amphibian PBY-5A on a partially cleared airstrip, even though he couldn't take off and had to return home on a navy supply ship. His advice on our bringing in a chartered Lan-Chile DC-6B would make it possible to conduct our first tour there.

In the United States, there was Dr. William Mulloy, head of the Department of Archaeology at the University of Wyoming. He had discovered the precise stonework of the altars on the southeastern shore of the island. None of these stone monuments had been found on any of the thousands of other Polynesian islands in the Pacific. Dr. Mulloy's carbon dating of fire remnants at the sites showed them to be dated in mid-800 A.D. There was also Carleton Smith, the archaeologist from the University of Kansas, whose carbon-dating measurements unraveled more rich information on the culture.

Without such expertise, the tours I had planned would be shallow. What's more, I wanted to gather every scrap of information before setting up the first trip. Although it would involve tremendous expense on a risky venture, I flew all of these experts to New York in February 1967 to discuss the historical and archaeological background, and the practical aspects as well. I did not want to take some fifty tourists at a time into the unknown without thorough reconnaissance. I had not even solved the air transportation problem when we met.

From General Parrague, I learned that we would have to rebuild the DC-6B to install a dome for celestial navigation. Since the trip would be over nine hours from Chile, we would have to take out the seats and install sleeperettes. And since expert celestial navigation was so important in hitting this speck of dust in the Pacific, we had to borrow several Lufthansa navigators from West Germany to handle that assignment. Strangely enough, they all bore the title of "doctor."

There were absolutely no accommodations on the island. It was almost as bare as the Antarctic. But there was available the same idea I had put into effect in Africa: the tented safari. My only choice was to buy and equip a complete tent city for fifty people.

Not only would we have to build the tent city, but we also would have to transport everything there before the first tour, including silver, glasses, linen, beds, and mattresses. We would also have to build toilets and showers. Louis-Alberto Aldunate, the head of the Chilean National Tourist organization, suggested that we construct a "casino," a recommendation that almost stopped me in my tracks until I learned that this was a term used to refer to a dining hall, or more accurately, a mess hall. Furthermore, no vessel was available at the time to take all these supplies, especially lumber, which was nonexistent on this almost treeless island. To solve this problem, the Chilean military authorities, who were cooperating with the U.S. Navy to bring supplies to the U.S. base, successfully arranged to ship our supplies on a U.S. navy transport called the *Wyandot*. It would sail out of New London en route to the Antarctic, with a stopoff at Easter. Without Chilean approval of this accommodation I would not have been able to ship a teacup.

These arrangements took months of conferences and cables before I could learn if we had the volume of business that could support the operation. I advertised these unique tours widely and waited. It didn't take long to find out that the response was overwhelming. Reservations for the tours poured in. We were booked solid to bring forty-eight clients every two weeks for months in advance, except in the rainy season of June and July. The cost for the land arrangements in the late 1960s was $570 for thirteen days, which provided a gross of over $50,000 a month.

But the advance supply problem was difficult in the face of Easter Island's rugged coastline. Supply vessels have to remain in the open sea in heavy swells. When the *Wyandot* reached there, supplies for what amounted to a complete hotel had to be unloaded. When I got word that this had been accomplished, I breathed more easily.

Our first expedition was set up for April 3, 1967. It would consist of a contingent of forty-six passengers and several Chilean officials who had never visited the island before. Lecturers on our expedition would be Bill Mulloy and Gonzalo Figueroa. Neither of them had visited there for some time, and they were anxious to get back to the site of their initial research and studies. The Lindblad group would arrive in Santiago first for a cultural tour of museums and sites before boarding our chartered Lan-Chile plane.

There was a lot at stake. Lan-Chile planned a test flight in our chartered plane under the supervision of the Chilean air force one week before our first tour departure. No plane of this size had yet landed on the new airstrip, and the test alone was of more than casual interest.

This advance flight would consist only of Chilean military officers, including General Parrague, and myself and Esperanza Rivaud, my then researcher and constant companion from Argentina. She had been of enormous help in making arrangements not only for Antarctica, Easter Island, and later the Galápagos Islands, but also for extensive tours deep into the little-known parts of South America. Her knowledge of the offbeat areas of the continent was invaluable, as was her ability to speak fluent Spanish.

The test flight in the Lan-Chile DC-6B took nine hours, flying by celestial navigation at night, sighting by stars to arrive just after sunrise. The view at dawn was spectacular, with rugged cliffs sloping steeply into the deep ocean water, with no customary barrier reef. Triangular in shape, the island has three major volcanic cones rising up some 1400 feet from the bottom of the Pacific. The talus slopes of these cones intersect to form the central part of the island—beds of coria and tuff interspersed with extensive lava flows.

We came in for a smooth landing at Hangaroa on the edge of the Pacific shore near the volcano Rano Kao, a barren sweep of land that welcomed this first arrival of a commercial plane. Esperanza and I waited in our seats until the military group had disembarked from the plane, then we gathered our luggage and stepped out onto the portable ramp. We were surprised to see that the military men had already dispersed, apparently having been whisked off to the barracks or village, neither of which were in sight.

We stood for a moment waiting for someone to show up, when suddenly a bearded man with a long white Capuchin robe appeared in the distance, walking slowly toward us with calm and dignity. When he introduced himself as Father Sebastian I felt as if I were meeting an old friend, for I had read about him at length in Thor Heyerdahl's book as a major contributor to the expedition. As a specialist in ancient languages, he had mastered more of the legends and lore of the islands than any other person, and was in the process of painstakingly cataloguing the moais and ahus.

We would learn more about his work later. Meanwhile, I looked for the tent city that was to have been set up by the labor force working for the Chilean navy at our expense. It was nowhere to be seen.

"Ah, yes," said Father Sebastian when I asked him about it, "the material did arrive, but it is all put in a storage shed. I'm afraid they have not been able to start the job."

This was a real shocker. The tour group had already reached Chile and was due to arrive in a few days. I could picture nearly fifty clients arriving for a week's stay with nowhere to sleep, wash, or eat except in the DC-6B.

The site for the tent camp was flat and barren, near the airstrip and the Pacific shore, a large open area sloping down to the sea. It was surrounded by archaeological remnants, including a fascinating cave with paintings that had been carbon-dated back 400 years. But the square pyramid-shaped tents were still in the storage shed, while the corps of workmen appeared to be waiting for some kind of cosmic signal to begin setting up the canvas city. With the imminent arrival of our first group, I drew on the aid of Father Sebastian and Mayor Rapu to initiate a crash program.

I got one of the tents out of the storage shed and showed the workers how to put it together. They began setting up the rest of the twenty-five tents, while I supervised the building of the "casino" mess hall, and expedited the installation of flush toilets, showers, and a septic tank. Fortunately, there were no glass windows required for the mess hall, and we were able to complete the job, including benches and tables, within forty-eight hours. To accomplish the task, we worked through two nights in the light of jeep and truck headlights.

In exchange for our transporting extra supplies for the U.S. tracking station, we were able to bargain for ice cubes and coolers. The station formed a strange contrast to the primitive atmosphere of the rest of the island. Because of its sensitive electronic instruments, the base was equipped with three generators that were able to supply the island with electricity. In spite of the poor supply situation, there were mobile homes and a three-story prefabricated structure for housing the personnel and the complicated tracking equipment. The U.S. commander was friendly enough, although wary of how our intrusion would affect his operation.

By the time the DC-6B bearing our first clients was due for arrival, I was confident that we had all our problems well in hand. We had already shipped a large supply of canned and dried food months before, along with enough wines and liquor to celebrate the occasion. Most important, the arriving plane would be carrying a full week's supply of fresh food, meats, pastry, and all the staples for the menu.

All the villagers of the central settlement of Hangaroa appeared as excited as I was about the pending arrival. Hangaroa is a small village with tidy white houses of cinder block or wood and tin roofs that serve to collect water. It houses most of the 1200 islanders. The church is also of white cinder block, and an impressive but modest school was on the drawing boards to be built two years after we arrived there in 1967. The islanders were known as Pascuenses, as they had been so dubbed by a Chilean naval officer. Over two-thirds are of Polynesian stock, sprinkled with Chilean, French, English, German, or Italian blood from the lusty visits of seamen over the years, some of whom remained. Unlike other Polynesian islanders, they have a minimum of dark pigmentation or fuzzy hair. Nearly a third are relatively recent arrivals from Chile, encouraged by incentive pay to colonize the island. In general, the Pascuenses are a hardy stock, many of whom are as fair as Europeans, and most of whom are cheerful and ingenuous. They dress in a mixture of Chilean modern and flowered Tahitian classic, plus trade-offs from rare visiting ships.

The night before our first group was to arrive, I went over the plans for a rousing welcome. I was intent on making the Easter Island project one of Lindblad Travel's best ventures.

Thanks to Father Sebastian, we were able to line up genuine historical festivities. He had been on the island since 1935, and as a linguist had dug deeply into the legends, arts, archaeology, and sociology of the people. He had patiently numbered all the statues—over 600 of them—plus every ahu on the island, and was continuing to probe how this totally isolated land had ever become populated. Scientists who came to study leaned on him for help.

He had done much to keep alive the music and traditions that were becoming eroded by Chilean discouragement of the Pascuense language and customs. He prepared both dancers and musicians for the plane's arrival, including costumes and guitars that were reminiscent of Tahitian dancers and musicians. The girls wore grass skirts adorned with white chicken feathers, with garlands of frangipani flowers around their heads. They wore breast covering of the same material as the skirts, although this was not the general rule for their own free-spirited festivals. The boys wore loin cloths and flower crowns on their heads.

Just after dawn, the DC-6B appeared in the sky on schedule, making a lazy circle over the island to give the passengers a preview. By this time, almost the entire population of the island, over a thousand strong, had assembled, most of them on horseback. When the plane touched down, the guitarists and dancers sprang into action, singing Polynesian songs and dancing not unlike the hula dancers of Hawaii. The passengers were more than surprised at the colorful reception, as the dancers placed garlands of flowers around their necks.

After I had greeted them all, I spoke with the crew to check on the vital supplies that were to arrive, including all the fresh food, pastry, and staples. At this point I learned that the plane had been overweight before takeoff, and they had had to offload all of the supplies. Mrs. Mary Barada, a retired secretary from Baltimore, and her brother, Dr. James McC. Finney, had watched the food being unloaded at Santiago with a measure of sadness, since the butter for all the sandwich lunches for the entire week had to be left behind with the rest of the delicacies. Later in the week, they were pleasantly surprised with the substitute we used: mashed avocado, setting a whole new trend in sandwich making.

We were now in a bind. There were forty-six ravenous passengers with only our supplementary food available. Esperanza went scurrying around the island, and was able to buy up enough local eggs for breakfast, and we had adequate supplies on hand to make sandwiches for lunch. But one of the highlights of the trip was to be a festive welcoming dinner not only for the travelers but also for the mayor, governor, and several officers from the U.S. tracking station, including the commander, the medical officer, and the chief of the construction team. I went immediately to the cook to see what we could possibly serve for this gala affair out of our limited supplies.

He looked at me sadly and said, "Spaghetti, sir."

I said, "Spaghetti with what?"

He said, "Spaghetti with nothing."

The menu looked rather dim until I was able to borrow from the U.S. base a supply of frozen chopped meat that we would replace on our next trip. We mixed this with our ample stock of preshipped spaghetti, and then proceeded to turn the event into a festive occasion regardless, with cocktails thanks to the base station's ice, and plenty of wine for the diners. The wine presented a bit of a problem. I had told the waiter to chill the white wine by filling the cooler with ice and putting the bottles in it. When the governor ordered white wine, the waiter ceremoniously opened the bottle and promptly poured it into the cooler on top of the ice cubes.

On the following day, the food situation became critical. I could not expect our group to continue eating nothing but spaghetti for the entire week, and we set out to see what could be done. Esperanza discovered a large sheep farm on the island, but the sheep were slaughtered only on certain days. The next few days were not among those. When she went to the farm, however, she discovered that sheep could be bought on the hoof. Without ceremony or experience, she set about slaughtering the animals herself with the help of expert skinners who were willing to work with her.

I was able to go ahead with my idea of arranging a traditional dinner for a representative group of some twenty Pascuenses selected by the mayor and governor. I had always made it a point to entertain in this way where it was appropriate, especially in remote places where personal contact with the people could be made in a mutually pleasant way. I counted on the local leaders to pick a democratic assortment from as many different groups in the area as possible, providing a congenial way to share ideas and customs.

I knew that Easter Islanders often held the equivalent of the Hawaiian luau, called here a sau-sau and similar to an old-fashioned New England clambake. At a sau-sau, there would be dancing and singing of traditional songs in addition to the feasting. Father Sebastian, as the outstanding scholar of the culture of the island, was enthusiastic and volunteered to organize not only the music and dancing, but the event itself. A special treat would be the local lobsters that could be caught at night along the shore with lanterns. These were actually large crayfish, without claws but tasty.

While Father Sebastian organized the affair, I went to Mayor Rapu to determine the cost. We talked about what would be served. The menu would include sweet potatoes, corn, pork, lobsters, lamb, and beef, to be steamed in open pits covered by wet banana leaves. When I asked him about the cost, he took out a pencil and did some figuring. Then he smiled and said, ''This will come to about $3000, Señor Lindblad.'' I could not understand this amount, and I pointed this out to the mayor. ''How could this be, with only forty-six passengers and a few invited guests?''

The mayor smiled again and said, ''You see a sau-sau is for *everybody* on the island. We need several hundred kilos of food to serve all the people. There will be at least 800 people on the island who will come. I'm sure you will have no less.''

When night arrived the pits were steaming and the fires burning to create a strange and exotic atmosphere on this tiny island, which in its original ancient tongue was called Te Pito-o-te-henua, which translates into ''Navel of the World.''

In the glare of the fires, it was almost impossible to tell how many Easter Islanders were gathered in a ring outside in the darkness. You could sense them there, rather than see them. I asked Mayor Rapu, and all he said was, ''There must be hundreds.'' I was told they had come from all over the island. Nearly everyone on Easter Island has a horse, and you could occasionally hear a whinny on the periphery of the fires. Aside from that there was mostly silence. Later, as we waited for the cooks to remove the steaming banana leaves from the pits, a few strains of a Polynesian song sprang up in isolated pockets of the almost invisible people as they grew bolder and moved closer to the fires. There was still no way of knowing how many there were, and the atmosphere was somewhat eerie.

Soon the helpers began removing the banana leaves. As they did the crowd pressed in closer. The mayor was right, there must have been hundreds. They were of all ages and sizes, including children, some in Pascuense clothes, others in garb brought over from the mainland. Then, as if a silent signal had been given, the crowd leaped around and over our group toward the pits.

The feast was devoured by them in minutes, as they ate in great good spirits, laughing and singing as they did. None of the tourists and guests was able to salvage as much as a single bite.

But by the time the Polynesian music and dancing began, all was forgotten. The performances were enchanting, even on an empty stomach. As the guitarists played, the dancers clapped their hands softly, moving their bodies gracefully and singing in soft, rich tones. Occasionally they would hop on one leg, as they jerked the other in rhythm with the music. It was often monotonous and in minor tones, with phrases repeated many times to create a trancelike effect.

Father Sebastian's work in resurrecting the fast-disappearing art of the island shone brightly throughout the evening. After it was over, our group retreated to the dining pavilion, where we enjoyed the only food we could assemble: mashed potato flakes with dry milk and water. It was not quite the lavish sau-sau feast we had anticipated, but no one complained and everyone seemed content.

Under Dr. Mulloy's and Dr. Figueroa's guidance, our itinerary would take us by truck to the crater of Rano Kao and to the ceremonial village of Orongo, inhabited once in prehistoric times, where nearly fifty stone houses remain and elaborate petroglyphs reveal in high relief the god Makemake and a strange man wearing a bird mask. On the following day, we would visit the volcanic cone of Punapau, where the huge cylindrical hats that topped many of the statues were carved and fashioned. On the third day, there would be a visit to the quarry of Rano

Raraku, where most of the 1000-odd statues were carved. Each day of our exploration would reveal something new, until all the important features of the island were seen and explained.

We started out on the first day, and approached the shoreline along a new road that was just being built to eventually circle the island. It was being constructed under the supervision of the governor as part of his five-year plan to grow citrus fruit and pineapple, and to generally improve the lot of the islanders. The engineer governor was an intelligent man, a good man, but seemed not too perceptive about the value of the archaeological treasures.

Figueroa had arranged with the Chilean officials that the road would not be built closer than a hundred feet to the priceless ahus along the shore. There were at least 450 of these, mostly overlooking the sea. What lay near or under them had never been fully explored, a project for the future. But the Chilean government had failed to define what these ahus were, or where the ruins extended. We suddenly came on the road under construction and found that the workers were scraping up archaeological debris as a foundation for the road.

Bill Mulloy and Figueroa went into shock. I joined them in dismay. We got together that same evening to figure out what could be done. Learning of our anger, the governor became furious. He refused to stop the road building, and somehow we couldn't get it across that the damage being done was unthinkable. Because of the pricelessness of the threatened sites, we decided to take urgent action. There was a civilian radio transmitter on the island, and we sent a message to Chile's President Frei, telling him of the crisis and imploring him to take fast action. We waited impatiently until the next morning, when his reply arrived. Fortunately, he proclaimed an immediate moratorium, and the road building was stopped. Our popularity with the governor sank to a new low, but he was replaced shortly afterward. He was a conscientious man, but his blindness in this regard could have caused a major archaeological tragedy for the world.

Our first journey to Easter Island was a marked success, in spite of the problems. Departures every two weeks continued. Minor mishaps continued too, but the spirit of the Lindblad passengers always remained high. On one of the early trips, Mrs. Alva Gimbel, the sprightly eighty-year-old widow of Bernard Gimbel, of the famous store chain, jumped up to join the dancers at the traditional sau-sau and promptly twisted her knee, almost breaking it. Treated by the German doctor on the island, she was told that she had to stay off it completely and dispense with the rest of the tour.

"I'm sorry, doctor," she said, "but if you will just tape this up, I'm going to visit every place on this island, come hell or high water. I came here to visit Easter Island, and you forget that at my age, the likelihood of my coming back isn't all that great!"

She continued with the rest of the group under great difficulty but with indomitable cheer. To add to her difficulties, the tent she occupied collapsed in a heavy rain, and the only way to untangle the mess was for me to slit the canvas carefully. When I had finished, Mrs. Gimbel poked her head out roaring with laughter and enjoying the adventure. She went on several of our tours and always set an example for the others. Whenever things went wrong, she looked for the best side of the situation.

On another tour in our second year, we faced the same sort of invasion that took place on our first sau-sau. This time I decided to give just a small private dinner in our dining pavilion for the governor, a few Chilean officials, and the wife of the American ambassador, Mrs. Edward Malcom Korry. I had known the Korrys when he was ambassador to Ethiopia, and I had invited her as a special guest on this trip. In contrast to our first sau-sau the year before, in which the islanders enjoyed the food so much, this dinner was to be a bit formal, with engraved invitations and a rather elaborate Swedish smorgasbord. The group also included members of the Archives of American Art who were used to a touch of elegance, and I brought with us on the plane beluga caviar, smoked salmon, herring, and all kinds of special delicacies to satisfy a gourmet palate.

As we sat down at the tables, I noticed shadows looming outside the open windows of the dining hall. I could sense what was coming, even though this was not the traditional sau-sau. I was sitting next to the governor and the wife of the ambassador, and I warned them that we would have to serve ourselves quickly if we were going to have anything to eat at all. I told them to pass the word along that I would stand up at the proper time and clap my hands, so that the guests could reach the smorgasbord before a possible onslaught. It was not that I wanted to exclude the gentle people of Easter Island or be rude to them. It was simply that this was a special occasion and we weren't prepared for extra guests.

The moment I clapped my hands, the Polynesians emerged, leapfrogged over us, and devoured everything in a hand-to-mouth rush. Fortunately, we had an ample supply of canned pork and beans, and again the invited guests took everything in good spirits.

I learned several things that evening. The first was that you simply don't give private parties on Easter Island. If you invite the officials you invite the populace. The second was that no one on a tour gets disturbed by an unavoidable upset. People get angry only if they think they are being shortchanged. The third thing I learned was that Easter Islanders still maintain the long tradition of sharing things, even to the point of what could be considered purloining. But it is all done in the most amiable way.

Through the 1960s, I continued to improve the facilities of our tent city, and then began an intensive program to try to restore the moais and ahus and bring the island back to its original splendor with the help of Father Sebastian, Bill Mulloy, and Gonzalo Figueroa. What we needed most was to carry the effort to the attention of the world. In 1969, I was able to persuade a team from *Paris Match,* together with Francisco Jose Oyarzun of the Chilean Foreign Office, to come there in an attempt to raise public interest in the restoration. They came and photographed all the important sites, and started to fly back to France by way of Chile and the Caribbean. As their Air France 707 approached the airport at Guadeloupe on March 6, 1968, it crashed into the side of a mountain called Soufrière, carrying fifty-one passengers and eleven crew members to their deaths. The entire team and all the film were lost. It was a tragic loss of able and dedicated journalists.

I continued to work hard in trying to persuade UNESCO to contribute to the restoration while Mr. Oyarzun did likewise through official channels, but without success. Finally, I was able to interest the International Fund for Monuments, which had done remarkable work in stabilizing the Leaning Tower of Pisa and helping to preserve Venice in the face of intruding waters. It was headed by a retired army colonel, James Gray, a former paratrooper who was dedicating all his efforts to preserving historical sites. He had raised the funds to bring back the twelfth-century churches in Lalibela in Ethiopia. With his help, I was able to set up a special Easter Island committee within his organization to create funds for the work urgently needed there.

From the first tour, I had decided to turn all of the profits from our Easter Island operation over to the project to restore the monuments on the island. Several Lindblad clients contributed on their own. Eventually, we were able to gather over $500,000 for the project. With the Chilean government contributing to the fund, it became possible to make an archaeological inventory of the treasures and bring many of the major sites back to their original condition. My conviction is that intelligent tourism can preserve the past by this kind of restoration, so that instead of damaging a historical site, tourism can enrich it. As the Lindblad tours continued, I was able to establish a permanent post there to handle the tours on location as they arrived. My love for the island grew so much that I never regretted putting back more into its preservation than I took out in profit. The dedication of men like Father Sebastian, Gonzalo Figueroa, James Gray, and Bill Mulloy made all this possible. There is no way to measure the work they did there in money.

The obstacles we faced in establishing and continuing the tours were many. We eventually brought in our own fishing boats to implement our food supply, plus several four-wheel-drive trucks to cover the island and aid in the restoration. I remember when our trucks were first being unloaded from the supply ship to the barges in the ocean swells of the unprotected anchorage. The ship had to wait for almost a week in the rough seas before the unloading could even be attempted. I watched as the ship suddenly rolled and pitched in a wave, and one of our trucks smashed against the side of the ship and broke to pieces. The ship had to wait at anchor for several more weeks until the other trucks could be lifted off. Later, on shore, I was standing on the back of one of the trucks when it passed under a low-strung electrical wire. My back was turned to it, and it caught the back of my neck and sent me sprawling on the ground with a severe neck burn.

For the first two years, our lumbering chartered DC-6B carried Lindblad Travel visitors to share the Easter Island experience. With improvements on the runway and with a new instrument landing system, the 707s began to arrive en route to Tahiti. Of course this was a mixed blessing. Prudent and intelligent people have to realize that the unlimited exploitation of a tourist site is not progress. It might make one generation rich, but it will impoverish future generations.

If anyone felt this way about Easter Island it was Father Sebastian. In his late seventies, he was working spiritually and physically for its welfare and resurrection. He continued to work with us in raising the funds that were desperately needed. It cost between $1000 and $5000 merely to lift up a single moai to its original position. To restore the priceless ahus ran higher: $20,000 or more. In spite of failing health, he volunteered to come to the United States in 1969 to help raise more funds. He would be escorting a ten-ton moai head that we could display in New York City to encourage more donations. His journey came to an end in a very sad but inspiring way.

Just before his trip was arranged, I had hired Geraldine Hotchner, the former wife of the writer A. E. Hotchner, to work with the International Fund for Monuments on the Easter Island project. She had told me she was suffering from cancer and did not have long to live. Her dream was to work on a worthwhile project during her last days. In spite of her illness, she was lively and capable, and went down to Easter Island to work with Father Sebastian.

She and Father Sebastian became inseparable. She accompanied him on the trip back and set up the arrangements for a new fund-raising campaign. Father Sebastian had never been to the United States and had never flown on a jet before. With his enthusiasm and natural charm, he appeared on the *Today* show and traveled to several cities. A portion of the moai was set up in the plaza of the Seagram building on Park Avenue, where it attracted enthusiastic attention.

But shortly after her arrival back in the United States, Geraldine Hotchner entered the hospital. It was during the Christmas season, and Father Sebastian came to visit in Connecticut. He asked about her health, but I evaded the question because she did not want him to know that she was dying. At the same time, however, Father Sebastian was stricken with pains in his stomach. He too was taken to the hospital for what was thought to be a gallbladder infection. Instead, it turned out to be incurable cancer.

A short time later, on January 8, 1969, both Geraldine Hotchner and Father Sebastian died within the same hour. Father Sebastian's body was flown back to Easter Island by the Chilean air force to be buried there. John Dos Passos, who had come to the island twice with our tours, was so fond of Father Sebastian that he returned for the funeral. "They lifted up their voices and sang in grief," he wrote of the services. "I never attended a burial service where such sincere grief was so beautifully expressed. It didn't sound like any mass we had ever heard." Later, the giant moai head was returned by ship from the United States to Easter Island for its own burial. It was put back in exactly the same position it had been found in, face forward with its mystical features buried in the ground.

I never regarded Easter Island as a business enterprise. I believe that the only way we live on in the memory of others is by what we have been able to accomplish. I know that what all of us did on Easter Island will live on. It is one of the things I have done in my life of which I am most proud.

After Father Sebastian's burial, the political climate in Chile began to change. President Frei could not succeed himself in the 1970 elections. Ambassador Tomic was running, as was Salvador Allende. A right-wing candidate joined in to create a three-way race. I met Allende in Chile at the start of his campaign, and found him to be a very civilized and charming person. He was a Marxist, but entirely independent of Moscow. Tomic, a middle-of-the-roader, was balancing the Right and the Left.

During Allende's campaign I flew with him to Easter Island. He had run many times as an opposition candidate, and I don't think he had any thought of winning. With a three-way race, however, there was a distinct chance. Chile's problems were so deep that none of the aspirants had any real answers to them. Allende convinced me that if he was elected he would run the country on a democratic, constitutional basis. He had no taste for Soviet support, and was planning to follow President Frei's lead in instituting social programs and extending gradual nationalization of foreign mining companies.

He was deeply concerned about the right-wing forces in Chile that were threatening to destroy its constitutional government, unquestionably with CIA, ITT, and industrial support on the part of the copper companies. He indicated that he would be a good friend of the United States and would turn to the Eastern bloc only if he were forced into it by lack of U.S. support.

I was impressed with his sincerity, even though his election would actually spell doom for the Lindblad operation. "I like what you have done for Easter Island," he told me, "and am grateful for it. You realize, however, that we can't have an outsider completely dominate the tour industry, in spite of all you have done. If I win the election, it's only fair to tell you that I'm going to have to ask you to leave and have our government run the tourist operation there."

He spoke without acrimony, only with regret. Although it would amount to a tragic loss for me, I could not feel bitterness for the man. From his point of view he was right. After he was elected in 1970, the inevitable happened. We had to sell our tents, boats, trucks, and equipment at great loss. All of this cut deeply, because my personal joy in what we had accomplished there was greater than in any other project. Now there was nothing but sorrow, but the greatest sorrow was when Allende was toppled by the military in conjunction with the CIA. He was a man who had a deep love for his country, a beautiful country whose democracy and constitution were brutally crushed.

We are still able to continue our tours there, though not as frequently. There are only six departures a year by air, and the *Lindblad Explorer* has included an annual stop there most of the time. Whenever

I return to see the restored monuments and remnants of the island's grand and mysterious culture, I am grateful that I had a chance to contribute. The culture of Easter Island is unparalleled in the world. The cultures of Greece, Rome, Egypt, and other historically rich countries have left splendid treasures. But Easter Island's monuments and undeciphered writings grew in total isolation on a flyspeck of land, with no riches or resources to account for them. To lose Easter Island would be to lose a total civilization unique in the world.

VIII

Darwin's Galápagos
Days of the Iguana

I CONSTANTLY carry in my head a map of the world. I also seem to be able to recall easily airline and shipping schedules, distances and time estimates, and the itineraries of all the concurrent tours that we are sending out all over the world at any single moment. In the days of our expanding explorations, one of my main problems was having my laundry catch up with me. I continued to spend only about thirty days a year in the office.

At the time I was opening up Easter Island in 1967, we had completed two Antarctica cruises with fifty-six passengers each, for a total of thirty-one days each. Simultaneously, we were running twenty-one-day archaeological tours of Scandinavia at a cost of $1395; the Explorer's Tours of Central Asia for forty-four days at a cost of $3650; and Dr. Cyrus Gordon's tours to retrace the route of Abraham from Turkey to Egypt.

Sonja was concentrating on Africa in conjunction with Tony Irwin of our Nairobi office, with almost all the departures sold out. With Fernando Maldonado and Jaime McMahon as tour directors, we were sending monthly tours called On the Inca Road for twenty-six days at a cost of $1835, or to Mato Grasso in Brazil for $2135, all at 1960 prices.

Meanwhile, we were launching our seventh annual Garden Tour, with Fritz and Elizabeth Legler conducting. At the same time I was preparing to scout a score or more islands in the South Pacific, and then move on to Australia and New Zealand to prepare to extend our Antarctic expeditions from down under. I was also expanding our Antarctic expeditions from the South American end, with wildlife tours in Patagonia, Tierra del Fuego, and the Falklands—at that time very peaceful and serene.

Our clientele was becoming more international than ever. Departures were being booked from Argentina, Canada, Chile, Denmark, France, Germany, Great Britain, Guatemala, Italy, Japan, Mexico, Norway, Spain, Sweden, Switzerland, Turkey, and Venezuela. At the time of our first tour to Easter Island in April 1967, I was simultaneously going through the same sort of peregrinations to set up the first historic tour to the Galápagos Islands. These comprise a small archipelago sitting some 600 miles west of Ecuador and are almost as lonely as Easter Island. They are irreplaceable, living laboratories of evolution. On this baker's dozen of islands that straddle the equator, life developed unhindered by man after the land had risen up from the sea in volcanic fury millions of years ago. The islands range in size from the eighty-mile-long Albemarle Island to the tiny Tower Island, barely 25 square miles in area. Overall, the islands cover some 3000 square miles and have a scattered population of only 1300, mostly Ecuadorians.

In the Galápagos, Darwin found the first compelling evidence that led to his 1859 work, *The Origin of Species*. Seabirds, sea lions, and fur seals had changed little from their ancestral types. Giant iguanas looking like miniature dragons swarmed over the rocks and lava. Darwin called them "imps of darkness." Some never moved more than ten feet from the shore and lived on algae. Others stayed on land, munching on unfriendly cactus, and grew up to four or five feet in length, somewhat larger than the marine iguana. Describing the latter, Darwin wrote: "It is a hideous looking creature, of a dirty black color, stupid and sluggish in its movements." But, more significantly, they had learned to adjust to either their land or sea environment, and thus survived.

The first land tortoises he came on were enormous: over 200 pounds each. They were apparently deaf, because they did not hear him approach. Once they saw him, they hissed loudly and pulled in their heads. He climbed on the back of one and rode it, finding it hard to stay on top, carefully measuring the rate of its walk: 360 yards per hour. He watched the tortoises replenish their water supply in a marshy pond, heads fully submerged, gulping great mouthfuls at the rate of ten every minute. But his most startling discovery was that each of the five major islands had separate species of the giant tortoises.

There were other clues to the theories Darwin was to form. Of fifty species of land birds, he discovered twenty-six different varieties of finch, all of them confined exclusively to the Galápagos. Each had a different type of beak for a different sort of foraging. From these observations, Darwin developed his premise: the world and its flora and fauna had not sprung up in a single instant of time, but had evolved. His most important evidence still remains to be examined there by the curious observer.

When Darwin first visited the desolate islands on the H.M.S. *Beagle* in 1835, the principal human inhabitants were Ecuadorian convicts who were the constituents of a Devil's Island prototype in the Pacific. Based on Charles Island, the prisoners were toted to Chatham and other islands for forced labor in raising sugarcane, and were often starved and beaten. It was not surprising that they rose up and hacked their chief oppressor to pieces, a questionable gentleman by the name of Manuel Cobos. The seventy-eight convicts then commandeered a sloop and sailed to Ecuador, where they were put on trial and reconvicted.

In the 1920s, the American naturalist William Beebe brought the archipelago to the attention of the world with his book *Galápagos, World's End*. He wrote so engagingly about the islands that a Norwegian promoter sold the idea of a large colony on Charles and Chatham islands. The idea died in a scene of infighting and murders not long after the colonists discovered the islands to be nothing more than lava, cactus, and weeds, instead of the promised Garden of Eden. Many nationalities tried their hands at colonizing the islands. Pilots, whalers, and eccentrics have come and gone over the years. The Germans came there in 1929 to form a meager colony punctuated by their own set of murders and violence.

But none of this could override the fact that in few places could such a generous selection of wildlife be observed at close range. One of the most charming characteristics of the Galápagos fauna is their fearlessness. Unmolested by predators (except for the tortoises that were harvested by the hungry seamen of the early whaling ships), they have never had to flee for their lives. They accept humans as equals. Nesting seabirds sit for close-up portraits. Sea lions and their pups romp in friendly sport with snorkelers. The only drawback is that sometimes an affectionate sea lion might want to get too affectionate. Mockingbirds and finches will land on your hand and stare at you. The birds will sit and peek at your camera, or unfortunately land on your lens, where you can't film them.

In the spirit of great curiosity, I approached the islands on our first cruise there in July 1967, only a few months after our first foray to Easter Island. I utilized the *Navarino* for the Galápagos run, using Lima, Peru, as our takeoff port. She was a seaworthy ship, comfortable but without frills, and could handle sixty-six passengers, but for comfort I kept the total to forty-six. She had been healed from her wound caused by rudder difficulty en route to the Antarctic.

When I chartered her, inflation was rampant in Chile. Their monetary base, the escudo, ran several hundred per dollar. There was better value in paying cash, and I came from the bank with two suitcases filled with escudos. I drove to the ship at Valparaíso, where I delivered the suitcases and signed the contract. From Valparaíso we cruised to Lima to pick up our forty-six passengers.

The expedition would last twenty-one days, including five days in historic Peru and at sea, at a cost of $1900 per passenger.

I was very pleased with the expert staff I was able to line up for the Galápagos. Not only did we have Roland Clement, vice-president of the National Audubon Society, and Guy Mountfort, international trustee and director of the World Wildlife Fund; we would later add Sir Peter Scott, Renaissance man and naturalist, and again Dr. Roger Tory Peterson with his unsurpassed background in ornithology. Roy Sexton would also be with us. Added to this would be the staff scientists of the Charles Darwin Research Foundation at Academy Bay on Santa Cruz Island, who had years of local experience. No passenger could take our Galápagos trip without gaining vastly expanded scientific knowledge.

Our first port of call was a small Ecuador navy base at Wreck Bay on the island of Chatham. The *Navarino* slipped into the bay cautiously and dropped anchor, while the Chilean captain and I went in by small boat to clear the ship. Even though we were a Chilean vessel, we had sailed from a Peruvian port, which was not likely to endear us to the Ecuadorians. Relations between Ecuador and Peru were strained at the time, after a squabble over Iquitos on the Amazonas River. There had actually been a shooting war only a few months before this. Ecuador was claiming that Peru had conquered the territory and should give it back. Every letter that went out from Ecuador bore a bold rubber stamp across the face reading: AMAZONAS WAS, IS AND WILL FOREVER MORE BE ECUADORIAN TERRITORY.

The commanding officer of the Ecuadorian navy base greeted us stiffly, as we presented the ship's papers. Both the Chilean captain and I were sure they were all in proper order. But in the eyes of our Ecuadorian friends they weren't. They maintained that one important document was missing. We had to admit to the Ecuadorian commander that we did not have it and were at his mercy.

He cleared his throat and said: "Gentleman, I do not like to say this, but I have no other choice than to put you under arrest for entering Ecuadorian waters without the proper papers. I am afraid that you cannot leave this room. I have no other choice."

My thoughts, of course, went immediately to the forty-six passengers on the trip who had made the long journey all the way from North America and had paid out nearly $2000 each for the voyage. The situation did not look good, especially when the commander added, "The regulations are inescapable. The punishment is imprisonment and confiscation of the ship. If you will excuse me, I shall confer with my officers and return. Meanwhile, you must remember you are under arrest."

The Chilean captain and I sat there for half an hour, trying to figure out what we could possibly do. We were obviously at the mercy of bureaucratic red tape, but this could be serious with our limited time. There was no direct recourse to higher officials back in Ecuador, and the commander indicated that he followed the book down to the last line.

When he returned he appeared more affable. He explained that the problem could be solved by payment of a tax, very similar to an airport landing fee. The tax would be based on the tonnage of our ship. Our captain with great alacrity described the *Navarino* as nothing more than a sardine can and quoted a ridiculously low tonnage figure. I don't think he fooled the Ecuadorian commander one bit, but he accepted the figure at face value, perhaps because he felt he had been too stiff with us.

The only other problem was figuring out how much tax we owed. The commander came up with a bewildering formula that neither he nor we could understand. The fine and the tax had to be paid in gold "sucres," and none of us knew how to translate this into the Ecuadorian paper "sucres." It was worked out, however, and we were released.

Back at the ship, there was considerable consternation among the passengers about the long delay. I laughed it off and explained it to them, not revealing my horror at what would have happened if bureaucracy had ruled and we had had to turn back. I always make it a point never to alarm people except in dire emergency. I invited the formerly recalcitrant commander on board for dinner that night, where he grew mellow and happy. He revealed that his wife was Chilean, a factor that had worked to our benefit.

I had already developed a theory as to how we should approach our visit to the Galápagos. The islands were so rich in flora and fauna that a superficial visit would mean little.

Even with a few intrusions since Darwin's time, the Galápagos have remained relatively unmodified by man. Like Antarctica, they have been afforded natural protection from the customary scars left by man. But through the establishment of a national park and the Darwin Research Foundation on Santa Cruz Island, the hope is kept alive that the plants and animals will continue to survive in their original state.

Darwin's finches are the most abundant land birds on the scene. About the size of sparrows, the males are often black and the females brownish-gray with a speckled belly. At first, they look singularly uninteresting, but this group of birds has provided a particular thrill ever since Darwin brought back a collection of them. Darwin postulated that they all came from a common ancestor, but their dissimilarities arose from competition. Each species had been forced into a different ecological niche and had had to adapt to different feeding habits.

Up to ten of the twenty-six species of Darwin's finches are present on a single island, but their adaptation must have taken place after the arrival of one ancestral stock. On our tour, we would be able to observe directly the most dramatic example of adaptive origination of species and to study a working demonstration of evolution.

The giant tortoises, or land turtles, are no less interesting. There are two main types: those with dome-shaped carapaces and short necks, and those with saddle-shaped carapaces and longer necks. The dome shapes are found on Santa Cruz, Chatham, Charles, and south Albemarle, where the highlands support the most lush vegetation on the islands. The saddle shapes exist on Duncan, Abingdon, and the north of Albemarle—arid areas where they feed on cactus pads, stretching their long necks upward.

As on most of our tours, we would be studying all the species of birds on the Galápagos. The most common seabirds are the boobies—"clowns" or "dunces" from the Spanish *bobo*. They have earned the name by their varicolored faces and apparent stupidity in allowing themselves to be robbed of their food.

Boobies and gannets together comprise the family Sulidae. Nesting habits differ widely among the various species. The red-footed boobies on Tower Island sometimes sit on their eggs for as long as 144 hours. In contrast, the masked boobies average only 28 hours. The blue foots on Hood Island sit for a mere 18 hours. Along with the albatross and frigate birds, the boobies dominate the islands. But there are many other exciting birds: petrels, shearwaters, and gulls, the stiff-legged mockingbirds running across the rocks, the herons and the pink flamingos that zoom over calm waters. There are also the Galápagos cormorants, heavier and larger than any others of their kind, but unable to fly. They stand about pathetically and touchingly on the beaches, flapping their stubby, useless wings.

The marine iguanas may enable us to observe the rate at which differentiation proceeds and how evolution works. Hundreds of iguanas, each three, or even four feet long, bask or swarm all over the rocks. It is a weird experience to see them crawl about the shore, with the surf breaking over it. "The chief sound of life here," Melville wrote, "is a hiss."

With little or no food on shore, they slide into the sea and crawl along the shore, chewing the seaweed from the rocks like a dog with a bone. They supplement this with crickets, which they hunt with great skill, along with shrimps and worms. They are fearless and can be approached within inches.

My goal was to have our passengers feel and experience all these fellow creatures with a sense of intimacy based on sound knowledge provided by our experts. Tourism in the Galápagos archipelago must be done from a ship that covers the scattered islands and allows the passengers to disembark in small boats. Arriving there by ship gave us an opportunity to educate the passengers en route on what to observe. The lectures on shipboard also gave us a chance to brief the passengers on respect for the delicate environment.

Roland Clement, an ardent conservationist as well as vice-president of the National Audubon Society, was a biologist whose talks on wildlife management, technology, and land ethics were enriched by his writings on these subjects, which had particular application to the special ecological problems of the Galápagos. Guy Mountfort's talks were drawn from his vast studies in dozens of countries and his expertise in coauthoring *A Field Guide to the Birds of Europe,* which has been translated into thirteen languages. His international experiences brought a broad perspective to the specialized conditions found on the archipelago.

In one way, visiting the Galápagos has had more impact on people than any other journey. I have had people tell me that the visit changed their lives radically because of the experience of observing so closely the interdependence of living things. There is a tremendous feeling of peace. You also have the feeling of communicating with the animals. Somehow there is a curiosity in them about you. They come to you and you come to them, and you meet. For people with sensitivity, the tranquillity that exists here is very marked.

In addition to our own naturalists, we were helped immeasurably in our understanding of the islands by those of the Charles Darwin Research Station. Dr. Roger Perry, a British biologist of great erudition, was the director of the international project. He was a close friend of Eric Shipton's. Like Shipton, he was a mountain climber and bird lover, and carried the British tradition to the bleak islands as some of the Kenya safari veterans did to Africa.

Perry dressed as a British country squire, with everything but a black tie for dinner. He went about his work in a Harris tweed jacket, shirt, old school tie, and suede shoes, while his staffers went about in cutoffs and T-shirts. At one time, he and Shipton had climbed to the top of the 1127-meter-high Alcedo volcano on Narborough Island to explore the fauna there. When their party reached the top, everyone was dripping with sweat and coated with grime. Unfeazed, Perry slipped into his tent and emerged in moments in his tweed jacket, tie and shirt, and suede shoes, with his pipe in his mouth.

Another staffer who was of great help to us was Miguel Castro, conservation officer. He was a self-taught Ecuadorian who had settled on the island and married a Swiss woman. Industrious and hardworking, he had developed a system of breeding the tortoises after collecting their eggs and bringing them to the incubator at the station. As a result, he had been able to repopulate those islands where the land turtles had become extinct.

The station at Academy Bay consisted of a main cinder-block office building, a one-room museum, and a few modest homes for the staff. There were stone-walled pens for the adult tortoises, and cages for the small ones to keep out rats that could attack and kill them. The staff worked not only on conservation, but also on trying to determine the exact age of the islands. This was an important question. Some fossils date back to the Pliocene epoch, some 7 million years ago. Potassium-argon dating indicates the oldest lava on Hood Island to be 2 million years old. The presence of the land tortoises and land iguanas is particularly puzzling. There was clear evidence that the islands had emerged from the sea by volcanic action in comparatively recent geological times, and that they had never been connected with the American mainland. How did these species arrive there?

One theory is that the Humboldt Current that moves up from the coast of Peru brought them on chunks of vegetation. The problem is that no such tortoises or iguanas are found in Peru, although there are slightly similar breeds in parts of the West Indies and Central America, where no such current could sweep them down. But the Humboldt Current is credited for the strange presence of almost exclusively Antarctic birds—penguins. The Galápagos penguin is a small breed, but it is the only penguin that has been found above the 45th parallel.

We had much to cover in the eight brief days we had to spend in the archipelago. All the islands have two names—Spanish and English—but for our tour we used the English terminology for those islands that were uninhabited and Spanish for those inhabited. There is San Cristóbal, or Chatham, with the tiny village of Basquerizo Moreno on Wreck Bay, our port of entry. Most of this island is barren and desolate, except for the higher part that is densely covered with vegetation.

There is South Plaza Island, which is the best place to see the land iguana. This is one of the prettiest of the lot, covered by a low red or yellow plant, the *Portulaca lutea,* and cacti, giving it an alpine appearance. Here, the iguanas burrow in the soft soil. In the southern cliff area, the swallow-tailed gulls nest, as the sea lions play around little pools on the north shore.

Tower Island abounds in seabirds. The island is the top of a volcano, with a lake in its floor. The walk inland over an arid terrain with low trees and shrubs provides a view of finches, mockingbirds, and doves.

Sullivan Bay, on the east end of James Island, features a white, shell sand beach to land on, with a beautiful red-cinder cone rising to several hundred feet at one end. Climbing the beach, you are suddenly confronted with a landscape of fiery, unearthly desolation. There are cones and craters of every size and description up to 6000 feet above sea level. Hundreds of playful sea lions are found on the beaches around Sullivan Bay.

Jervis Island has a cluster of many types of lava rocks and is a home for nesting pelicans, masked and blue-footed boobies, and a flamingo lagoon.

Albemarle Island, the largest, has the shape of England, with neighboring Narborough to the west serving as Ireland. Tortuga Point is the nesting place of the pathetic flightless cormorants, plus the Galápagos penguins and seals. In addition, the marine iguanas are sprawled everywhere over the rocks.

The other islands—Floreana, Hood, and Champion—offer their own pastiche of color. Floreana has a special tradition: the historic Post Office Barrel, which was set up by passing whalers on their way to the Antarctic. During the War of 1812, Captain David Porter of the U.S.S. *Essex* intercepted a quantity of British mail here. As a result, he subsequently was able to sink thousands of tons of enemy shipping.

Even though our time was short, we learned much on that first trip. Roy Sexton was the first to step off on the beach on our first landing from our lifeboats on Hood Island. In seconds, a mockingbird was sitting on his hat, and another on his camera lens. A Galápagos hawk lighted on a branch and allowed us to pet it. Nonpoisonous snakes there will slide right up to you and stare you in the face. The sea lions will literally play with you in the water, and without coaching will play with an orange or balance a ball.

There were so many fascinating things that I immediately began planning fourteen-day cruises for the future. The temperature is comfortable, mostly running between 70 and 80° F, even though the equator runs through the islands. The upwelling of the Antarctic currents causes this, while mainland Ecuador remains miserably hot. Roger Tory Peterson said to me, "There are benign paradises in the world, and there are harsh paradises. This is a harsh one, but it is sad to think that it is the paradise it is because man didn't have a chance to cultivate this region for his own use."

It *is* sad. In many places I have visited, man has become the most destructive of all animals. He has brought with him cattle, goats, sheep, and dogs, cats, and rats. In the brief attempts at colonizing the Galápagos, the colonists found that the islands were not the promised land they expected, and left. They also left behind their domestic animals, which strangely enough became wild predators. Wild pigs rooted out tortoise eggs. Rats found nests of birds on the ground and ate the chicks and eggs. Cats decimated many rare birds, while wild goats destroyed the vegetation, leaving nothing for the tortoises. On Charles Island, the number of wild goats mounted to tens of thousands, while wild donkeys grew out of all proportion. In addition, bands of wild dogs even attacked sea lions. Because of all this one of the biggest efforts of the Darwin Research Station has been to eradicate the traces of man and the domestic animals that turned wild when they were left behind. The greatest success has been on the smaller islands, where all the former domestics have been eradicated and Darwin's creatures can continue to exist and develop.

Wildlife there is not confined to fauna. For some reason, the archipelago's turbulent human history continues in scattered form. One of the first inhabitants I met was a gentleman whom I came to call the Naked German. He was an odd sight, stripped to the altogether, with a long beard and a piercing gaze. He told me that he had served with the kaiser in the First World War and had come out to the Galápagos to escape the ravaged European scene. He lived in a house that was luxurious by Galápagos standards and had acquired a lot of land that he had sold off in parcels over the years.

He was the product of the many cults that had started in post–World War I Germany—a philosopher who had read a lot and likened himself to an Indian sadhu, although he knew little of India. He lived at war with the rest of the island, perhaps because of his bitterness about his wife. She had joined him there to live an Adam and Eve existence, only to run off with another German who came along with them. His liverish disposition inspired the young people to torment him by sneaking into his walled garden and stealing things. As a result, he had turned his home into a walled fortress with booby traps, shotguns, and World War I rifles.

I learned all this on my first visit to the islands. He seemed so desperate to revisit Germany that I offered to help him make a trip back. Time after time he seemed ready to go, but never could bring himself to do so. Instead, he told me about a hidden volcanic cave he liked to retreat to for meditation. One day he gathered some food together and went off to his secret cave. Several years later, they found his cave and his bones—the end of a legendary Galápagos figure.

But the islands have been constantly filled with strange people: extraordinary, gripping, comical, many connected with the same German wanderlust that brought my friend there. Since the Galápagos was supposed to represent the remotest place in the world you could go, it appealed to such nonconformists. On Floreana Island, I encountered Mrs. Wittmer, an enigmatic, jolly lady who, with her husband, had carved a thriving farm out of the cruel and unyielding soil of the lonely island, and somehow managed to make a go of it with common vegetables, tropical fruits, and field crops. I enjoyed many hours of illuminating talks with her. She and her husband had arrived in the early 1930s, disillusioned with the civilized chaos of post–World War I Germany. She bore two children, fought off the raids on her gardens by wild "domestic" bulls, and greeted curious navigators from all over the world who wanted to see how any family could survive under such grueling conditions.

At first, the only other inhabitants were a cluster of German emigrants that included a dentist who had turned into a philosopher and had come to the island with his female disciple to accept the universe. With a strange brand of dental foresight, he and his lady had all their teeth pulled, and had brought with them one set of steel dentures that they shared. Another strange constellation was a German baroness with two consorts who seemed determined to take over the island. The baroness had all the accoutrements of a pirate queen. She wore riding breeches, carried a whip, and wore two pistols at her sides.

The colony in the 1920s was not a happy one: feuds developed, people were mysteriously shot or disappeared without a trace, the baroness and her lovers also disappeared, the dentist died ostensibly from what may have been poisoned chicken. Either the desolate mood of the island or the grim struggle for survival brought raw emotions into play. Still spry and nearing eighty, Mrs. Wittmer has survived and likes to serve the orange wine she makes herself from her orange grove. She firmly denies having any part to play in the macabre convolutions on the islands.

Even the scientists have not been immune from strange and mysterious happenings. In 1968 local resentment against Miguel Castro's industriousness as conservation officer was so great that he became the target of some unknown fellow countryman who shot his Swiss wife through the head as she hung out the laundry. The only motive seemed to be a venomous resentment against Miguel's success, a penalty for being an intelligent and gracious gentleman. After this personal tragedy, we brought Miguel to the Seychelles when we opened up that archipelago in the Indian Ocean; his work there was invaluable and he was able to get away from the grievous scene of his wife's murder.

With Miguel's help, we had been guided through many of the smaller islands where it was possible to obtain a more accurate count of the tortoise population, thought to have been reduced to only eighty. By increasing the number of observers, we were able to show an increase in the number of tortoises—between 10,000 and 15,000 by 1976. In 1982 the estimate had jumped to 17,000.

The gruesome ambiance that has at times gripped the islands might be traced to the difficulty of living off the harsh land. When the Norwegians came there in the 1920s with the promise of milk and honey, they found hell instead. There had been a potato blight at home; in the Galápagos, living was worse. The few Norwegians who remain there today have conquered the adversities to become good farmers making a decent living for themselves. They seem to be able to put up with the oppressive isolation that can sometimes drive others mad.

But my own memories and experiences there are all pleasant. It is an exhilarating sight to watch the waved albatross as they arrive to nest on Hood Island. They come here mysteriously every April, huge birds with an eight-foot wingspan. They go through their elaborate courting dance, lay their eggs, rear their young, and then take off to sea.

On land, they are most awkward, waddling along to a cliff near their breeding ground, waiting for a strong updraft, then throwing themselves clumsily into the air, transforming themselves into soaring things of beauty. They are pelagic birds, living on fish and resting on the surface of the water. But no one has been able to determine exactly where they go as they fly off on their journey into the unknown. By leg-banding, it has been determined that individual birds return every two years. We know they go to sea. The question is, where do they go?

The blue-footed boobies have their own courtship dance, a very amusing set of calisthenics as they lift one leg and then the other in a charming, comical ballet. To watch the marine iguanas going in and out of the water is a scene of endless fascination. These former land animals must have landed here on their clumps of mainland vegetation in a state of exhaustion. Now they have learned to survive by diving for seaweed, but with no webbed feet to help them, swimming by their oscillating tails. To get back on land, they wait for a high wave that takes them near the edge of a cliff and keep trying until they make it after dozens of futile attempts. Although they feed in the sea, they stay there only a short time, and come quickly back to shore to warm up. Here they mate and lay their eggs. On land, they literally carpet the ground, yet you can walk among them without being molested or nipped.

One of the most interesting places is Punta Espinosa, on the northeastern section of Fernandina or Narborough Island. Here we spent a day ashore among the marine iguanas, flightless cormorants, penguins, and sea lions. Fernandina is dominated by an active volcano over 1500 meters high that erupts sporadically and spews its lava down the sides of the mountain. Most of the island is covered with immense sheets of frozen black lava.

On one visit, we stood on the deck of the *Navarino* and one of the lady passengers asked me, "Is the volcano dead?"

"No," I replied, "it's merely dormant."

"You seem to be able to arrange anything, Mr. Lindblad," she said. "Why can't you arrange for a small eruption?"

"Well," I said, "let me think about that. I'll try to arrange it."

I had almost forgotten about my little joke when we suddenly heard a loud hiss followed by a tremendous explosion. Fire and smoke rose in the sky from a rupture on our side of the volcano. It looked at first like blood spurting from a severed artery.

The lady turned to me in awe. "How did you ever arrange that?" she asked.

Completely startled myself at the coincidence I said, "You remember Moses and the Red Sea?"

It turned out to be one of the major eruptions of the century, and we remained at anchor to watch it. By the time we steamed off, the entire sky was covered by a sulphuric cloud of hot ashes and cinders that, after cooling, was to fall on us for days to come. The eruption lasted for several months.

In doing my homework in preparation for our first Galápagos trip, I learned that one of the highest concentrations of tortoises could be found a few hundred feet up in the highlands of Santa Cruz Island and could best be reached on horseback. These giant beasts cluster around watery mud holes to slake their thirst. I also found that the trip from Academy Bay to the site was a long one, and had cabled ahead to reserve some horses for those who wanted to give the rugged trip a try.

When the horses were being made ready for the journey, I discovered that only a dozen of them were available, although most of the passengers wanted to go. The horses were scrawny. All were bad; some were worse than bad. All the saddles were unkindly wooden. I wanted to screen those who were going to take the trip to make sure they were hardy enough.

Because of the length of the trip, the riders had to get under way in the predawn darkness. As I was checking out the group, I discovered that one of them was a striking elderly lady, a Gibson Girl in the early 1920s, whose name had been at the top of the list of those wanting to take the trip. With memories of Mrs. Featherstone still in my mind, I gently took her arm as she started to mount the saddle. "I'm really terribly sorry," I told her, "but I don't think you realize how long and difficult the trip is. Especially on horseback."

She laughed. "Mr. Lindblad! You don't need to tell me about horses. I've been riding all my life."

"On a wooden saddle?" I asked.

"Nonsense," she said. "I'm going to reach the top of that mountain, and I'll be back fresh as a daisy!"

I pleaded with her, but she would hear none of it. I watched her as she rode off in torchlight, just behind Miguel Castro's horse. I was glad a local man was beside each horse.

I felt a bit edgy during the day, waiting for the riders to get back. Optimistically, they were due back at sunset, about six o'clock. At dusk, there was no sight of them. But quite suddenly a lonely figure on a horse came out of the bush and rode up to me. It was my Gibson Girl friend.

"Did you give up and turn around?" I asked her.

"I turned around, all right," she said. "But not until I reached the top. Delightful trip."

"But where are the others?" I asked.

"They're a bit slow," she said. "I imagine they'll show up in an hour or two. Some of them preferred to dismount and walk."

Then she jumped off the horse, took my arm, and said, "Let's go back to the ship. I'm in grave need of a dry martini."

The others did arrive, saddle sore and weary, about four hours later, most of them walking beside their horses in moonlight.

The following year I made sure that the long trek would be done more sensibly. It was obvious that the journey could not be completed in one day. I brought in comfortable saddles, tents, sleeping bags, and electric torches to make it an overnight excursion, and ordered more horses so that everyone could go if they wished. But my foresight was not enough. With such a long caravan on the trail, it turned out that almost every other horse was a stallion, while the others were mares—some in heat.

The caravan moved up the mountain, with the distinguished Roger Tory Peterson and naturalist Nigel Sitwell ready to bring their expertise to the journey. It didn't take long for the stallions to become restless and enamored. Neither conscience nor bridle could prevent several of the stallions from plunging up on the mares ahead of them. Several riders were pitched off into the bushes and, worse, cacti. Nigel Sitwell felt as if he had become a living pincushion. Roger Tory Peterson was thrown onto a rock, and for a moment he felt sure the end had come. He struck so hard that the works of his gold watch were stripped, and all that was left was the casing. If it weren't for several injuries to the group, it would have been almost funny. But it wasn't.

Later, I received a moving letter from Mrs. Beatrice Green, of Augusta, Maine, who recalled her experience vividly a dozen years later: ''I appreciate even now the kindness of the staff and cruise members following my unfortunate accident on Santa Cruz Island while we were on the overnight trip to the area of the giant tortoises. When thrown from the horse I was riding, I received four broken bones (rib, back, and pelvis) and except for my arms, complete paralysis. Tender loving care from Dr. Roy Sexton, Ruth Hanscomb, and Barbara Peterson, and many cruise members was there for me constantly. After prolonged hospitalization and therapy I have recovered completely, and since that time have joined in an expedition to the Arctic on the first such trip made by the *Lindblad Explorer*. I guess I just wanted to say thank you for making what might have been a nightmarish experience a warm memory of Lindblad Travel.''

Others who were injured also took the incident in remarkably good spirits.

We had had another sad occasion on our first Galápagos voyage. An elderly lady suffered a stroke in her cabin, and Dr. Sexton worked frantically to save her life. I radioed the U.S. Embassy at Quito, which arranged to dispatch a DC-4 from the U.S. air base at Panama to the airfield on the island of Baltra, from which she could be flown to a hospital for intensive care. We steamed all night and anchored at sunrise. The DC-4 arrived at that same moment. Tragically, however, the passenger died almost at the same time.

Abruptly, the rules and regulations changed from an emergency to that of transporting a deceased. All the arrangements we had made were useless. The new regulations were stringent. We had to wash the body and wrap it in sheets and a tarpaulin. Then we took it to shore in a lifeboat where the Ecuadorian officials made us stand offshore for several hours until they could arrange to fly the body to the mainland for an autopsy. The regulations created an almost impossible situation; we could not touch land nor could we take the body ashore—or out of the country until several days later.

After our first expedition to the Galápagos, I had dinner in London with Captain Sir Thomas Barlow, a descendant of Charles Darwin. We talked at length about the possibility of creating an impact study of the increasing number of visitors. We decided that Lindblad Travel should create a grant for a two-year study, and approached Dr. Michael Harris and his wife whom I had met on my first visit to Tower Island. A young British couple who were naturalists, they had been working in isolation there for two years. Michael was a top authority on seabirds.

His laboratory on Tower Island harbored over a million storm petrels, among the other extravagant birdlife. The storm petrel includes many species. They are robin-sized birds with a tubular beak and web feet. The storm petrel got its name from St. Peter, because it appears to walk on the water as it skims along the surface.

Michael was not only conducting the definitive study of the storm petrel, but also of the frigate bird, with its great wingspan and light hollow-bone structure that enables it to soar in the most graceful way. It lives on fish, but strangely enough, if it falls into the water it drowns because it carries no oil on its feathers. It has a deadly capacity to get around this drawback, however. Like a piratical jet fighter, it flies on the tail of boobies and other seabirds, diving and gliding after them, after they have caught fish for themselves. The in-air battle goes on with a fury, until the hapless booby is so harassed that it regurgitates its half-digested seafood dinner. At this point, the frigate bird snatches the re-gurgitated fish out of the air, depriving the booby of his meal. Meanwhile, its wings remain dry. Like the booby, the frigate bird has quaint mating habits. The male has a large red throat pouch that swells up during the mating season to attract watchful females.

The wandering albatross, one of Antarctica's many fascinating birds, has become the symbol of Lindblad Travel as tourists have followed Lars-Eric Lindblad, literally, to the "ends of the earth." (Photo by George Holton)

Pygmies of Zaire in Africa are among the greatly varied peoples of the world with whom Lars-Eric Lindblad has visited. (Photo by George Holton)

Dr. Roger Tory Peterson (left) and Keith Shackleton (center), both renowned wildlife experts/artists, have accompanied Lars-Eric Lindblad and Lindblad Travel on expeditions to the four corners of the world. Here, a trip to Antarctica aboard the M.S. *Lindblad Explorer.* (Photo by George Holton)

Capt. Robert Falcon Scott, British explorer who reached the South Pole, stayed in this hut at Cape Evans in Antarctica during his arduous journey. (Photo by George Holton)

Penguins! Colonies in Antarctica sometimes have populations of more than a million individuals. And the variety — from Emperor to Adélie (shown here) to Chinstrap — is as fascinating as their marvelous, friendly personalities. (Photo by George Holton)

This huge stone carving of Mulbekh, the Maitreya (future) Buddha, greets
visitors to Ladakh in the Himalayas. The magnificence of statues and
other carvings throughout India is overwhelming to a first-time visitor.
(Photo by George Holton)

Tenzing Norgay (right) and his wife, Daku, are close friends of Lars-Eric
Lindblad (center). Tenzing and Daku host Lindblad trekkers in Nepal and
Tenzing has escorted many trips to other parts of the world.
(Photo by George Holton)

Egyptologists accompany Lindblad tours to Egypt's historic monuments (here, a group visits Seti's tomb), enriching the visitors' understanding and appreciation of the nation's great contributions to civilization of the Western world.
(Photo by John Lazarus)

This magnificent statue on the exterior at the Luxor Museum is part of the greatness of Egyptian monuments.   (Photo by John Lazarus)

A Lindblad safari to East Africa takes you as close to the animals as safety of passengers permits. Special vans provide each passenger with a window seat — and an open roof for splendid photo opportunities. (Photo by Sven-Olof Lindblad)

One of the most magnificent sights in all the world is the migration of Africa's great animals as they battle for survival. While poachers still take their toll in some places, many African nations have adopted farsighted conservation laws. (Photo by Sven-Olof Lindblad)

In China's remote Xinjiang Province, Kazakhs on horseback are highlighted against the Nan Shan mountains. Displays of skilled horsemanship are a highlight of tours to the area.
(Photo by George Holton)

The mighty Amazon River — cruised many times by the M.S. *Lindblad Explorer*. Because of its compact size and shallow draft, the ship can enter remote coves and visit tiny villages, enabling passengers to learn, in depth, about the natives, the flora, and the fauna of one of the world's greatest rivers. (Photo by George Holton)

Most of the giant moais of Rapa Nui (Easter Island) were carved at Rano Raraku — and many were left in various stages of completion. The visitor leaves the island wondering whether monoliths and temples were influenced by cultures of South America, or whether they are strictly Polynesian. (Photo by George Holton)

When Lars-Eric Lindblad first visited Easter Island, he struck up a long friendship with the late Father Sebastian Englert, the Bavarian priest who was
instrumental in preserving the Polynesian culture of the island.
(Photo by George Holton)

The late Dr. Albert Schweitzer (left) also became a good friend to
Lars-Eric Lindblad and the two often met when Lars-Eric visited Africa.
(Photo by George Holton)

The M.S. *Lindblad Explorer*'s sturdy Zodiacs permit passengers to visit shore areas off shallow waters such as Sullivan Bay on James Island in the Galápagos. (Photo by George Holton)

The close approach of a visitor to this red-footed booby on Tower Island in the Galápagos is typical of the lack of fear of the islands' birds and animals. They seem as curious about their visitors as the humans are about them. (Photo by George Holton)

The M.S. *Lindblad Explorer* has traveled the farthest south — and the farthest north —
of any passenger ship. The walrus colony greets visitors to Spitsbergen and the Arctic.
(Photo by George Holton)

After years of chartering ships for cruising expeditions — and never finding quite the perfect
ship — Lars-Eric Lindblad commissioned construction of the M.S. *Lindblad Explorer*, a very
special ship specifically designed to reach those remote areas where large cruise ships simply
cannot go. (Photo by George Holton)

The M.S. *Lindblad Explorer* is at home in warmer climates, such as the Seychelles, where she anchors off a coral reef on Frigate Island and is framed by coconut palms. (Photo by George Holton)

Passengers from the M.S. *Lindblad Explorer* reach a remote shore in Antarctica via Zodiac, permitting a visit to Scott's hut on Cape Evans. (Photo by George Holton)

Lindblad Travel passengers enjoy the rugged, as well as the luxurious. A husky sledging expedition in Greenland took this group across Angmagssalik Fjord. (Photo by George Holton)

Natives in war canoes greet visitors to Agats in West Irian, Indonesia. (Photo by George Holton)

A Balinese dancer performs the Legong dance for visitors to Bali. (Photo by George Holton)

In Bhutan, too, dancers perform for visitors from around the world. These masked dancers are the royal troupe in Thimphu, capital of the tiny Himalayan kingdom. (Photo by George Holton)

Fortress monasteries (dzongs) in Bhutan are among the world's most impressive buildings. This is the Monastery of Tachichhodzong in Thimphu. (Photo by George Holton)

The children of Suzhou helped greet Lars-Eric Lindblad when he inaugurated cruises along China's famed Grand Canal. Their warmth and friendliness is typical of the way Chinese people invariably greet Westerners. (Photo by Cary Ann Lindblad)

The Harrises had completed an extensive study of these and other birds on Tower Island. Since the preservation of nature is actually one of Lindblad Travel's most valuable assets, I was pleased that the Harrises were willing to undertake the impact study that resulted in developing careful regulations for future tourism. While the study was going on, I was informed that the Ecuadorian national park service had only a small budget for the Galápagos Islands, and we helped by paying the salaries of the national park officers, as well as by supplying saddles and tents for the patrol officers.

Twelve years after the first impact study, a similar one was conducted, with encouraging results. It was determined that the impact of tourism had not been detrimental to the wildlife, thanks to the restrictions that were laid down as a result of the earlier study.

We were able to use the *Navarino* only up through 1968, when the ship had to be used as a Chilean naval transport. It had become too expensive to continually refit it for travel groups. It had served us well, however, and the Chilean crew was one of the best I had ever worked with. In addition to the Galápagos cruises, we had used the *Navarino* three times to the Antarctic—one of them being its aborted trip in 1968, when the rudder had broken, and we had been forced to send the disappointed passengers back to the United States. But the disciplined crew had then saved us from a major disaster.

I had had such a close relationship with the Chilean officers aboard the *Navarino* that I would miss them. In 1968, in the second year of our Galápagos voyages, news came over the radio that all the Chilean merchant marine officers were to go on strike immediately. The *Navarino* passengers had all been boarded, and we were ready to sail. I thought again of having to send a whole shipload of passengers back to the States, and the financial loss it would involve.

The Chilean officers called me into a meeting and told me, "Look, we haven't received the official notice on the strike. So we suggest you get all the visitors ashore, and we can then leave."

One officer went on to explain that once we had left port, they would not be required to strike, at least until our return to Guayaquil. Then he could find us Chilean naval officers on leave who could take over the ship, since they were nonunion members. We dropped the lines and took off from the docks at once, and were able to carry out our next cruise without delay.

Meanwhile, I had been going ahead with my dream of building the best small cruising ship I could conceive for Lindblad Travel. My preliminary inquiries and planning had been continuing all through the hectic times on Easter Island and in the Galápagos. Because of details involved in those projects, I had to attack the preparations for the new ship piecemeal. I could visualize it so clearly that it seemed almost as if it were already built.

The idea of the ship sprang from the problems we had had with the *Magga Dan* and the *Navarino* in Antarctic waters. I came to the conclusion that in order to continue the Antarctic voyages, we needed our own ship: first, she should be able to navigate safely in ice; second, she should be able to carry close to a hundred passengers; third, she should have a speed of fifteen knots.

Safety would come first, especially in those Antarctic waters. The ship would have to be ice-strengthened so she could push the pack ice to the side or slice through it. She needed that double hull, so that if we were pierced, we would float. In the Antarctic, you can be very far away from help—or even if help is close by, it might not be able to make it through the ice to your side. I also wanted the ship to be self-sufficient—to store enough food, fuel, and supplies to sustain passengers and crew through an entire winter if necessary.

The fifteen-knot speed was necessary to cross the oceans in minimum time. The roaring 60s and 70s southern latitudes down near the Antarctic Continent brought winds that could almost bring a ship to a standstill. I wanted to cross the treacherous Drake Passage from the tip of South America in thirty-six hours, instead of the two and a half days required by the *Navarino*. The run from New Zealand to McMurdo took nine days on the *Magga Dan*. I wanted to cut that to five days.

Sorting out the bids from several Scandinavian shipyards, I finally was able to interest some Norwegian partners in offering their financial participation and expertise, and I came to terms with a Finnish shipyard named Nystad Varv as builders. This firm in Swedish-speaking

Finland has been building sailing ships since 1800 and super-strength icebreakers since the early 1900s.

The matter of risk included the big question of whether I could fill the ship month after month, year after year. But then what was a risk compared to a dream? What was possible financial disaster compared to new adventures that had never been offered before—learning adventures that would be as exciting as they were informative? What was the $2.5 million it would take to build the ship compared to the thrill of seeing the *Lindblad Explorer* slide down the ways?

In October 1968, I signed the contract with my Norwegian partners, confident that the *Lindblad Explorer* would be a thing of beauty and a joy almost forever.

IX

THE LINDBLAD EXPLORER
A Very Special Ship

DURING the last half of the 1960s, I was concentrating on establishing firsts for Lindblad Travel, out of pride and the necessity to keep growing, plus an irresistible itch. I enjoyed the challenge when people would tell me that my ideas were impossible. Taking tourists to the Antarctic, I had been told, was not only impossible, but outrageous. Easter Island and the Galápagos were supposed to be foolhardy. The Wing Safari in Africa was a hopeless idea. Yet they were all working well. Now I was working on a new first—the first tour operator to commission his own cruise ship.

By 1968, our staff had grown to over seventy throughout the world. In association with Tony Irwin, the staff in Nairobi had grown from five to twenty-eight. Hanns Ebensten had come from England to handle the Galápagos operation. Anabelle Moscoso came from the Canadian Government Travel Bureau to concentrate on the African tours. Rosalie Howard arrived from Devonshire to specialize in preparing recommended reading lists. Myriam La Rotta, from Bogotá, Colombia, devoted her time to Russia, the Middle East, and South America.

Other specialists joined the company: Stella Howland, for Africa and the Amazon; Olga Sorokowsky, for special groups; Henry Van

Scofield, for special promotions; Barbara Dahn, who became West Coast representative, and later a utility executive; Babette Liebman, for special projects. We had grown to the point of specialization, and with this help I was able to go on with my dreaming, which sometimes drove my associates up the wall, especially Kevin McDonnell, who was in charge of the treasury.

When the contracts for the *Lindblad Explorer* were signed, I took a globe of the world and studied it. There were many inviting ideas. What could be more exciting, for instance, than to circumnavigate the world *vertically?* Not that the ship could cross the poles directly, but perhaps come close to it. This could be a new sort of "round-the-world cruise." On the globe was Spitsbergen, high north of Norway and above the Arctic Circle. To circumnavigate that with a passenger ship would be a rare adventure. What about Clavering Island, on the east coast of Greenland, and the remote and lonely Scoresby Sound—a spot where no tourist had ever thought of going?

There were the tropical islands, too, rarely visited: the island of Tristan da Cunha, halfway between Africa and South America; the 13,000 islands of Indonesia, scattered through the Banda and the Flores seas; the Seychelles, in the middle of the Indian Ocean; and the Amazon, all 4000 miles of it. I could picture these cruises in detail, even before the keel was laid.

I was lucky to get the services of the famous Danish marine architect, Knud E. Hansen. He was a designer of vast experience and great empathy for the unusual qualities we needed. I also brought in Captain Edwin MacDonald again. His Antarctic experience was needed. He went over to Finland to live during the year the ship was being built. Because of their dedication to the job, the *Explorer* was able to slip down the ways and be christened by Sonja on schedule in July 1969. The ship would be ready for final delivery in early December.

Since I was continually being asked, "What next, Lindblad?" I proceeded to work out the itineraries for the *Explorer* when she would finally be ready for her shakedown cruise. Christopher Powell, who worked with me on this, was an expert who knew the ground—and the sea—well. My primary target was to bring the *Explorer* to Antarctica, where its design would enable us to penetrate farther into the ice than before. We would also avoid some of the international jealousies, since we would be flying a "neutral" Norwegian flag. In addition, there were the sub-Antarctic islands, the Falklands, known also as Islas Malvinas, and South Georgia. The "forgotten islands" of the Indian Ocean were of real fascination and could be best visited by small groups living on shipboard and avoiding heavy tourist impact.

The progress on the construction of the *Explorer* was superb. She would be ready on the delivery date of December 10. I planned the maiden voyage with Powell for its ultimate Antarctic target in the most interesting way possible. We would take over the ship at the Finnish port, Nystad, with a shakedown through the Baltic to Southampton, where we would pick up our first regular passengers. The first voyages of the ship were sold out far in advance, simply by an announcement to our regular clients: a month's cruise at an average cost of $1500 a person, 1969 prices.

From Southampton, we would sail to the west coast of Africa to visit the Madeira Islands, off the Moroccan coast. From there, we would move to the Canary Islands, closer to the African coast. Moving down the coast of Africa, we would stop at the Cape Verde Islands, almost 400 miles off Senegal. This is the least-known group in the Atlantic, once a Portuguese colony, that produces coffee, oranges, and sugarcane.

We would then move across the equator in the South Atlantic to Rio de Janeiro and finally to Buenos Aires, where we would begin our Antarctic cruise. It was an ambitious schedule for a maiden voyage, covering more than 8000 miles. Joining me as a leader of the cruise would be Keith Shackleton, one of the most universally liked persons I've ever known.

I arrived in Helsinki in December with Sonja, Kevin McDonnell, and Christopher Powell. I have to admit I was tremendously proud. The *Explorer* was trim, sleek, and beautiful. With a red hull and white topsides, she was a miniature gem of an ocean liner, all 250 feet of her. In some respects, she had the qualities of a private yacht. She displaced only 2300 tons, and her draft was a little under 14 feet, so that she could slip into narrow fjords, shallow lagoons, and remote harbors that no other cruise ship could visit.

Her top observation deck was spacious, with a crow's nest for passengers high above it. The bridge was equipped with the most sophisticated navigational equipment, twin radars, depth finders, and echo sounders. There was all the safety equipment required by new U.S. Coast Guard requirements just established the year before. On the bridge deck was a small hospital complete with X-ray and full medical facilities, especially designed by Roy Sexton and Dr. John Stubenbord, a Washington colleague of Roy's. The boat deck just below it had ten compact but comfortable staterooms, each with private shower and toilet, as were provided for all the staterooms on the decks below. There were a total of 50 one-class cabins—twin-bedded, cozy, and each with its own temperature-control switch. All were outside cabins, with music, news, and announcements piped into them electronically.

The swimming pool on the aft deck was small and charming, but hardly for Olympic swimmers. It would be refreshing in the tropics. Also aft was the Penguin Room, equipped for lectures and films, with a broad counter and stainless-steel sink for dissecting specimens. There were also microscopes, centrifuge, and other equipment for serious study of marine biology.

The dining room was a favorite of mine—modern, bright, and cheery. It could seat seventy passengers at a time for the gourmet meals and wines I insisted on, imagining myself an unwavering gourmet. A large buffet table allowed for informal luncheons and breakfasts. The Explorer Lounge was another favorite, with an inviting bar of weathered driftwood. Just off the lounge was a small well-stocked library, filled with carefully chosen books on the anthropology, ornithology, geology, and marine life of the places we would be visiting, plus a supply of current best-selling fiction.

Technically, her special features were critically important for the regions we would be exploring. Although the *Explorer* was not a full icebreaker, she was what is called an ice-working vessel, cleared by Lloyd's of London for sustained operation in ice and designated as Ice Class-1A. Her reinforced hull, ice-knife on the rudder, and protected variable pitch propeller enabled her to push through heavy pack ice. Her two engines generated 3800 horsepower. For docking and turning in her own length, she had special bow thruster propellers forward. The roll-dampening device operated on the action of the free surface of liquid contained in two opposite tanks. The evaporators for distilling seawater assured an ample supply of water for drinking and cooking.

But one of the most important features of the *Explorer* was the rubber outboard Zodiacs. They could be swung down from the upper deck in minutes to carry the passengers directly to the shores of tropical islands or Arctic ice floes. Six of these would be in constant use. The Zodiac fleet actually became the key to our entire operation, combining a "go-anywhere" ship with a "land-anywhere" capacity. They were safe, stable, and excellent in pack ice or tropical surf. They were perfect for snorkeling and scuba diving. The more timid could snorkel among coral reefs holding on to the safety line around the sides. Each day in our later cruises, we would be instructing the passengers for a "wet landing" or a "dry landing," depending on surf conditions. To me, the Zodiacs changed the entire art of cruise ships, enabling us to see the world from an intimate eye level.

On the eve of our shakedown cruise from Finland to Southampton, we had a festive party with our Finnish and Norwegian colleagues before we set off through the Baltic Sea under the command of the Norwegian Captain Jestead. There was still a lot of final trimming to be done when we reached England, but the important part was that we were off to fresh adventures that promised a whole new spectrum in the travel world.

Although I expected some misadventures on the shakedown and maiden voyages, I wasn't quite prepared for all of them. You have to expect things to go wrong with a spanking new ship. It is not like breaking in a new car. A ship often takes several years to break in, and ours was no exception. There was generator trouble by the time we reached the Kiel Canal in West Germany, where we stopped the ship and brought up two new generators from Bavaria by truck. We took them aboard to be installed at Southampton. In spite of the delay, we were able to board the passengers and move out into the Atlantic for our first leg to the Madeiras and the Canaries.

After pleasant visits there, things began to pile up. The *Explorer* had two engines for its single prop because if one stopped the ship would still be able to make port under reduced power. Not far from the Canaries, one of the engines stopped. We had no other choice but to divert our course and head into Dakar, Senegal. We now discovered that the builders, in order to deliver the ship on time, had neglected to put a primer on the hull, and a serious rust condition was developing. Again, I was facing a crisis. The repair work at Dakar would take us five days, making a very tight schedule to join up with the passengers in Buenos Aires for the forthcoming Antarctic trip. Miraculously, the paint touch-up and the engine work were rapidly completed, and we took off again.

I was beginning to feel very content as we moved across the Atlantic. Both engines were now running well, and the ship was handling the seas, with her stabilizers making the ride comfortable and steady. The Antarctic passengers would be arriving in Buenos Aires soon, and we would be able to pick them up on schedule. I was in my cabin typing up the program for the day, in a state of relaxed concentration.

Christopher Powell suddenly poked his head in the door and said calmly, "The ship is on fire." I told him to run along because I wasn't in any mood for a joke. Then it occurred to me that Powell didn't go in for this kind of joking. I got up from my desk to go out into the passageway. Then the fire alarms went off all over the ship. I met Powell outside, and he said apologetically, "The ship *really is* on fire." I could see smoke billowing toward us from the direction of the galley.

We discovered that one of the cooks had left a deep fryer unattended. The oil had ignited, and the fryer had become a flamethrower. The flames were so high and hot that the deck above was melting. The sprinklers were unable to cope with this sort of fire—only the chemical extinguishers would work. As the officers and crew battled the flames, I assembled the passengers quietly in the bar behind a fire door. After a few drinks, the expressions of concern were replaced by a gallows humor. The thought of abandoning ship in the middle of the Atlantic was not attractive. I went out to check the lifeboats, where I found three of our crew members. Each was standing at attention, staring straight ahead, with a Singapore passport in one hand and a transistor radio in the other. I wasn't sure whether it was fear or great discipline they were exhibiting.

The entire crew worked desperately to fight the flames. Then another complication developed. The steering cables passing above the melting ceiling had been destroyed, and without warning the ship went into a tight turn, listing hard to port. Fortunately, the seas were calm in perfect weather. The crew was able to straighten out the rudder manually, using walkie-talkies to communicate with the bridge. The crew finally got the fire under control, and we limped directly toward Buenos Aires, eliminating the stop at Rio.

The rest of the journey took nine long days, with food served from hot plates. By now, we were far behind schedule. The entire group of Antarctic passengers—nearly a hundred—was waiting for us in Buenos Aires. Since the ship would have to go into dry dock, there was no other choice but to fly them back to the United States and reimburse them for the trip. This cost was staggering; the cost to lay the ship up at Buenos Aires for complete repairs and repainting was worse. For the first time in Lindblad Travel's history, I was facing a disastrous loss for the year. At least two Antarctic trips, fully booked, had to be canceled.

Passenger John Redfield summed up the state of mind of the cruise group in a way that indicated the importance of keeping up everyone's spirits in the face of the setbacks on the *Explorer*'s first voyage. "The *Explorer* had had troubles on her maiden voyage," John wrote in his recollections. "Burned out wiring would require extensive repairs. We were days late docking at Buenos Aires. We spent hours waiting through customs formalities. Hotel accommodations were confused. Elevators were erratic. The group was tired, hungry, and irritable. Tension was in the air as we boarded buses for the drive to the restaurant for a very late meal. Another delay, and then Lars swung aboard and slid open the section of roof permitting a view of the starlit evening sky. 'What a wonderful evening,' Lars exclaimed. Suddenly, the tension was gone, and relaxed and smiling we drove off to a splendid Argentinian steak dinner.''

When I reflect on the incident, I wonder how I summoned up the courage to make that remark in light of all the passengers had gone through. The *Lindblad Explorer* meant more to me than anything I had created in my life. To see her, proud and new, sitting in the dry dock was almost like looking at a sick child in a hospital bed.

In the face of the loss of three major trips, I was determined to have the repairs completed in time for our already booked sub-Antarctic cruise in February 1970, a month away. This was scheduled to go from Puntas Arenas at the southern tip of Chile to the Falkland Islands, South Georgia, Gough Island, Tristan da Cunha, and on to Cape Town, South Africa. After that would come The Forgotten Islands of the Indian Ocean cruises, a special love of mine, because the territory was so fresh and such a rare setting for the traveler. I had all the faith in the world in the *Lindblad Explorer*.

With the *Explorer* now over her growing pains, we left Puntas Arenas on schedule and headed east toward the Falklands. Aboard were three distinguished staff experts who were becoming regulars with the Lindblad expeditions: Roger Tory Peterson, Captain Edwin Mac-Donald, and Roy Sexton. In addition, we were fortunate in having with us Dr. Robert Cushman Murphy, emeritus and research associate of the American Museum of Natural History. He was considered an unsurpassed authority in the field of natural sciences. His two-volume work *Oceanic Birds of South America* is ranked as a classic. Beyond that, he was an adventurer. Before his numerous expeditions, he served his apprenticeship as a naturalist back in 1912 on the brig *Daisy,* the last wooden whaling ship to sail out of New England for South Georgia.

Bob Murphy was not only revered for his scientific works, but also is credited with naming many of the glaciers, mountains, and bays of South Georgia. He named one of them after his wife, Grace, who accompanied him on the trip. She was quite a personality, testy and a bit of a spitfire. She never stopped reminding her husband that she had let him take the long schooner cruise to South Georgia right after they had been married in order to advance his career. Perhaps out of guilt, Murphy had written a most informative book on whales and wildlife in the sub-Antarctic and had named it *Logbook for Grace.* I'm not quite sure she appreciated such a dedication. When we finally reached South Georgia, Murphy pointed out a glacier he had named after her, and being deaf, she spoke high and shrill, "Bob, this is a *very* small glacier!" Retaining his courtly demeanor, Dr. Murphy replied, carefully enunciating his words, "It has *shrunk,* dear. It has *shrunk!*"

The Falklands, or Malvinas, are so remote that they had never been visited by tourists until we brought the *Navarino* to visit two years before we arrived on the *Explorer.* The people of the islands are very British, although some insist they are Scottish. The 2000 inhabitants live in great comfort on their sheep farms and in the town of Port Stanley, the capital. By some measurements the Falklanders enjoy one of the highest standards of living in the world. Most families own their homes, often with several Land-Rovers, and with all the conveniences of modern life. At Christmastime, all work comes to a standstill for a two-day *ghymkhana* with horse races, competitive games, and dancing. Falklanders play hard and work hard. Some of the farms range up to 400,000 acres, with shearing sheds, cookhouses, and even a general store. In the summer, most men work in the fields and shearing sheds; in the surprisingly mild winters, they repair fences and buildings to prepare for the next summer season. If ever there was a picture of peace and prosperity in 1970, it was the Falklands and their serene and prosperous capital, Port Stanley. When William Myers, one of our passengers from Boca Raton, Florida, discovered that the full hospital rates per day were only $5, he came back aboard the *Explorer* to tell Keith Shackleton, "Do you know the hospital rates here are only five dollars a day? I'm thinking of getting a mild chronic disease and moving down here!"

The islanders are a rare, salty, and congenial people. When the *Lindblad Explorer* pulled into Port Stanley, we were greeted with an enthusiastic welcome. The people invited us into their homes. In return, I arranged for a buffet lunch that we served in the church for over 400 islanders, and then invited a group of the eighty leaders—including the British governor—aboard the ship for dinner.

When our guests arrived, I suddenly remembered that for 365 days a year the Falklanders eat nothing but lamb, their most abundant and virtually exclusive meat. While everyone gathered in the lounge for cocktails, I went down to the galley to check our menu for the evening. It was hard to believe, but the main dish was lamb. It was already cooked and almost ready to be served. I quickly told the chef to put the lamb on ice (we would serve our own passengers double orders of lamb later), and we rushed out a hundred frozen steaks from the freezers. These were hosed down with lukewarm water to defrost. The enjoyment that our guests took in the steaks was worth all the frenzy.

The mix-up in the dinner menu was distracting. I had looked forward to visiting the Falklands for many years because of their unique flavor and character. I stood up at the end of the dinner to tell our guests just that, and how proud I was that the *Lindblad Explorer* would make this sort of visit possible on a continuing basis for many years. Concluding the speech I said, "It is such a joy for us on this lovely evening to welcome all of you from the Galápagos Islands who have come aboard."

The minute the words were out of my mouth, I realized the mistake I had made. No group of people likes to have its homeland called by a wrong name. After a roar of laughing protest, I went on to finish the speech. But when I wound up my final lines, I again repeated the same mistake.

There was another friendly roar of disapproval. Then the governor rose to thank us for the dinner and hospitality. He took the microphone and said, "As Her Majesty's representative of the Gilbert Islands, I'd like to thank Mr. Thomas Cook for his hospitality!"

We ran into an incredible coincidence on our second visit to Port Stanley that season. As before, I invited island guests to come aboard for dinner, after having warned our chief chef that we were not to serve lamb to them under any circumstances. But that same day, the chef took sick, and the second chef took over. This time I did not feel any need to check the menu, but when I sat down with our guests I discovered the main course was lamb chops and it was too late to do anything about it. I made another allegedly humorous speech about what had happened, and our guests accepted it in good spirits.

But the Falklands are much more than the charming people there. Scientists have been continuously fascinated by the countless numbers of penguins. The Gentoo, Chinstrap, Jackass, Macaroni, and King all move through the water like porpoises. A chain reaction can result from one pesky penguin jabbing at another. Suddenly, a whole massive rookery can burst into a frenzy of apparent grudge battles, with shrieking noise and pandemonium. Then, just as suddenly, the carpet of penguins will return to calm, and even fall off to sleep. The Falkland Island penguins never take direct routes anywhere. They hop along meandering trails that have existed for centuries. Coming out of the surf, they seem to explode and land stiff-legged or flat on their bellies. Some of them skid and somersault to a stop. Then they quickly regain their dignity by pretending to preen themselves.

As in the Galápagos, the tameness of the Falkland birds is astonishing. Kelp geese, with the ganders garbed in snow-white plumage and the females in plain dark feathers, merely stand politely aside when you stop to look at their nests. The rare steamer duck merely waits and looks you over as you approach. Pipits cheerfully sing directly at you. The winter plover, black-throated finch, and Falkland robin fly about you with great indifference. Unusually high concentrations of albatross invite close scrutiny. Herds of sea lions, elephant seals, and fur seals lie in masses on the beaches in self-contentment, while dolphins play in the waters. For the discerning bird lover, there are plenty of chances to observe the kelp gull, skua, blue-eyed shag, Fuegian oyster catcher, and several varieties of ducks and geese.

The journey from the Falklands to South Georgia is over 900 miles, almost due east across the South Atlantic. You can sense the loneliness and isolation of this island in the two days and nights of steady sailing toward it. But the *Lindblad Explorer* was running as she should, after her shakedown misbehavior, warm and cozy and handling the open seas admirably. When Captain James Cook on the H.M.S. *Resolute* discovered this 110-mile-long, 15-mile-wide island in January 1775, the weather was undoubtedly bad. He wrote in his log: "Not worthy of discovery, lands doomed by nature to perpetual frigidness, never to feel the warmth of the sun's rays, whose horrible and savage aspect cannot be described.''

But the island is not always that bad. The land and ice often stand out in the sharpest detail against the bluest of skies. Sparkling waterfalls leap from lofty mountain crags. Glaciers—blue, green, and sapphire—branch out into pinnacles sheathed in ice. There's a mysterious beauty and enchantment about the scene.

England's great Antarctic explorer, Sir Ernest Shackleton, is buried at the edge of the small settlement of Grytviken. His saga ended here in 1916 after he and his crew were stranded in the Weddell Sea. His vessel *Endurance* had broken up in a fast ice pack. The crew pushed small boats for miles across the ice, then rowed and sailed over a hundred miles to Elephant Island. Here most of the crew stayed to live on seal meat while Shackleton set out to row and sail in an open boat toward South Georgia, over 700 icy miles away. He made it—only to find that the Stromness whaling station was on the other side of the island, with towering mountains in between. Shackleton staggered across them on foot, and soon mounted a rescue expedition to save the men on Elephant Island, still surviving more than two years later, after the world thought they were dead.

Gone now are all the whaling stations that were set up in South Georgia, stations once famed for capturing whales from the fat humpback to the 100-foot-long blue whale that thrived in the waters swarming with krill. They could be harpooned from small, fast whale catchers and pumped with air to be towed to shore to the whaling factory. Then the blubber strips would be flensed and made into oil in large steaming vats. The industry was so lucrative that financial backers frequently made fortunes on their investments.

When we arrived in 1970, the whaling stations and factories were remarkably preserved, while skeletons and whalebones littered the beaches, testimony to the unrestrained slaughter of these beautiful mammals. Few whales could be seen in the surrounding waters.

All the stations had been manned by Norwegians and most bore Norwegian names, even though the stations had been owned by Argentine, Scottish, and some Norwegian interests. They had flourished during the 1920s and 1930s, and several thousand people worked there during the whale-catching season. The quite elaborate ghost towns still remained, with churches, cinemas, dance halls, and two- or three-story buildings. Like the frontier towns of the Wild West, they had been scenes of fighting and feuding, especially between the Norwegians and Scots, who bore no love for each other.

One of the strangest sights we found was the way nature was reclaiming the land. The huge elephant seals, weighing up to three or more tons, had almost become extinct, since their blubber, too, had been boiled down for oil. But they had now come back with a vengeance. Walking through a deserted village, we found them everywhere: in houses, up and downstairs; between church pews; along the streets; on doorsteps—everywhere, both inside and out. When man abandons, it seems, nature takes things back very quickly.

Like the Falklands, South Georgia is the nesting place for millions of seabirds and penguins. Albatross, petrel, whalebird, and skua fly about in the greatest profusion. Rarer birds such as the upland goose, teal, and pipit are often seen, as is the showiest of all penguins, the orange-throated king penguin. He struts about in arrogance, showing off his brilliant-colored throat and towering over the smaller of his breed. Along with the elephant seals that have come back in great numbers are the leopard and fur seals.

Just as the sporadic settlers of the Galápagos brought and deserted their domestic animals and pets, so did the Norwegian settlers of South Georgia in the 1920s. To the Canterbury Plains of South Georgia, bordered by glaciers and tassuck grass, the Norwegians brought reindeer. The small domestic reindeer herds took to the tassuck grass and began proliferating. The reindeer spread to other parts of South Georgia, and the herds continued growing in the absence of the former whaling owners. By the time we reached there in 1970, more than 20,000 were roaming the island. A project was under way with professional hunters to thin the herds down.

About the only occupants of the island when we arrived in 1969 were the twenty-five members of the British Antarctic Survey Station. They were as lonely and isolated as if they were stationed down on the Ross

Ice Shelf. About the only fresh meat they had was reindeer meat, the equivalent of lamb in the Falklands. The entire base was elated when we sent the Zodiacs in to pick them up for dinner aboard the *Lindblad Explorer.* Before their arrival, I had told the chef that we must make this dinner the finest possible for the scientists. After so many months of isolation, they deserved a banquet. But I had forgotten one thing. When we left Finland, we had put aboard as a rare delicacy the carcasses of several reindeer from that country. And it *is* a delicacy if you don't have to eat it day after day throughout the year. It is actually better than venison, a true gourmet's delight.

I wasn't aware that the chef had caught my enthusiasm and had brought out the reindeer from the freezer for this special occasion. After the cocktails and hors d'oeuvres in the lounge, we all marched into the dining room to face an extravagant banquet of reindeer steak, beautifully cooked and served.

I shall never forget those three almost consecutive incidents as long as I live — two in the Falklands and one in South Georgia. The men from the base could barely hide their long faces when the meat was placed in front of them. We kept them in a good mood with plenty of wine and a long session at the bar until the smallest hours of the morning. While they were letting down their hair in a hearty evening of drinking, I had the crew slip ashore in the Zodiacs with several sides of beef to make up for my oversight.

It didn't take them long to retaliate. The next morning I came topside to go to the dining room. All along the gangway was one long row of reindeer carcasses, dressed and ready to cook. The scientists had slipped aboard just before dawn to return our hospitality, and to replace what for us was a delicacy and for them an anathema. They also repaid us with their guidance around the island. Nearly a hundred of us went ashore several times in the Zodiacs in rough seas, an undertaking that was difficult but safe. On the second day's exploration ashore, we were preparing to come back to the *Explorer* when the wind suddenly began to shift from a dead calm to gale force, bringing cold rain, snow, and heavy breakers with it. But I didn't find anyone who didn't enjoy the experience.

On our last day on South Georgia, after our visits to the great rookeries, we went to the grave of Sir Ernest Shackleton to place a wreath on it. This was a particularly meaningful moment because he had been the greatest of all my heroes as I grew up, and still remained so. I had always wanted to be an explorer such as he. Now, with the world completely revealed and uncovered, I was doing the next best thing—bringing people to the scenes of the unusual accomplishments of man, especially in those remote regions where people rarely think of traveling.

We left South Georgia Island and headed northeast across a wide and seldom-traveled stretch of the Atlantic, toward the tiniest pinpoint halfway between Cape Horn and the Cape of Good Hope, Gough Island. Stop a hundred people on a street corner, and I don't believe you would find a single person who had ever heard of it. Eight miles long and four miles wide, it rises like a perpendicular castle from the sea, its high cliffs broken by several startling cascades that have carved deep fissures. Like Tristan da Cunha, 250 miles to the north, it sits above what is known as the Mid-Atlantic Ridge. The only thing due south of it is the Antarctic Continent. There is only one lonely beach halfway along the eastern side where you can find a toehold to examine its high interior, 2000 feet above the sea. Here is an undulating flat area, with broad swales, marshes, and some pastureland.

No serious attempts have been made to colonize the island, although survey expeditions were made there in 1922 and 1955. The only inhabitants today are those at a South African weather station, set up during the International Geophysical Year of 1957–58. We dropped anchor and went ashore in the Zodiacs to spend only half a day there looking for the twenty species of seabirds. It was a brief but interesting stop on our way to Tristan da Cunha, just an overnight sail away.

This group of volcanic islands consists of a strange and interesting colony of some 200 people who subsist mainly on potato growing and fishing. The islands were first settled when a British corporal brought his family there in 1816 and decided to stay. There are no harbors, but the population began to grow, mainly because of shipwrecks. They were an assorted lot, British, South African, Portuguese, African, and

Spanish—though they remained British in character. When the twentieth century arrived, they remained in the nineteenth. Their speech patterns developed so uniquely that linguists studied them. Even the place-names reflected this: Down Where the Minister Land His Things, Ridge Where Goat Jump Off, Noisy Beach, and others.

The colony remained as a time warp in history until 1961. Then suddenly a long-dormant volcano erupted. Lava began spilling down toward their croftlike homes beneath it. The Dutch ocean liner *Tjisdane*, bound for England, was nearby, and the islanders, who knew little of the rest of the world, were taken aboard and to England as refugees under the protection of the United Kingdom. Here they were taught the ways of the twentieth century, as linguists puzzled over their curious archaic speech.

They tried hard to adjust. One woman refugee said, "There's God's hand in this—we were meant to leave, and He will look after us." But many felt more inclined to look after themselves and get away from the contamination of modern civilization. Except for one who died, they all returned aboard the M.S. *Boissevain* to reconstruct and resume their simple lives. An advance party of men had gone ahead to assess the damage. They found wisps of smoke still coming out of a new 250-foot volcano. The island's only commercial venture, a lobster freezing plant, was buried in lava. But the volcano had added new ground: half a square mile where it had formed a slight natural breakwater they had never had before. And the croft homes remained much as they had left them, except for the thatched roofs that had to be replaced. All the sheep had died, but strangely, the cattle had increased several times over. Over 200 islanders were rowed ashore in longboats to be repatriated in a land they preferred to the glitter of civilization.

When our Zodiacs went ashore, we were the first passenger ship to be able to land all its passengers on the island. As we approached the lava breakwater, a man stood on its edge with a large red flag. He looked carefully from his vantage point to see which waves were high and which were low. We hove to our Zodiacs until he lowered his flag briskly; then we aquaplaned in. I don't believe they had seen anyone from the outside world since they had left England, and their hospitality reflected it. There was no airstrip on the island—they didn't want to give up any precious farmland. They spoke with a perfect British accent, but it was totally Victorian in cadence.

Probably the most important official on the island is the postmaster. Their issues are the philatelist's dream. The income from them supplies all the necessities of life, including free electricity, water, and sewage.

We invited a score of islanders out to the *Explorer* for lunch, and their enthusiasm was as overwhelming as their welcome. They inspected and admired every part of the ship, from the laundry to the engine room. Their visit pleased us as much as it pleased them. Captain MacDonald and I ferried them back, in past the natural breakwater, while our trusty friend with the red flag guided us through the breakers.

When we set out to return to the ship, we found a great wind had sprung up without warning. On shore, they warned us that this might last for a week or ten days, and that we might have to be their guests for at least that length of time. If this happened, the *Explorer* would have to go on without us, and no one knew when the next ship might pass by to take us off.

But the man with the red flag went to his station. The flag went down, and we gunned our motor. When the first enormous wave hit, both MacDonald and I went soaring into the air three or four feet high, holding onto the lifelines and engine mount. We came down with a crash, fortunately landing inside the boat. The next wave put us through the same gymnastics. We continued on out to the lee of the *Explorer,* airborne at least 25 percent of the time.

On the way to Cape Town, 1600 miles to the east, where our cruise would officially end, I was framing the best possible program for the *Lindblad Explorer*'s capacities. For the austral summer, we would go south past the Antarctic Circle—the farthest south any passenger ship had traveled. For the boreal summer, we would go north, past the Arctic Circle—the farthest north for such a ship. For the long fall and spring periods, there would be equally enticing journeys. I had already explored the Seychelles and other forgotten islands in the Indian Ocean the previous year, and that would be our next logical voyage. We would bring the ship up the east coast of Africa from Cape Town to

Mombasa, on the Kenya coast. From here our floating hotel would make over fifteen cruises to visit rare Indian Ocean islands, with minimal disturbances to the wildlife and peoples there.

In the years following the *Explorer*'s maiden voyage, her success exceeded my expectations, in spite of the early problems with the ship that brought us a severe loss in 1969. Fortunately, our business was growing swiftly, so that full recovery was eventually possible. By the end of 1971, the *Explorer* had completed five very successful journeys to the Antarctic. We planned two more trips there in the beginning of 1972. When they were completed, we would then be ready to cover the whole west coast of South America, the Galápagos, Panama, the Bahamas, the British Isles, the Baltic Sea, and the Gulf of Bothina, which reaches almost to the Arctic Circle where Sweden and Finland meet in Lapland. Following that, we would move the entire length of Norway, again above the Arctic Circle to the Soviet Arctic border, then on to Spitsbergen, only ten degrees south of the North Pole itself. In August we would sail to Greenland and Iceland, then back to England and Spain, before cruising the entire length of the Amazon, and down to Argentina for another cruise to the Antarctic at the end of 1972.

It was the most ambitious and elaborate schedule I had ever planned, with the *Explorer* doing what she was supposed to do: roaming the world over. For all practical purposes, we were sold out, signaling the most profitable year in our history. As far as the *Explorer* was concerned, I was beginning to think she was invulnerable. I figured 1972 would be a banner year.

Then the crack-up in Admiralty Bay, King George Island, occurred on February 11, 1972, in the middle of an Antarctic storm. All the extravagant plans for the year were gone in a single moment. Whether the *Explorer* could be saved or not, the cancellations for an entire year would be close to ruinous. If two tugs had failed to pull her off the rocky pinnacle spiked in her bottom, how could the single German tug steaming down from South Africa do any better? And if it could get her off, would the double bottom hold, or would she sink to become another Antarctic shipwreck? Or would she founder on being towed across the Drake Passage to dry dock—or on to Scandinavia, in the North Atlantic winter storms?

While I went back from the Antarctic to New York to pick up the pieces, and to go through the painful process of refunding hundreds and thousands of dollars worth of business, the German tug *Arktis* was steaming at over thirty knots toward the possible graveyard of the *Explorer* at Admiralty Bay. I waited, nerves raw, for word from the skeleton crew of what happened when the tug got there.

Finally, word came through by radio. First, with the help of divers, they removed some stones and rocks from beneath the ship. Then they put out a heavy hawser and secured it to the *Explorer*. The 36,000 horsepower engine of the tug went into action. In moments, they had pulled the ship off the beach as if she were a toy. Towed to the deep water in the bay, the ship lay at anchor while the crew waited.

There was no water in the bilge at the start. There was none after a day's wait. The second skin was holding well. But would she hold up in the punishment of the Drake Passage under tow? She did. Under tow, she was brought to dry dock and hauled at Buenos Aires. I flew down there with great apprehension. She had survived the trip so far, but was she capable of being fully repaired?

I watched as the water drained out from the outer plates. There were gaping holes wide enough to drive a truck or bus through, but the inner hull was completely intact. The yard was able to weld temporary steel plates over the holes so the ship could be towed all the way up and across the Atlantic to Norway for repairs. In spite of the agonizing losses, I thanked whatever gods there be for our planning and design that permitted the *Explorer* to stand up under conditions of stress that few ships could have survived. The repairs were made in Norway, and we were able to pick up our schedules in August of that same year, as I concentrated on increasing our volume of business to make up for the massive losses. At the same time, I marveled at the capacity of the *Arktis* that had been able to tow a 2500-ton displacement vessel almost halfway around the world from south to north, almost in line with the vertical meridians. At the end of 1972, I found that our gross had grown to over $4 million, and thanks to that growth, our recovery would be swift.

During 1968, the year before we accepted delivery of the *Lindblad Explorer,* I had been concentrating on the research and development of those forgotten islands of the Indian Ocean, over ninety of them spread across a thousand miles of ocean. My object was to find the best possible parts of the world for the *Lindblad Explorer* to visit in between her cruises to the polar regions, north or south.

No outsider had really seen much of these islands, the principal group of which is the Seychelles, sprawled about a thousand miles east of Zanzibar, sturdy granite masses rising out of the sea just below the equator. To reach the government seat of Port Victoria on Mahé, the main island of the Seychelles, you had to take a ship running from Mombasa to Bombay that occasionally would make a stop there. There was no airstrip yet, and I discovered that the only way to research such widely separated islands was by the sluggish chartered schooner called the *Iron Duke.*

Knowing very little about the area, I was not at all sure that such a long and strenuous survey would be worthwhile. The time element was critical, and it would be a tremendous gamble to spend weeks on a small schooner and not come up with anything productive. However, I had flown blind many times before. There would be many reasons to question my decision after I became embroiled in this venture. But without hesitation, I was off for Mombasa to board the slow boat to the Seychelles, and the even slower schooner through the little traveled waters of the Indian Ocean.

X

SEYCHELLES
Bypassed Islands

I CAME to learn about the Seychelles in a roundabout way. In 1968, I had been invited by the government of the now independent island of Mauritius, at that time still a British colony, to assess its potential as a tourist attraction. It lies in the Indian Ocean, due east of the island of Madagascar.

Mauritius is easy to reach by air. This made it a good starting point in my search for the best possible area to cruise when the *Lindblad Explorer* headed north from the Antarctic. At Mauritius, I learned more about the Seychelles and how their rare loveliness was mostly unvisited since there was no airport.

I also learned of a curious island southwest of the Seychelles, known as Aldabra. It is the largest raised atoll in the world, a massive coral reef that contains the only other breeding ground beyond the Galápagos for the giant land tortoise and teems with other rare wildlife. There were other scattered islands in the area, too, present or former territories of Britain or France. They all were in an area of clear blue seas and inviting climate. This part of the western Indian Ocean was obviously ideal for the *Lindblad Explorer* in between her icy polar voyages.

We got together an exploratory team. Roger Tory Peterson would appraise the birdlife. George Holton, who had now joined Lindblad Travel, would bring his photographic talent. Jimmy James, of British Airways, then known as BOAC, would come along to assess the future possibility of air travel to an area that had no airports. Tony Irwin of our Nairobi office would join me in laying out a practical cruise schedule through the islands.

We flew to Mombasa on the Kenya coast. Here, we boarded the British India Line's M.S. *Kampala* on her Africa-to-Bombay run. The ship was to make an almost grudging stop at the Seychelles. She was a venerable vessel with no less than four classes of cabins, plus a steerage that was not built for comfort. We left on the journey not sure whether our expectations exceeded reality.

When the island of Mahé hove in sight, however, there was no doubt in my mind that we had found some of the most beautiful islands in the world. As we passed the isle of Silhouette, Mahé rose out of the turquoise waters with high granite cliffs. It was even more beautiful than Morea in Tahiti. I wondered why these islands had been bypassed over the centuries.

Once ashore, we were taken to the Hotel des Seychelles, the only hotel on the island at the time. Modest and charming, it seemed to reflect the nature of the Seychellois people. They represented a melting pot, a grand mixture of many races that had only arrived there some 200 years before.

Arab traders must have brushed by the islands many times, as long as 1000 years ago, but there are no written records. An expedition of a British East India Company put in there in the early 1600s for water and ship repairs. But they found nothing but coconut palms and alligators, along with tortoises and fruits. There was not a sign of human life anywhere.

Even the pirates and privateers of the 1700s found no evidence of human habitation. The French decided to annex the archipelago for strategic reasons. Following that, French settlers began to arrive from Mauritius, which at that time was known as Île de France. They brought slaves with them, and the nucleus that created the newest race in history began to form, augmented by pirates, adventurers, slave traders, exiles, dissidents, and shipwrecked seamen. Intermarriage was frequent, with no distinction between whites and blacks. The emerging new race embraced every color, from pure white to the darkest black.

In one of the more friendly takeovers in history, the French finally relinquished their rights to the British on the demand of Captain Henry Newsome and his flotilla of four British navy vessels in 1794. The French governor, Jean Baptiste Queau Quinssi, hauled down the French flag and hoisted the British in its place. At times, Newsome would raise the French flag when a French ship arrived in port, but the British finally predominated. So skillful a diplomat was Jean Baptiste that the British begged him to remain governor in their service.

When we arrived at Port Victoria, the capital of the Seychelles, in 1968, the islands were still under the British flag, but Britain had decided to turn the islands over to self-rule. Jimmy Mancham, a young, vigorous lawyer educated in London and Paris, was gunning for the status of an independent British protectorate on the model of Gibraltar. He led the Seychelles Democratic Party. He was opposed by Albert René, another sophisticated lawyer, who had had a brief career as a European banker. René headed the Seychelles People's United Party, which leaned to the Left under the influence of the Organization of African Unity. He wanted outright independence from Britain and was willing to fight if necessary. Both were members of influential Seychelles families. Albert René was quiet and introspective. Mancham was charming and flamboyant, a playboy by both Eastern and Western standards—but with a sharply contrasting seriousness of political purpose.

Mancham was chief minister of the newly elected Legislative Council when I met him at the hotel on our 1968 arrival. His mother was a Seychellois of French descent; his father of Chinese descent. Jimmy Mancham had an engaging personality and a passion for both beautiful women and his country. He immediately made it evident that the Seychelles needed tourism to vitalize the precarious economy of the country—*if* it could be done without destroying the wildlife or scenic beauty. Of course this was my objective, so we hit it off from the start.

Waiting for us on Mahé was Tony Beamish, brother of Lord Tufton

Beamish of the British House of Lords. Both had been trying to generate enthusiasm and support in England for the islands, but without much success. Thanks to Tony Beamish, our team was able to set up an exploratory cruise, first to the immediate islands near Mahé, and later to the atolls to the south—the Amirantes and Aldabra.

We headed out in a comfortable cabin cruiser for the islands known as the "granite group," as contrasted to the coral and volcanic islands we would be visiting later. Most of them were privately owned; all of them have sparkling, uninhabited white beaches and wildlife that includes some species found nowhere else in the world.

One colorful Seychellois named Harry Savy owned several islands: Frigate, Des Noeufs, and Aldabra. The first is a granite island, surrounded by a coral reef, with magnificent beaches. More important to Roger Tory Peterson was that it harbored one of the world's rarest birds, the magpie-robin. There were only supposed to be a handful in the world, yet when we arrived there we were able to count fifty-six of them—more than twice the reported world population. The bird's survival may have been due to the pigs that Harry Savy had brought there. In uprooting the soil, they exposed lavish quantities of earthworms that made life easy for the magpie-robin. This may be one case where a domestic animal has helped the wildlife.

Harry Savy was cordial, granting us permission to bring the *Lindblad Explorer* to his islands on our cruise there in 1970. In a territory of mercurial and formerly isolated landowners, it was important to get permission well in advance. In his sixties, Savy had quite a reputation. Rumor had it that he had sired some 120 children on his islands, with 70 or 80 of them on Frigate Island, amounting to about half the population. Once the law came down on him when he was accused of having a child by his own daughter. His defense was that he thought she was just another pretty girl, and he had no idea that he was her father. He was also accused of having intercourse with one of his granddaughters. His defense was the same. Whatever the circumstances, he was a man of irresistible charm.

Nearby Des Noeufs Island in the Amirantes has an extraordinary population of 2 million pairs of sooty terns and noddies. Savy was not exactly a conservationist. Each year he would harvest these nutritious eggs and carry them on his schooner to the Mahé market. They had thin shells and were difficult to transport, but he brought them through the surf to his waiting ship with great commercial success. To assure a supply of fresh eggs, he would have his men trample the old eggs and then collect the new batch that the terns would obligingly supply the following day.

We sailed on to Praslin, the second largest of the Seychelles and an island of such beauty that the British General Charles Gordon of Khartoum became convinced in the late 1800s that this was the original Garden of Eden. Praslin's Vallée de Maie, a forest of unique palm trees called coco-de-mer, has the enchantment of a cathedral. The trees tower 100 to 200 feet above you, with the largest leaf and fruit of any known tree. The nuts can weigh up to forty pounds. These coconuts were first discovered on the shores of India and the Persian Gulf, where legend had it that the trees must have been growing under the sea.

The large double shape of the coco-de-mer looks amazingly like a female form, downright erotic in appearance. The male tree appears to have a phallus. Legend has it that at night the male tree uproots itself and visits the female to make love. However, a stern warning abounds: if you see this happen you will die. Perhaps this feature is responsible for the myth that the meat of the coco-de-mer is the most powerful aphrodisiac in the world, greater even than the powdered rhino horn. However, I have tried it and can certify that it simply doesn't work. It is reported that before the island source had been discovered, in 1602, one Hapsburg king paid 4000 gold florins for one of the nuts that had drifted onto an African shore. In this magnificent forest, the slaty black parrot is found exclusively, along with the Seychelles flying fox, a bat with a three-foot wingspread. Its wing beat is more like that of a heron than a bat.

Just half a mile from Praslin is Cousin Island, which is truly ''strictly for the birds.'' Its seventy acres have been turned into a permanent nature reserve as the result of a concerted effort by the International Council for the Protection of Birds. One of the granite islands, its features include tens of thousands of fairy terns, the brilliantly colored long-tailed tropic birds, petrels, and pryons, as well as a type of brush warbler endemic only to this island.

La Digue, a sleepy sort of paradise on its granite base, invited a restful tour on the only form of vehicle available—the ancient ox cart. Later, I built fifteen new carts to transport our passengers from one end of the island to the other. Bird Island, the northernmost of the Seychelles group, has a coral reef that not only inspires snorkeling and fishing but supports a million and a half sooty terns that screech at the decibel level of a dozen jet engines.

Our consensus after two weeks was that the Seychelles could provide one of the most beguiling attractions we had ever scheduled—if the environment could be protected. Later, Roger Tory Peterson wrote of his visit. ''In search of an earthly paradise, no one can come closer to that vision than in the archipelagos of the Indian Ocean.''

Cousin Island was being administered by the International Council for the Protection of Birds. There was a natural concern about what could be done to protect it from eventual tourism. In my discussions with the council, the need for establishing a resident warden came up. They had in mind a young and talented scientist, Dr. Malcolm Penny, and his wife, who seemed ideal for the job. Malcolm had done an excellent job as leader of the first Royal Society expedition to Aldabra, and both were expert on wildlife. With the cooperation of the council, I set up a grant to enable the Pennys not only to carry out the conservation work, but also to compile a definitive field guide to the birdlife of the area. By the time the first tourist expedition arrived two years later, we had already established the procedure for the protection of the environment through the efforts of the council and the Pennys, a fact that became especially important when the Seychelles were eventually opened up to jet travel in 1971.

The Indian Ocean is of strategic value to the United States and Britain, as well as to Russia. At the time we were making our survey in 1968, the Soviets had established a base in Somalia. The Western alliance was still without a naval or air base in this part of the Indian Ocean. Furthermore, with the Suez Canal then closed, the western Indian Ocean sea-lanes became a primary artery for the flow of oil from the gulf, around the Cape of Good Hope to the United States and Europe.

The United States together with Britain was casting around for a suitable island for a strategic air and naval base in the region. Meantime, Jimmy Mancham was pushing hard for a commercial airport, which he considered a must to put the Seychelles on the map. He was well aware of both the U.S. and British aspirations for an air base, and used this knowledge in eventually getting the commercial airport established.

A survey team had already visited Aldabra and found that the island would be ideal for a military base, with ample room for long runways and a large lagoon that could be blasted out for the naval base. This caused considerable concern among people interested in the natural sciences and the whole ecology of the area. Aldabra, twenty-one miles long and nine miles wide, is the only other place in the world besides the Galápagos where the giant tortoise exists. It also features other rich wildlife, especially birds, some of which are entirely endemic to this island. The tortoises were important symbolically, too. The coat of arms of the Seychelles features it prominently as part of the islands' heritage. Through Mancham's conservation efforts, it had become a protected species, a step applauded by wildlife experts throughout the world.

The voyage from Mahé to Aldabra is the same distance as from New York to Detroit. Our ship was to be the sixty-foot schooner *Iron Duke,* a clumsy old wooden craft with a 65 horsepower engine and a set of dubious sails. She was commanded by a salty old Cornish captain named Tregarthen, assisted by a young cabin boy and a deckhand. As the ship was being provisioned, I wondered how we were going to make it. Eight of us, including the captain and his crew, were to be on board. Six double-decked bunks were squeezed as tightly as firewood into the superstructure.

Forward was a galley with a wood stove, along with a supply of wood for cooking. Forward of that were the fuel barrels and water tanks with only a single hose, so that the water was flavored with diesel oil. Also forward were our live chickens and piglets, which would have to be slaughtered en route whenever we wanted fresh meat. Aft was the toilet, literally hanging over the aft rail, but probably the most comfortable perch on the ship. From there, everyone was encouraged to cast out the fishing line, because we would depend a greal deal on fresh fish during our six-week voyage of exploration. Surrounded as we were by supplies, an inflatable Zodiac, two outboard engines, and gasoline, only a six-by-six-foot hatch was available to us as deck space.

The cruising speed of the *Iron Duke*, with full power in a calm sea with no current, was three knots. With a following sea, we could probably build up to five knots. Later we found that under certain conditions of wind and current, the ship actually went backward.

On our route to Aldabra, we visited many islands in the Amirante group, including Des Roches, Bird Island, Farquhar, and Astove. Life on the *Iron Duke* was hardly serene. In addition to the cramped quarters, we hit several severe storms that put the creaky timbers of the boat to a vicious test. To survive them, we wedged ourselves between the Zodiac and the foremast and hung on for dear life. I instructed the captain to trail lines just in case anyone went overboard. No less than half an hour later, both the cabin boy and George Holton were swept overboard. Luckily, they were able to grab the safety lines.

After each encounter we found that the fourteen-foot-high waves had flooded many of the chickens in their cages, cutting sharply into our food supply. When a chicken is drowned it becomes inedible, and we had to throw the dead ones overboard. Whenever we decided chicken was to be on the menu, my assignment was to slaughter them, not the most pleasant job. We did it by grabbing the chicken around the neck and swinging it overhead. This renders the chicken unconscious before its throat is slit, and we hoped that it died quickly and painlessly. Slaughtering the small pigs was even more unpleasant. As I had learned in my farm tours of Europe, pigs seem to have an unearthly premonition that their end has come.

We finally approached Farquhar after our battle with the seas. The *Iron Duke* had a twelve-and-a-half foot draft, which made shallow coral reefs precarious. All through our trip we were to have trouble with the captain's navigation. Using charts and the Indian Ocean pilot book, he worked with a stubby pencil, while his eyeglasses, which had only one temple, kept falling off. He had a wobbly sextant and a chronometer that ran six minutes slow. Beyond that, the captain snored so loudly every night we could barely get to sleep. Tony Irwin's attacks on him with a pillow did little to help.

To get into the lagoons of Farquhar, or any of the islands, was a major challenge. We would line up a couple of tall trees to use as range finders along a charted channel. Then, with our three-knot speed, we would try to keep on the range. But half the time we would be swept hopelessly off course. If it was close to sunset, we would have to retreat to open water and wait for daylight. The anchoring ground was usually dangerous. It was either too deep or too close to the coral shelf that rose up so steeply. The following morning, bone tired, we would try to beat our way back.

We finally inched into Farquhar to find it an unlikely place to bring the *Lindblad Explorer.* We were welcomed at the house of the copra plantation manager there. As we had not had a freshwater bath in weeks, we longed for a shower or tub full, but none was available. We settled for a cool drink on the veranda of the manager's house. Suddenly, a brief but intense rainstorm hit the island, and water was gushing down from the roof gutters. Within moments, we put down our drinks, stripped, and splashed in the rainwater for the length of the storm.

Before we left Mahé, I learned of John Veevers-Carter and his wife, Wendy. He was a Briton who yearned for idyllic isolation on the island of Astove, where he was in the process of building a Moorish castle. His wife was the daughter of the late Clarence Day, whose *Life with Father* brought him worldwide acclaim. They were raising their children there, and Wendy worked as an artist. So marked were her talents that she had been commissioned to design the currency and postage stamps of both the Seychelles and the British Indian Ocean Territory. In fact, we were carrying with us the latest issues of the stamps she had designed, as well as a complete set of the new banknotes.

The Veevers-Carters had sought their paradise island in the most remote area they could find. Although Astove is a beautiful island, I'm afraid I couldn't share the Veevers-Carters' idea of paradise. Handling a small boat there was highly dangerous. Veevers-Carter had destroyed his boat intentionally, so that he wouldn't be tempted to use it in the treacherous local waters.

We found other drawbacks. One of the workers had just murdered one of his companions by smashing his head with a coconut, and Veevers-Carter pleaded with us to take him to Mahé for the meting out of justice, a request that we denied without hesitation.

Various shipwrecks had brought rats to the island, and they had practically taken it over. These rats were ferocious and habitually bit off the feet of the chickens. Consequently, most of the chickens were balancing precariously on their wretched stumps. The other paradise killers were the mosquitoes. They bred in the coral, and at night we had to retreat to the *Iron Duke* so we could sleep.

The family had been waiting for literally a year for the supply of salt and sugar we brought them. They welcomed us graciously, and of course invited us to dinner. I could not count the menu they served in the gourmet class. They had slaughtered a donkey for meat, which was served with rice sprinkled with some sort of black condiments that I couldn't identify. Roger Peterson mentioned that I apparently didn't like the condiments. Suddenly, I realized that the rice bins had been swarming with rats, and the little black pearls I was putting aside were rat excrement. Veevers-Carter calmly informed us that we had nothing to worry about—the excrement as well as the rice was thoroughly cooked.

During our stay we visited the large lagoon of the atoll, which had an opening on one end that Veevers-Carter planned to close off for his fishery. He was no amateur at this, having been in charge of the fisheries for both South Yemen and the Seychelles. But he would have to face a plethora of sharks, manta rays, and sting rays that swarmed throughout the waters of the lagoon. You could see the manta rays mating in huge numbers offshore. They thrashed in great frenzy, so that the waters appeared to be boiling. It was one of the more spectacular sights I've encountered in the world.

In spite of many attractions and my great respect for the pioneering spirit of the lonely family, I had to cross Astove off as a stop for the

Lindblad Explorer. We crowded back into the *Iron Duke* and took off for Aldabra and its great coral lagoon, not only the home of the giant land tortoises, but also of rapacious coconut crabs that can tear off the husks of coconuts with their large claws. We knew that the only inhabitants on Aldabra were those at the Royal British Society's scientific station and that the entrance into the lagoon was extremely precarious. Veevers-Carter had also reminded us that the approach was even more difficult than that at Astove. But our first job was to find Aldabra under our extremely slow headway and dubious navigation.

With his stubby pencil, rickety sextant, and sluggish chronometer, the captain one morning pointed out a large atoll on our port. He said it couldn't be Aldabra since in accordance with our charts, we were to approach the island from the south. We decided to take our Zodiac and land on its shores anyway. After a few steps we stumbled on our first giant tortoise, and we knew we were clearly on Aldabra. We calculated that the British station was on the other end of the atoll, some twenty-two miles away. Since the speed of the Zodiac was almost ten times that of the *Iron Duke,* we decided to cruise to the station along the shore and let the slow schooner catch up with us the next morning.

The fishing en route was incredible, and as we followed the shoreline we quickly filled the little boat with fish of many kinds, including four-foot-long barracuda. We arrived at the station by midafternoon, where it was low tide and we had to wade ashore, dragging the rubber Zodiac behind us. After about ten feet, I felt a sharp sting on my leg and discovered that I had been attacked by a large moray eel. I pried him loose with great difficulty and proceeded with much greater caution to the shore.

Here we were met by a clearly astounded group of the eight scientists at the base, who obviously could not understand where we came from in such a small boat. The schooner, of course, was nowhere in sight. Before they even greeted us, they wanted to know where we had come from. I told them that we had come from Mombasa, some 700 miles away. Since the Zodiac was the only boat in sight, they had no choice but to believe me and seemed full of admiration for our braving such a long stretch of sea in such a small craft. They were also pleased with the fish that we brought them.

But after a few minutes, an uncomfortable silence fell over the group. When they suggested that we immediately put back to sea, we were greatly puzzled. The reason became clear when they told us that at about ten that morning, their cook had died in convulsions, screaming in pain. They had buried him promptly with no diagnosis other than that his death must have been caused by a powerful virus. But we were exhausted and in no mood to leave. We then told them the truth about the *Iron Duke*. There was really no other choice than to stay, and they invited us for dinner with considerable apprehension. When dessert was being served, we heard a strange whimpering sound from the kitchen. It came from the newly appointed cook, and our first reaction was that here was a second fatality in the making. It turned out to be something equally macabre. The new chef, stricken with guilt, wanted to confess a heinous crime: he had put rat poison in the chief cook's dinner. He threw himself at the mercy of the scientists.

We had now faced two murders in one week and found ourselves with another request to transport the murderer from Aldabra, which we were fortunately unable to do. But with the confession came a certain measure of relief. At least the cause of the tragedy was known, and no mysterious plague was lurking in the background.

We stayed several days on Aldabra, identifying birds, stalking the tortoises, and snorkeling in blue, crystal-clear waters. In surveying the mangrove shores of the lagoon, I got nicked again by a moray eel and suddenly discovered a colony of stone fish under my feet. I knew they could be nasty, but didn't learn until later that if you step on one, you'll be dead in fifteen seconds. There were also plenty of shark, barracuda, and sting rays to worry about. I decided that our future visits would be confined to cruising and exploring in the Zodiacs, with snorkeling and fishing confined to designated safe places.

We studied the incredible colonies of birdlife inhabiting the mangrove thickets: egrets, night herons, frigate birds, and red-footed boobies in rare concentrations. The tortoise population was plentiful, and the fact that the former estimate of 2000 had now grown to a hundred times that number was most encouraging. We all applauded the campaign that Tufton and Tony Beamish were carrying out in England to preserve the atoll.

To enter Aldabra's enormous lagoon from the sea is an adventure in itself. At times the tide pouring through an entrance can reach up to twenty knots, which is more like a cascade than a tidal current. On one occasion we approached the narrow entrance when the tide was slack, the only time when it is safe to do so in a Zodiac. Even then, the water can boil out of the lagoon with a vengeance. We took great care to stay in the center, away from the razor-sharp coral reefs on each side. One false move left or right, and the rubber sides of the Zodiac can be sliced from bow to stern, sinking the craft. On later trips this happened with uncomfortable results.

As we edged into the mouth of the lagoon, the coral bottom became so shallow that we could no longer use our outboard motor. We jumped over the side and began pushing the Zodiac through the coral heads against the current. Up ahead I noticed one of the islanders of the station staff standing in a dugout canoe and fishing in the more quiet waters. He was holding a harpoon in his hand, about thirty yards away from us.

Suddenly he raised the harpoon and threw it with tremendous force in our direction. It landed in the water not more than five feet away from us. When I recovered from shock, I saw that he had struck and killed a twelve-foot tiger shark just in front of the boat we were pushing. In spite of the clear waters, none of us had seen it approach. As the fisherman prepared to haul the shark into shore, we thanked him profusely. Later, when the jaws were removed, they formed an archway large enough to walk through.

Our visit convinced us that in spite of its hazards, Aldabra would become one of the most exciting places to bring the *Lindblad Explorer*. We would be able to enter the lagoon in Zodiacs as long as it was slack tide through the Grand Passe, or Passe Hourow, and safely observe the sharks, dolphins, and other large fish, as well as the tortoises and birdlife ashore.

The eight British scientists were sorry to see us go. They were as concerned as we were about a possible military base of any nation there, a step that would wipe out another treasure of natural science that ranked with the Galápagos. The island was technically owned by the ubiquitous Harry Savy, but was part of the British Indian Ocean Territory, which held political control.

We left Aldabra on the *Iron Duke* and headed for the port of Diego Garcia, in the north of Madagascar. We had gathered all the material needed to plan a program of compelling interest. We all wanted desperately to get off the *Iron Duke,* with its six-by-six-foot deck space and a bunk room almost as small. In addition, the cockroaches had grown almost as big as mice. Nearly six weeks on that schooner was about as much as we could take.

On the chart, we found an island group that I had not noticed before, called the Comoros. It was close enough that we changed course and headed in that direction. The main island was called Grande Comoro.

The harbor town of Moroni was typically Arabic, with narrow lanes and small market squares. The harbor was filled with native dhows, and their crews stared intently at the sight of our strange appearance. The Comoro Islands were a French possession at that time, and they were very strict about our papers and clearance. I quickly learned of an air service back to the African mainland, consisting of one Piper Aztec large enough for our team. I chartered it for departure in a few days; this would give us a chance to say good-bye to the *Iron Duke* and charter a local boat to prowl around the nearby islands of the Comoros. Although there were no tears whatever in my eyes on leaving the *Iron Duke,* I felt a strange nostalgia as we disembarked.

I was glad we had stumbled on the islands. They had their own enchantment and warranted a scheduled stop for our future *Explorer* trips. It was interesting that one of the Comoros held the last outpost of the French Foreign Legion.

On the way back to the States, we agreed that our survey had accomplished all we had set out to do, and that the forgotten islands of the Indian Ocean were ready to be rediscovered. They were completely fresh territory, and no one had ever researched the area in depth before. In between our adventures and misadventures, we had been able to gather a large amount of scientific data on birds and marine life, part of which we would put to use in mounting our fight for the preservation of Aldabra. We had even discovered entirely new species of birds.

My next visit to the Seychelles would not be until the *Lindblad Explorer* arrived several months later, but I was anxious to get back to work closely with Jimmy Mancham and Tony Beamish in their efforts to save Aldabra.

At this stage, I felt that the Seychelles from Bird Island in the north to Aldabra in the south would offer the visitor much value. The establishment of the commercial airport at Mahé would be important, of course. Mancham was convinced that the air service would bring genuine prosperity to his area. But he was also firm in wanting to protect the wildlife of the islands and the seas surrounding them. He worked with the remnants of the British colonial rule to set up a code for stringent control of future tourism which would forbid the building of high-rise hotels, spear gun fishing, shell collecting, the killing of tortoises, and other obvious threats to the ecology. But it remained clear that tourism was essential to the economic future of the islands.

In anticipation of the certain interest in the underwater reefs, I purchased a fifty-six-foot converted Norwegian coast guard cutter named the *Christian Bugge* (irreverently referred to as the Holy Queer by the Seychelles' fine British governor, Sir Bruce Greatbatch), which could take small groups of travelers who arrived by air around the islands. She had been built in 1905 with teak decks and was full of character. Later, I also bought a beautiful, sleek 125-foot schooner, replete with a lounge with a crystal chandelier and a piano. She was called the *Dwyn Wenn*, Welsh for the Goddess of Love. She had five double cabins and would provide two-week cruises for those who flew in after the airport was completed. Both ships served us for years in taking people with a special love for the sea, snorkeling, and diving.

Meanwhile, the fight was shaping up to keep Aldabra from becoming a military base. Roger Tory Peterson and I contacted every opinion maker we knew to emphasize that Aldabra was one of the most important wildlife areas in the world. Tufton Beamish continued to lobby in the British Parliament. Jimmy Mancham cajoled all the British and

American officials he could collar. Sir Peter Scott did the same. Christopher Cadbury, staunch Quaker and chocolate manufacturer, provided major funds and effort. But the British and American military commanders continued to be confident they would win out.

As protectors of the Seychelles, the British had the major influence, of course, although they planned to lease the islands to the U.S. Air Force if legislative approval was given. But they failed to realize the power of the voice of the tortoise. In England, millions of determined women with gray hair and knitting needles carry tremendous clout. When aroused, they can spoil the chances of any well-meaning MP, especially if the issue involves dogs, cats, other animals, or rose gardens. We not only aimed for their support but for that of every wildlife and conservation society over the world.

We were now scheduling the *Lindblad Explorer* to arrive in the Seychelles on her first cruise there in April 1970. The big commercial jetport on Mahé would not be completed until eighteen months later. By now, both British and Seychellois officials were looking forward to the economic boost that tourism would bring and pressed me for the date the first Lindblad tours would arrive. Other travel organizations had made promises to them, but none had been kept. I told Governor Greatbatch and Jimmy Mancham that I would bring two full tours there, both by land and by sea, precisely on April 19, 1970. They were more than surprised at this, because the new jet airport would not be ready.

But as part owner of Wilken Air in Kenya, I was sure in the back of my mind we could find a good location on the site of the big airport under construction to clear an airstrip that could handle a small plane. Tony Irwin became greatly involved in the flight venture and proceeded to arrange for building another landing strip on the Veevers-Carters' Astove Island where small planes could stop and refuel. I arranged to put into use two bulldozers: one to make the primitive landing strip at Mahé that could handle one of our Wilken Air Twin-Engine Navajos, and the other to create a strip on Astove for the refueling stop. In this way, I was able to bring the Seychelles the first air service they ever had.

I'm sure my promise was heard with a great deal of skepticism, so when both the *Lindblad Explorer* and our Wilken Air Navajo arrived at Mahé exactly on schedule on April 19, the surprise and elation were marked. The isolation of the archipelago was broken, but I continued to work on protecting its values. For two years, the *Explorer* carried out twenty-four cruises between Mombasa and the Seychelles, with the naturalists on board emphasizing the need for protection of the locations we visited. The struggle between civilian and military control of Aldabra still was going on. I continued to invite as many conservation leaders as possible from England, France, West Germany, the United States, and other countries to visit Aldabra on the *Lindblad Explorer,* and I found that once people saw the island and learned about it, they became passionate advocates of saving it.

The *Explorer* also played a part in one of the more dramatic sea rescues of the Indian Ocean. On July 1, 1971, the *Explorer* was cruising toward Aldabra in the vicinity of a small island named Bijoutier, some 400 miles northeast of Madagascar. We discovered that a Taiwan fishing vessel named the *Chin Fu* was hard aground on a coral reef, and that none of her crew of twenty-two could swim. Enormous waves were breaking over the stranded vessel. Although it was impossible to pull alongside, four of our Zodiacs under the command of Chief Officer Karl Torseth pulled in close enough for nine staff and crew members of the *Explorer* to swim through the waves, board the ship, and tow the nonswimming Taiwanese crew to the shallow waters of the lagoon.

The hull had been sawed open by the reef, and hundreds of bloody fish were spilling out, drawing a large number of sharks to the sinking ship. Some of the *Chin Fu* crew were being swept out to deeper waters and larger sharks, as the Lindblad rescuers hauled them into the Zodiacs. Aboard the distressed ship, Keith Shackleton and Rod Salm pulled a badly injured Taiwanese crewman out of the hold and lowered him to a Zodiac manned by Kim Morton, who managed to maneuver the rubber craft up to the hull and out again through eight-foot waves.

So rough was the water and weather that the overall operation, including ferrying the shipwrecked sailors to the *Lindblad Explorer,* took a total of eighteen hours. Later, the British naval survey ship H.M.S. *Beagle* arrived at the scene to take the shipwrecked crew to port. Sir Peter Scott, who watched the rescue from the *Explorer* deck through binoculars, later said that the work of the *Lindblad* crew was one of the most spectacular displays of individual courage he had ever seen.

The new commercial jetport opened on July 4, 1971—the final link between the Seychelles and the rest of the world. A BOAC VC-10 landed on the runway surrounded by most of the population of Mahé. With great ceremony, Jimmy Mancham stepped out of the plane on returning from one of his international trips to bring his region to the attention of the world. Speaking to the crowds he said, ''The landing of this giant bird on this strip of tarmac marks the momentous beginning of a new era for our islands. We are suddenly and irrevocably thrust forward into the twentieth century.''

Playboy or not, Mancham was an astute politician with charisma. With independence from Britain looming as inevitable, his rivalry with Albert René intensified. With the arrival of the jets, Lindblad Travel was swamped with requests for our tours to the Seychelles, and we were hard put to keep up with them. It was obvious that our operation would have to become much bigger than we had anticipated. Europeans and South Africans were booking our tours heavily. To meet all this demand, I decided to open an office, setting up Mark Gross and his wife as managers. They had worked successfully for us on Easter Island. I also brought Miguel Castro over from the Galápagos to be in charge of the *Christian Bugge*. But with the increased demand, this still wasn't enough. We began handling tours for other agents not established in the Seychelles, and finally Sonja decided to go to Mahé to coordinate the new operation. She planned to stay only a short time. But as the traffic increased, she eventually remained there for over eight years. I was lucky to add Dr. Lyall Watson as both a naturalist and a survey specialist for future itineraries. Not only did he have a vast knowledge of biology, but he had lived for some time in the Seychelles and Indonesia, and knew the islands and islanders well.

The Seychelles were so attractive that they drew tourists like a magnet. We were to take as many as 42,000 there in one year. I tried to match every increase in business with some kind of effort to preserve what might be destroyed. I served on a committee for the preservation of the islands and spent a great deal of time on its work. The Aldabra fight remained the center of attention, but it did not come to a head until the mid-1970s, when the joint U.S.-British military finally conceded defeat and agreed to place the U.S. base on the more distant island of Diego Garcia. I took a lot of pleasure in discovering that giant tortoises and a few million birds could chase away B-52s that threatened their existence.

In 1971, when Jimmy Mancham was running for reelection in the second election in the Seychelles, I sailed on the *Christian Bugge* to Des Roches Island, southwest of Mahé. Mancham asked if he could hitch a ride with me on our schooner to campaign among the small islands while I continued my survey.

Regardless of how remote the islands he was going to visit, he dressed as if he had just stepped out of the shop of a prestigious London tailor. We put into several small atolls, landing in our Zodiac, with Mancham stepping off on the beaches to give his election messages. On some of them we were forced to wade up to our knees to reach shore. By the time we got to shore, there was no longer a press in Mancham's elegant, soaking-wet trousers, but he mounted a palm stump and gave his speech to the handful of people on the beach as if he were talking to a packed stadium.

But the problem with Mancham was that he was first a lover of his country and beautiful women, and second a politician. He had become very attracted to one of the stewardesses on the *Lindblad Explorer,* and his impatience in getting to our rendezvous with the ship was getting the best of him. When the *Lindblad Explorer* finally hove in sight, I was fishing off the stern of the schooner. Then Mancham spied the big ship. I had just hooked a huge tuna and was fighting the line for a long time. But Mancham unceremoniously cut the line and ordered full speed for the *Explorer.*

What eventually happened to Mancham is part of a history that was still continuing in 1982, when a mysterious contingent of mercenaries arrived at the Mahé jetport in the guise of a rugby team, purportedly bringing toys for children and posing as members of a beer-drinking club known as the Ancient Order of Foam Blowers. The roots of this abortive coup go back to the granting of independence in 1977.

Mancham, being head of the new country's largest party, was appointed president. His rival Albert René, as leader of the opposition party, was appointed prime minister in accordance with the new constitution to form a coalition government. Mancham welcomed this solution and political peace seemed assured. When Jimmy Mancham left for London to attend the Jubilee in 1977, René embraced him and wished him godspeed.

Once Mancham was out of the country, René staged a coup and took over the reins while Mancham remained in exile. This coup had already been planned when René kissed Mancham good-bye. I had grown to like Jimmy enormously and knew how bitter he was about being deposed. At the same time, he told me that he would never go back to the Seychelles and live as a prisoner in his own country. He was still a lover of life number one, and politician number two.

René's government remained paranoid about Mancham's trying to come back and organize a countercoup. When the headlines broke in late 1981, it was obvious that the countercoup was taking place. The disguised mercenaries had come out of South Africa under the leadership of the notorious sixty-two-year-old South African mercenary Mike Hoare. A tape recording of a speech by Mancham was found in the possession of the mercenaries, who were defeated with one killed and two wounded.

The coup failed because some of the mercenaries got drunk on the plane that carried them to Mahé. One of them started to make his exit through the customs gate marked SOMETHING TO DECLARE, as opposed to the other gate marked NOTHING TO DECLARE. The customs official opened his suitcase to find an automatic weapon right at the top of the suitcase, and the cat was out of the bag.

When René accused Mancham of staging the coup, Mancham replied, "Who are you to cry wolf?"

I have often reflected on this tragic struggle between two very capable and dedicated men. They both come from the same background and have a deep love for the Seychelles. There is no question that each wants the country to prosper. At the beginning of independence, Mancham was granted the opening moves, just like a chess player who chooses the white pieces gets the artificial option of moving first. His opponent has no other choice than to play the black pieces, whether he wants them or not. In other words, he has to take the opposite stance from his opponent. In this small country of 60,000 people, Mancham stood for continued cooperation and communication with Great Britain because he was convinced that tourism was the only viable industry the economy of the country could be based on. René, with basically the same goals as Mancham, was forced by the situation to choose a different direction. The result was that the "loyal opposition" had to become the "disloyal opposition." The regrettable part is that they are both patriotic and accomplished men who have been forced into an artificial enmity.

The roots of this struggle were evident at the time of my first visit to the Seychelles in 1968. My own battle then was to preserve the natural resources there, as well as to build a profitable business. I had to switch my attention at that time to several projects on many different fronts that demanded great care. Many of them involved keeping the *Lindblad Explorer* on productive cruises that would take it to the Amazon, Indonesia, New Guinea, the Pacific Islands, and the Arctic—all of which would require the most careful scouting and research.

The probing of the Arctic, never before undertaken by a passenger cruising ship, especially would need meticulous planning and imagination. It would be as challenging as the Antarctic, and I was hoping to keep our misadventures down to a minimum. I cannot say that we were successful.

XI

THE ARCTIC
Northwest Passage and More

THE *Lindblad Explorer* finally reached the dry dock in Norway in April 1972, nearly three months after the Antarctic crack-up. This was the same time that we had scheduled her first voyage toward the North Pole, moving far above the Arctic Circle.

The repair work at the shipyard moved ahead fast—so fast, in fact, that I was able to set up the first Arctic cruise in August, only a few months behind the original schedule. Thanks to the nucleus of intrepid travelers who seemed always ready to strike out for new territory, we were able to sail on our August schedule from Kristiansund, on the west coast of Norway, with a full complement of passengers. This would amount to a second shakedown cruise. The engines had been rebuilt and the ship completely refurbished; it was like sailing on an entirely new vessel. This was both good and bad—good because everything was spanking new again, and bad because we still had to check everything out.

Since we were proceeding up the Norwegian coast toward Bear Island, or Bjørnøya, we would be able to double-check the performance as we cruised through the fjords before we got into open ocean. But within a day, as we entered a spectacular fjord, the generators failed us.

This created a complete blackout and caused the engines to stop. We drifted slowly toward the ominous rocks in the narrow fjord. They seemed to be coming up to meet us. I forced myself to stop thinking the unthinkable—that the *Lindblad Explorer* would go aground again. Below, the engineers worked frantically to get the auxiliary generator going, which they succeeded in doing only minutes before we would have struck the rocks. We proceeded northward and were lucky to find two tugs that could tow us into port. Here we radioed the shipyard for assistance, and on the following day, the generators were repaired. From that time on, the *Explorer* has been functioning like a Swiss watch.

After a thorough inspection and testing, we headed out toward Bird Island, just below the Arctic Circle and almost due south of Spitsbergen. Here we would spend a day and a half inspecting the rich plant and bird life and the relics of an early whaling station, and visiting a lonely Norwegian meteorological outpost. Unlike the Antarctic, which has practically no vegetation, Bird Island holds fifty-three different species of plants and many species of birds, such as the fulmar, auk, and gull; these birds share the island with the Norwegian puffin, guillemot, northern eider, purple sandpiper, and Arctic skua.

The polar regions of the north and south have much in common, but the details are figuratively as well as literally poles apart. The Antarctic is a continent surrounded by ocean; the Arctic is an ocean surrounded by continents. The ice even has a different character. Eskimos and Arctic Indians form the native population of the north; the south has no native population whatever. Penguins are never found in the north, just as polar bears are never found in the south.

Our first landfall at Bear Island provided a spectacular sight with its high, steep cliffs jutting out of the water—an isolated speck in the distance, much farther north than the top of Alaska and most of Greenland. Coming ashore in our Zodiacs, we found the Norwegian weather station in a state of shock. Two days before, one of the young meteorologists had left the station building in the early morning for a routine check of his instruments. He had returned only to find that the door had slammed shut, locking him out. Before he could act, a young polar bear came at him and ripped him to death instantly. Arrangements were being made to send his remains back to Norway that day.

The incident was not only a tragedy for the weather station; it was also a grim warning to us. There is little you can do about a polar bear attack in the open. One expert told us the only thing to do is to drop part of your clothing as you run. Theoretically, the bear is supposed to stop to investigate your clothing while you continue running away. Another theory is that you should throw yourself on the ground and roll up into a ball. The rounder you wrap yourself, the safer you are supposed to be.

Neither technique was appealing or reassuring. We issued a stern warning to beware of the danger of an approaching polar bear. We also planned to do any polar bear viewing from the safety of the ship. Since we would be going through pack ice and many floes, we would surely sight some bears from a safe vantage point.

We continued northward toward the Pole, heading to the east of Spitsbergen, with the pack ice scraping constantly against the bow and sides of the double hull, a strange, hollow, and resonant sound that re-minded us we were now in the Arctic. As in the Antarctic, the waves and swells of the ocean were gone; the huge pancakes of ice flattened the waters and kept them calm. At the edge of the ice pack, the problem is that of "growlers" and "bergy bits"—big chunks of ice that float on top of the sea and are swept up at high velocity and smash hard into the ship. These are a greater danger than icebergs, which can be detected well in advance. They are made of ice several years old that has melted and been refrozen until it becomes hard as steel. Fortunately, we were built to withstand them. In the north, there is less salinity in the sea than in the Antarctic, which makes the growlers harder and more dangerous.

We approached King Karl's Land, which is noted for harboring polar bears. The weather was beautiful when we arrived. Shortly after the Zodiacs were ashore, however, we were surrounded by a deep fog. I became concerned quickly because I assumed there might be polar bears nearby, and I moved inland to check how far in our people had gone before the fog set in. Lady Scott and her son Falcon accompanied me. In a short while, however, we became lost. We plodded on, trying to keep an eye out for polar bears, which would be barely distinguishable in the murk.

Quite suddenly, we came on a small hut no larger than an oversized tent. I was startled to see fresh polar bear footprints, to say nothing of their droppings, equally fresh. I bent down and looked in through a window and saw two young men sleeping inside. They woke when I tapped on the window, and they sat up, apparently horrified at the sight of us. They quickly let us in the entrance, which was so low we had to bend down to enter. We discovered they were Norwegians manning a Decca station for ship navigation in the polar region. They told us that only a few minutes before, several polar bears had surrounded the hut, and that the day before they had counted seventeen of them on the small island. The pack ice surrounding the shores had broken up and drifted away, stranding the bears there. There was no way they could be shooed off the island until the pack ice drifted back to shore. With the thick fog, there was no way of knowing where the bears might be lurking.

They had a chart, compass, and two rifles, and we rushed back toward the beach to notify the crew to sound the emergency call on the horn. The fog was fortunately lifting somewhat. Coming over a small ridge, I stumbled on an extraordinary sight. Beneath me in the snow were two elderly ladies from the ship, each rolled up in a tight ball. Standing just a few feet above them, we discovered another passenger, Evelyn Scott of Okemos, Michigan, wearing a large white fur hat that in the murk of the fog appeared to the cowering ladies as nothing less than a polar bear.

Ms. Scott recalls the incident vividly: "Arctic trips always bring forth hopes of seeing polar bears. An advance notice on the bulletin board warned that the island we were to visit the next day had some polar bears wandering around. We had been told the safest action to take was to sink slowly to the ground, turn to the side, and curl into a fetal position and lie still. The bear would probably sniff around a little, but would do no harm.

"The next day, I walked up quite a steep hill. Reaching the crest, I looked down to see two little ladies, fellow passengers, on the ground lying on their sides. Very slowly, I looked around, not daring to breathe, thinking surely a bear was about to inspect the prone victims, but there was no bear around. Then understanding dawned.

"I was wearing a huge white fox hat, and they had seen it coming up the other side of the hill. I laughed to let them know I was there. They were understandably embarrassed, but I think a bit disappointed. What a story that would have been!"

After the incident, we herded the passengers back to the Zodiacs for a hasty retreat to the ship. Here we had a system that we follow on any Zodiac expedition to the shore. As the passengers go down the ladder to the Zodiacs waiting to bring them ashore, they take with them a tag with their cabin number on it from a peg board. On their return, they hang the tags back up so that the officers can make a complete check for any absentees.

In this case, one tag was missing after all the other passengers were safely back aboard. The conspicuous open space indicated that a sixty-year-old lady from Cabin 308 had not returned with the others. I have learned from experience that the older passengers consistently show more sense of adventure than many half their age—and women often more than their husbands.

Polar bears are dangerous enough when you can see them and have a place to run to. To have a group of them sidle up in a thick fog was not a planned feature of adventure travel. Keith Shackleton, the two Norwegians, and I took off in a Zodiac to return to shore. Since the lady passenger had not responded to the ship's horn, we were convinced that the worst had happened. We brought a stretcher with us.

We lost no time in beaching the craft, shouting at intervals, and waiting for a response. It wasn't long before we found her, sitting quietly on a rock completely unruffled.

"I didn't know you had gone back to the ship," she said. "I just found the atmosphere here enchanting and mysterious—even in the fog. I was enjoying myself so much, I had no idea anything was amiss."

We whisked her back to the ship. We could see the shore plainly now, and not far from where our passenger had been sitting stood a whole group of polar bears who were waving their paws at us. I shuddered as I thought to myself, we must never have been more than a hundred yards away from them.

It wasn't until we proceeded north past the 8oth parallel to circumnavigate the island of Spitsbergen that we had another experience with a polar bear. We are always ready to act spontaneously to make a detour while we're under way, if the weather is right and something unusual is at hand. In the South Pacific, it might be a desert island that looks attractive and may never before have been visited. We'll drop an anchor, and go ashore to explore it or snorkel and swim on a virgin white beach. In the polar regions, if the ice is safe and tested, we may disembark all the passengers on a sturdy ice floe and stage a complete barbecue. It's a simple matter to drive dead man anchors into the ice and drift along with the floe.

We did just this off the coast of Spitsbergen under a crisp blue sky. As we were finishing up, a curious polar bear appeared in the distance and began slowly moving toward us. Everyone climbed safely up the ship's side and gathered on the deck or by the portholes that were eye level with the ice, as the bear came up and tried to get aboard. It is one thing to see one in a zoo; it's another to see one up close in his own environment. We lowered him a bucket of steak, which he enjoyed immensely, along with a pail of Coca-Cola, which he drank with zest. He stayed by the side of the ship for over an hour, then finally decided that he had had enough. He loped away, ran across one floe, then jumped into and swam across open water to several others before disappearing. He would have made a great commercial for Coca-Cola.

Passenger Hazel Hansen of La Mesa, California, recalls the incident, and on a later *Lindblad Explorer* trip in the Pacific she was greeted by Captain Hasse Nilsson, who said to her, "I know you have been with us before, but I can't remember which cruise."

Ms. Hansen replied, "I was on the Arctic expedition when we met the polar bear."

"Oh, I'm glad you're here," the captain said. "No one believes me when I tell them we stopped the ship in the ice and fed the bear Coca-Cola and beefsteak. Now you can back me up!"

The captain expressed a common complaint among Lindblad travelers. They run into so many strange experiences that when they get home, half their friends have trouble believing them. Even I have trouble believing some passengers.

All the islands of the Spitsbergen archipelago are tucked inside the Arctic Circle, surrounded by Arctic ice and 400 miles north of the tip of Norway. Nearly half of the few people living here are Soviet citizens. The Vikings discovered the land in the twelfth century, but it was five centuries later that the English got serious about it, in trying to find the famous Northwest Passage to the Orient and its riches.

In 1829, on the ship *Victory,* John Ross tried to find the Northwest Passage, but instead not only discovered the existence of the shifting magnetic North Pole—at that time northeast of Baffin Island—but also proved that men could spend four winters in a row in the Arctic. He further introduced to the world a race of people known as Eskimos, which proved that man could exist for generations in the Arctic wastes.

Our first targets in Spitsbergen were Danskoya and Amsterdamoya. It was from the former island that the Swedish explorer Salomon Andrée tried with two companions to reach the Pole by balloon in the 1890s. They were forced down on an ice floe in Russian territory, and their frozen bodies were not found until 1930. A few relics still remain.

On Amsterdamoya, we found the site of a seventeenth-century Dutch whaling port. All that remained were the ruins of what had obviously been a large city of several thousand inhabitants—the ghosts of tidy stone houses and neatly laid-out streets, along with the foundations of the old vats that were used for boiling whale blubber.

Along the sixty-mile coast of Spitsbergen are two unusual settlements. At Longyearbyen, over 1000 Norwegian coal miners live in barracks, eat in a common mess hall, and share a community center that provides entertainment, a library, and chapels, along with a gymnasium. There are 250 women here, including cooks and waitresses at the canteen, and wives of the foreman, engineers, and executive staff.

In 1920 the islands of Spitsbergen were ceded to Norway by the Treaty of Paris on the condition that the other signatories, including the United States and the Soviet Union, should have equal access to the natural resources there. No military installations could be set up, however. The Soviets had obtained coal-mining rights from Norway and had established the settlement of Barentsburg, just twenty-five miles away from Longyearbyen. No one except Norwegian officials had visited there. When we brought the brightly colored *Lindblad Explorer* to within fifty yards of the dock, we did not know what sort of reception we would get.

Peter Scott, Keith Shackleton, and I went ashore in a Zodiac, to be met by the Soviet settlement leader. He greeted us very cordially and responded with enthusiasm when he heard the names of my companions, who, it turned out, were well known in Russia for their work as naturalists. Without delay, the Russians invited the *Explorer* to pull up to the dock. In the settlement, we were treated to black Russian bread and sausages, along with ample quantities of caviar and vodka. Life is made more bearable for the Russians in this isolated outpost by a full orchestra and a cadre of professional entertainers who, together with talented amateurs, make up a 200-voice chorus. They are joined by a theater company that includes dancers and singers. For the privilege of mining here, the Soviets pay Norway a fee for each ton of coal mined, and the residents pay 4 percent tax on personal incomes, just as the Norwegians do.

When evening came, we reciprocated by inviting nearly fifty of the Russian staff aboard the *Explorer* for dinner. They had hearty appetites. It was a happy encounter, and we repeated the experience in the following years, as we continued to be the only passenger ship to visit this Soviet enclave.

From Barentsburg, we prepared to head north in the pack ice to reach the farthest north point we could for the record, keeping a sharp eye out for icebergs and growlers. Compared to the hardships suffered by the early explorers, our voyage was a luxury, but there was still that atmosphere of danger that greets anyone sailing above the Arctic Circle. We turned toward Greenland only after reaching latitude 82°, which still remains a record for passenger ships.

We made our landfall on the northeast coast of Greenland, the largest island in the world. Its length would stretch from New York to

Wyoming. Only 49,000 people inhabit its 840,000 square miles—four times the area of France. Seven-eighths of the island consists of an enormous ice cap, with a thickness of up to 14,000 feet, on a high plateau.

Because of this ice cap, many think that Greenland and Iceland should switch names. The nearest piece of land to the North Pole is Cape Jessup, only 400 miles below. One theory is that Greenland may be a collection of small islands covered up by the ice cap to form glaciers; these glaciers, in turn, break off into the sea to form tremendous icebergs. The glaciers move up to 100 feet in a single day.

All but 10 percent of the population live along the west coast, where the climate is considerably warmer. We edged carefully toward one of the few small pure Eskimo settlements on the east coast, at Scoresby Sound, at the entrance of a breathtaking fjord. With a clear blue sky, we cruised through a land of black peaks, white snow, and blue ice and water to eventually put ashore, where we greeted our first Eskimos.

They were smiling and friendly, awed by the sight of the *Lindblad Explorer.* Around us were tall wooden racks for drying meat, out of the reach of the huskies and wild animals. Also stored on the racks were upside-down kayaks used by the hunters to harpoon seals for their meat supply. Literally hundreds of howling dogs were tied up. They produced a characteristic sound, continuing day and night, a sound found in all northern Eskimo villages. The huskies are friendly with people, but often have the inclination to tear each other apart. The women— dressed in colorful clothing with jewelry, beaded collars, and hand embroidery—were beaming at us.

Before long, one of the men in the village began thumping on his sealskin drum, while another began a monotonous chant, swaying from side to side, his feet remaining stationary. Soon, the other villagers joined in with the song as the rhythm grew more intense. The music was shrill and eerie, creating a trancelike state among the group. At times the women joined in, dropping their quiet shyness, dancing and singing with unexpected abandon.

By tradition, Eskimo women are retiring. Dance is one of the few public outlets they have to release their emotions. Another is the cus-

tom of mothers' continuing to nurse their sons up through the age of puberty, or even beyond. One woman is reported to have nursed her son
until he got married. They seem to do this as a matter of pride and as a
symbol that they are still young enough to be procreative.

In 1823 Captain Scoresby must have found a less colorful picture
here when he arrived at the sound that was named after him. He
counted barely a dozen Eskimos on the whole east coast, and they
promptly scattered and disappeared from their dwellings, leaving their
smoldering fires as they did so.

In 1972 we found the villagers prosperous, with time to turn their
oars and harpoons into works of art, embellishing them with narwhal or
walrus ivory. They dislike being called Eskimos, preferring to be
called Greenlanders. They have developed an extraordinary culture of
their own. There is little question they arrived in the Arctic from crossing over the Bering Strait from Central Asia. Their mahogany color and
broad features closely resemble those of the Mongols. Under Danish
rule, their life became somewhat easier, with schools and buildings,
and even heat in some cases. There are few igloos left—we discovered
some on Ellesmere Island in 1973, but for the most part, these are
gone.

Traditionally the Eskimos are nomadic hunters. In the last few de-
cades, they have been weaned off hunting and have moved into settlements to be taught how to fish more productively.

In theory, this is good. But with the change have come disadvantages
like alcoholism and widespread gonorrhea—nearly universal afflic-
tions. In other words, not too much good has resulted from changing
the Eskimo into a village dweller instead of a nomadic hunter. The
United States has made the same mistakes in the Aleutians and North
Alaska, in the full belief that it has been doing the right thing, but blind
to the side effects.

We brought the headman and his wife aboard the *Explorer,* and his
hospitality suddenly became overwhelming. Speaking in Danish, he instructed his wife to sit on my lap and convey any favors whatever. With
bathing facilities nonexistent at the village, and with the habit of wash-
ing their hair in urine, Eskimo women are rather lacking in olfactory

appeal. The *Explorer* captain was sitting near, and I suggested to the headman that since the captain was the most important person aboard, it was for the captain to take advantage of his generosity, at which point she rushed over to his lap. After he explained that he also couldn't take advantage of this very generous gift, the headman and his wife went back to shore unperturbed. Later, a message arrived from the headman. It stated that he could understand that we might not have found his wife attractive enough and was dispatching his daughters. We again politely refused, although there were officers aboard the ship who were more than willing to accept the kind attention of these pretty girls.

Scoresby Sound had amazingly little ice in it, and we arranged the next day to circumnavigate a large island known as Milne Land with the help of Eskimo guides from the village. They had done so in a kayak; no large ship had ever cruised the waters. At this location, the Franz Josef and King Oscar fjords join with Scoresby Sound to form the largest ramification of fjords in all the world. Here some of the highest mountains in East Greenland show their lofty peaks. Keeping a sharp watch on our radar and depth sounders, we moved cautiously through the narrow waters, with the mountains 6000 feet above us, and the tongues of glaciers calving at unexpected intervals. We also had our first view of musk oxen on the island.

The calving of the glacier foot is dangerous because of both falling ice and the wave that follows. If you're in a Zodiac, you have to lie well back. The break explodes with the sound of cannon fire as the berg slips from its "dry dock," and brash ice scatters all around it. The big bergs break more serenely from the slower moving glaciers, and lie there as the sun and the waves resculpture their outlines. Eventually, they are carried by the Arctic Current down the Denmark Strait, where their prodigious mass makes them endure as they move toward the St. Lawrence sea-lanes.

As we moved out to the Denmark Strait and down the eastern coast of Greenland toward Cape Farewell, we put in at Angmagssalik, a larger settlement that even has an airfield with weekly flights to Iceland. Here the emergence of a new race becomes evident—a mixture of Danes and Eskimos, characteristic of much of modern Greenland.

Flowering plants—including Iceland poppy, *Cassiope, Cerastium, Potentilla, Dryas,* and *Epobium*—are everywhere during the summer months. It is also possible to see Greenland hare, ptarmigan, raven, wild geese, eider, skua, tern, and gull. Even polar bear or walrus show up regularly.

It was on our way southward toward Cape Farewell that we encountered one of the most heartening sights I have seen. The Sierra Club had estimated that the entire population of the largest living animal, the giant 120-foot-long blue whale, amounted to 80 or so. As we came close to the cape, we suddenly saw several enormous pods of the blue whale and were able to count more than 400. The official estimates of the number of blue whales now vary between 10,000 and 20,000. Often too many pessimistic reports are given on the survival of endangered species, but I like to see that some successes are stressed, and that the efforts of conservationists are applauded.

We have continued with many voyages to the Arctic since that first voyage in 1972, all of them stimulating and exciting to me, as well as to the passengers. We later extended our itineraries to the Canadian Arctic, including Ellesmere Island, Baffin Land, and sometimes the magnetic pole, which changes its position from year to year, nearly a thousand miles south of the geographical Pole. In Hudson Bay, the calving of the icebergs is particularly sensational, an almost constant process as you sail along the shores. It is hard to schedule voyages there because the bay is shallow and it is the last area where the ice becomes free after the winter freeze.

The lonely Canadian town of Churchill sits on the northwest shore of the bay, with a population of a few Eskimos and many Indians. Churchill is the terminus of the Hudson Bay Railroad, which carries grain for shipment abroad in the brief period when the port is open. Most interesting is that polar bears rim the shore in this region, and create a hazard for the town of Churchill in the spring and fall. When a bear approaches the community a siren is sounded, and a polar bear patrol immediately is dispatched. The bear is then tranquilized and put aboard a helicopter, flown a safe distance away, and released.

Our voyages in the Canadian Arctic were without incident, except for one time when we were frozen in solid at Pond Inlet and had to remain for several days jammed in the ice. But the *Explorer* survived admirably, and we expanded our trips even more by moving up to the north of Alaska, through the Bering Strait separating Russia from Alaska, to the Chukchi Sea and the pack ice of the Arctic Sea. We would be going far beyond the routes of the conventional Alaskan cruise ships on the Inside Passage, moving on from Glacier Bay and Skagway, where most other cruises end. The rarer sights are memorable: the Malaspina Glacier, larger than Rhode Island; the killer whales and beluga; the musk ox on Nunivak weighing up to 700 pounds; the many thousands of walrus on Walrus Island, the largest concentration outside the Soviet Union; and the largest fur seal herds in the world on the Pribilof Islands in the middle of the Bering Sea.

Here is another encouraging story. Avaricious hunting had made these herds almost extinct by 1911. But as a result of an international agreement for their protection, an amazing comeback took place. From a low of 300,000 the Pribilof fur seals have now increased to 1.4 million, with Saint George Island being entirely closed to hunters. Here can be viewed the young male seals in their "loitering grounds," as the large territorial bulls protect their territories while waiting for the arrival of the females.

At Little Diomede Island, you can look across two and a half miles of water to Big Diomede Island, which is Russian territory and a full day away because the international date line runs between them. All through these parts of Alaska, the early Russian influence still remains in place-names and architecture, as in the onion-like tops of the Russian Orthodox churches.

The successes of the Arctic tours showed that the *Lindblad Explorer* had justified herself fully after her unsteady beginning and her Antarctic contusions. The fact that she was able to come back strong and whole was of great satisfaction to me, and proved the worthiness of her design. Before our maiden Arctic trip began in 1972, while I was waiting for the repairs to be made, I turned to focus on South America again. As usual, it was only one of several simultaneous projects, but one of the most fascinating.

XII

The Amazon
River Across a Continent

BACK in the mid-1960s, when I had first begun to explore the more unusual places, I was fortunate in having Esperanza Rivaud as my companion. She knew her native continent well and could find those places
that few people knew existed. There is Salta, in northern Argentina,
where the mica surface of the mountains glistens in starshine, and the
gauchos dance with music and drums. There is a little village in Peru,
where Lindblad Travel was later able to restore a church that had priceless frescoes buried under layers of wall paint. There are Tierra del
Fuego and Lago Argentino in Patagonia, areas few North Americans
had ever visited. Here are lakes with enormous glaciers running into
them, which calve into icebergs as if this were a polar region. There is
the Beagle Channel, with a topography different in image than commonly thought, including fjords like those in Norway or Alaska. Here
is a passage that is regarded as the uttermost end of the inhabited
world—and one of the most spectacular.

In this package of surprises, Tierra del Fuego is a land of sheep and
farms inhabited largely by Scottish people who came here over a century ago to grow prosperous on their livestock. Few have ever been
close to their native Scotland or to England, yet they wear traditional

tweeds and British-tailored suits, and look un–South American in every detail. In Valdéz, you can find clusters of Welsh countrymen in their traditional costumes, speaking Welsh and relaxing in teahouses and pubs that look as if they have been lifted out of the countryside of Wales.

In Brazil, two villages in Mato Grosso, deep in the interior, are made up almost entirely of descendants of Confederate soldiers, speaking in a southern accent mixed with a Portuguese dialect. If you go into parts of Bolivia or Brazil on foot or horseback, you can suddenly stumble on a complete Japanese village, with meticulously laid-out gardens and fine fat cattle. South America is really not what people think it is. In addition to its own culture, with its Indian and Latin strains, it is also English, Welsh, Italian, and German, and full of kaleidoscopic pageantry.

My early surveys, however, were all just a prelude to planning the Amazon cruise of the *Explorer.* She would be working her way south from the 1972 Arctic cruise carrying several cruises en route and eventually would be ready for her 2300-mile trip up the Amazon in autumn. Here is the world's largest river system, so large that it is often called the river sea.

Its volume of water exceeds that of all the nine next largest rivers combined, including the Nile. The basin includes the world's greatest tropical forest, which is so large that it was once thought to be the main source of oxygen in the earth's atmosphere. Although this theory no longer holds, the river still has a profound effect on the atmosphere. Here trees grow to over a hundred feet in height. The forest harbors as many as 3000 different species of flora and fauna per square mile.

Estimates have been made that there are 500 to 2000 varieties of fish, including twenty-foot-long catfish, manatee, and pink or white dolphins. The last are never intentionally killed, because legend has it that the soul of any person who has drowned goes on to live inside a dolphin. The species of birds, insects, and reptiles are equally uncountable. There are over fifty different species of monkeys alone and more than 2000 different types of birds.

The *Explorer,* with her small draft and maneuverability, would serve as an ideal riverboat. She could make available inland waters that other large cruise ships could not handle. With our fleet of Zodiacs, we would be able to go ashore every day to explore remote lagoons, networks of streams and tributaries, and isolated Indian villages rarely visited.

The Amazon forest rests in and on rotted leaves and bark that lie in mushy ground and decaying layers. It is not really soil at all. The tree roots sprout out at the base and stand mainly on the ground, not under it, a very fragile support. Underneath the soggy layer is water.

The Transamazonica Highway and other roads reaching up from the new capital of Brazil, Brasília, are a noble effort for opening up and distributing new lands to the poor. The problem with these 200-foot-wide highway swaths through the jungle is that the adjoining lands have to be cleared, the stumps burned, and new vegetation planted. The first year, the result is good. The second year is fair. The third year, there is disaster. Then more land is cleared, and the process begins all over again. Instead of soil, a red clay called laterite appears. Once a red desert begins to form it can never be reclaimed. A process described as ''green hell to red desert'' takes place. The government is trying to fight this by prohibiting any more than half a holding from being cut, but the danger still remains.

Today, big freighters and Brazilian navy vessels move up and down the river with considerable ease in spite of tricky currents that can approach five or six knots. But I was not interested in merely cruising up and down the river. I wanted to scout where we could find the rare eagles and the bird called the pia, which screams in unbelievable volume; the crocodiles, alligators, and concentrations of piranhas; headhunting Indian villages; and other rare sights.

Oddly enough, I began my travel detective work in Liverpool, where the Bank Line that operates Amazon freighters was located. But, in spite of their experience, they were unable to give me any meaningful information. Their pilots had one thing in mind: to deliver the freight. They rarely looked right or left at the riverbanks except for navigation.

I went from Liverpool to Rio de Janeiro to check with the Brazilian navy. Here I received a great deal of help. Their navigation charts covered almost every inch of the river. They recommended that I talk to the Brazilian river pilots at Belém, the entry port at the broad mouth of the Amazon. They constantly made the 2300-mile run from Belém in Brazil to the Peruvian border, where pilots had to be changed. But they, too, had little information about flora, fauna, and people along the banks and up the tributaries.

There was a lot to learn from them, however. The variance of depth in wet and dry seasons is hard to believe—a sixty-foot differential. The pilots warned about the large floating logs, partly submerged, that could ram the hull like a spear. Later a friend of mine failed to heed the warning. In a new cabin cruiser, he first had the exposed twin propellers knocked off, and after that a log went through his whole ship and sank it. Some of the pilots told us that we might not ever complete a successful voyage; their freighters had constant trouble with this hazard. But again, we had something they didn't have: the reinforced hull and double bottom that would make us different from any other ship on the river. We also had our reinforced rudder and protected single propeller, built for ice-duty at the poles, but which appeared to be a distinct asset in the Amazon.

There were other warnings. The Amazon is an international waterway, and political situations were very volatile. By international agreement, Peru, Colombia, and Brazil were not permitted to close the channels of the Amazon, but Argentina, Uruguay, and Paraguay had been able to close off the Río de la Plata to meaningful international trade. Added to this problem would be the basic need of taking on potable water. The trip from the mouth of the Amazon to Iquitos in Peru would take some eighteen days. The Amazon is muddy, turbulent, and full of silt. The *Explorer* was basically designed for saltwater voyages. We could easily distill saltwater to replenish our supply, but were not able to distill sweet water. We would probably take in a lot of sand. We learned, however, to locate the tributaries that flowed with fresh, clear water, where you can see the bottom and where we could pump the tanks full. Adding chlorine, we could obtain a safe and ample water supply. These refilling stops would also provide excellent exploring on sandy beaches and inviting water for swimming and snorkeling.

With the help of Lyall Watson, who had scouted both the Seychelles and Indonesia with me, I began our survey to find those areas and anchorages that would be most interesting. We went about our scouting trips separately. Aside from the anchor points of Belém on the Atlantic end and Iquitos in Peru, a few hundred miles from the Pacific, there were three key focal points. These included the incredible isolated city of Manaus, almost dead center in the continent. There was Santarém, halfway between Manaus and Belém, about 400 miles from each. There was the city of Leticia, also isolated, where the boundaries of Brazil, Colombia, and Peru meet. Lyall and I began piecing together the segments of the river like a giant jigsaw puzzle.

I began in Belém, even though I had been told that the upper reaches would be more interesting. Belém is the major port at the mouth of the Amazon, where exotic fruits and vegetables and colorful fish of bizarre varieties are to be found at the market. Medicine stands sell potions for every ailment: herbs, barks, roots, snake tails, skinks, and lizard tongues. The Basilique in Belém has fine mosaic-covered walls, carved cedar ceilings, and magnificent stained-glass windows.

Directly across the bay from Belém is the island of Marajó, larger than Switzerland, where gaucholike cowboys herd the cattle of wealthy cattle ranchers. In the rainy season, a large portion of the island is under water, the reason huge herds of water buffalo flourish there. These animals are not indigenous. Back in the times when the British were importing thousands of East Indians to work in the sugar plantations in Guyana and Trinidad, they also brought water buffalo. A ship bearing a herd of them to the Amazon foundered on the shores of Marajó. These animals disappeared into the wilds to make their own way—which they did, very successfully. Today, tens of thousands of them roam the island, some of them domesticated, some not. Those that are not are very apt to attack an unwary person, and they vie for the land with the cattle. Since the water buffalo can survive on much less, and are at home in swampy lands, they thrive there.

The island is also full of wild pigs, which share the scene with many alligators and crocodiles. The latter have developed the nasty habit of biting udders off the cows. The channels around the island are very deep and very narrow—they would be just wide enough for the *Explorer*. Howler monkeys and raucous parrots frame both sides of the shore. There are plenty of butterflies, beetles, dragonflies, and mantis—but strangely enough, few biting insects. Marajó made an ideal jumping-off place for our cruises.

Continuing the survey, I flew by small plane to Manaus, 900 miles to the west, where the Rio Negro flows into the mainstream Amazon. Manaus is the capital of the Amazonas state, a large port for oceangoing vessels, an unusual city of over 100,000. Here in the middle of the great forest is a thriving city with beautiful homes and extensive culture. It was founded in the late seventeenth century, and a steamship line began regularly scheduled service from Belém in 1853.

It was rubber that changed Manaus from a handful of mud huts and set up a phenomenon that equaled the gold rush in Alaska. In fifteen years, rubber exports jumped from 70,000 pounds a year to over 5 million after the boom started in the 1830s. The rubber barons of Manaus changed quickly to robber barons. Indians were put into peonage. Foreigners swarmed in: English, Germans, French, Americans, Portuguese. The peons hacked through trackless forest to isolated trees, sliced into the bark with machetes, and drew the white milky fluid into buckets. Then they heated it over a fire until it coagulated enough to be made into a large, 200-pound ball. By 1910, the price had risen to nearly $3 a pound, most of it going to the barons. Manaus became a Paris in the forest. By 1900, it had electric streetlights, telephones, and running water. Some of the barons were so fastidious that they shipped their laundry to Paris.

By 1912, one-third of Brazil's export trade was in rubber, and Manaus was the principal beneficiary. But as the plantation growers in Asia discovered how to grow and harvest the product more efficiently than in the Amazonas, prices began to drop. The sloppy methods of the growers were no match for the techniques used in Asia. The boom was over for the rubber barons. For a while, Manaus became a ghost city, and it remained that way until expansionism and the new highway system through the jungles restored its economic blood.

The most striking improbability set in an area surrounded by jungle is the opera house that has been restored to its former glory. With pillars of Italian marble and a colorful tiled dome, it sits graciously behind a broad, tiled plaza, with elegant statuary in its center. Sarah Bernhardt once played there, Caruso sang, Pavlova danced, and full-dress audiences applauded. The edifice stands in sharp contrast to the busy commercial waterfront with its sheds and wharves, where jute, timber, and steel from local mills await shipment.

As interesting as Manaus is, it served mainly as a jumping-off point for my scouting expeditions above and below it. I arranged for a series of small boat and seaplane charters, and even canoes, to find out where we could take the ship or the Zodiacs off river. Sometimes as many as fifty streams run parallel to each other in certain areas. We could skim by boat at times directly into the forests, an eerie experience providing better looks at colorful birds, and iguanas that curl around a high limb and suddenly drop into the waters beside you. I found remote Indian villages that we could visit on future voyages. I discovered many original cultures still remaining, self-contained ethnic groups who had little dealing with the outside world. At one point, I found fascinating primitive abstract paintings on apparel colored with vegetable dyes and used as ceremonial robes and masks. Here also was a strange hair-pulling ritual for girls when they reached puberty.

There were many other settlements up and down the river, communities that eked out a living from this lush but fragile vegetable garden. There were small settlements made up of a mixture of Indians and Portuguese. The most prosperous were those of the Japanese. Their orderly gardens were highly productive, and they shipped their produce up and down the river by motorboat.

There were some things to watch out for. Piranhas, called roving teeth with a fish on their backs, could scavenge a cow or bull in a matter of minutes. Four-hundred-pound catfish were said to swallow up a child occasionally. Head-hunting Indian tribes still existed in some areas. But these were either easy to avoid or could be observed safely from our craft.

Esperanza, Lyall, and I scoured the river from April to July in 1972—very close to the time the *Explorer* was ready to leave her dry dock in Norway for her Arctic voyage. By the time we sat down to piece together the segments, we had pinpointed ninety-two different anchorages where we could encounter exciting birds, wildlife, settlements, dances and rituals, and a panoply of varied cultures. There would be ample opportunities for fishing and snorkeling en route in clear blue waters bordered by white beaches of silica sand. For the amateur naturalist, we planned continuous lectures on board ship and a checklist of 1700 species of birds that might be encountered over the eighteen-day cruise.

I joined the *Lindblad Explorer* in Belém in October 1972, after it had completed its voyage in the Arctic and an en route cruise through the Caribbean. She was running beautifully now, ready for her first freshwater 4600-mile roundtrip.

After braving the river in canoes and small motorboats it was a treat to relax on the *Explorer* as we started upstream through the narrow channels of Marajó Island. There was a particular thrill in standing on either side of the captain's bridge, which almost touched the trees. Just off Marajó, the mouth of the Amazon is nearly 200 miles wide, big enough to grow its own weather. Huge cumulus clouds build up over the island, while the sky above the river is blue and cloudless. The narrowing of the deep channels of Marajó creates a sudden contrast.

Beyond the delta and into the mainstream of the Amazon, we traveled mainly by night and through the steaming hot hours of midday in air-conditioned comfort. We planned our shore and Zodiac excursions in early morning and evening, when the weather was inviting. All along our course, the pink dolphins were going through their acrobatics with that mischievous smile that dolphins always seem to wear. Occasionally, rain would fall in one sharp, short rush, and afterward a gray mist would rise from the warm waters.

From the shores we could hear the howler monkeys—and they really do howl in a chorus, described by some as a "cascading roar." Most often you can hear their cries in the predawn hours, but often in the middle of the night. They have bulging stomachs requiring enormous quantities of leaves and fruit, and their howls apparently are intended to keep alien groups of monkeys away. They weigh up to twenty-five pounds and take the flood season in stride, as they are excellent swimmers.

Past the old fort at Óbidos, the river runs 200 feet deep, as the waterways connect, divide, and intermesh, forming a maze among the giant trees. We had to be careful in launching the Zodiacs from the overhead crane on the *Explorer* because of the swift current. The outboard has to be started the moment the rubber boat hits the water, and its bowline must be unhooked at the same moment. Our only serious accident happened in this way. The swift current dumped over a Zodiac with five passengers aboard, and within a short time they were swept a mile down the river before being rescued. Extra precautions prevented any repetition.

As the ship glided through the narrow channels, nothing was more startling to the remote villagers than to look up and see the bright red and white hull of the *Lindblad Explorer* five decks above them, for the ocean freighters never venture on many of these out-of-the-way channels, as we did. Some of the villagers rarely moved outside their own boundaries, or even had seen people from the outer world. At times we would drop anchor and visit the settlements by Zodiac; at others, we slid slowly by and observed their way of living at close range. We had full permission from Brazilian authorities to cruise the entire length of the river. What we did not realize was that at certain stops along the way, officials could be truculent or worse.

When we put into the town of Santarém, some 500 cruising miles after we had left Belém, we anchored near the shore and made plans to bring all our ninety-plus passengers ashore. The town lay at the junction of the Tapajós River, whose sparkling blue waters at its wide mouth blended with the chocolate turbulence of the Amazon. There were rubber plantations in the area, but they were skeletons of those in the nineteenth-century heyday.

In 1972 you could read a long sequence of horror stories about arrests and brutality that sprang up without apparent reason in Brazil, especially in remote areas where local officials were unrestrained and unconcerned about any impact of this behavior on the rest of the world. In this case, I was about to pay my respects to the local authorities, as we always do, whether it is at an Eskimo village or a remote Spice Island in the Banda Sea. I had with me our Indian guide, Moacir. Before I had a chance to inquire where the municipal headquarters were, Moacir and I found ourselves surrounded by police. We apparently had to have special permission to land at Santarém. Moacir and I were thrown into a police car and driven to jail. There was no chance to notify our passengers, the ship's officers, or Lyall Watson, who had remained on the ship to supervise the launching and return of the Zodiacs. At the jail, the officer in command was brusque. He said we were to be kept in jail until he was able to receive instructions from Brasília, a thousand miles away. He seemed so vituperative that I thought he was going to pull the ugly-looking revolver from his holster.

Moacir and I were put in adjoining cells. Over an hour went by. Then I heard the police come down the corridor and go into Moacir's cell. Without any motive at all, they began beating him up. His screams rang out in the corridor, as I listened with horror. My protests for them to stop were ignored. The police seemed to be enjoying the procedure sadistically. Finally, they left the cell, as Moacir continued sobbing. I tried to comfort him, but I couldn't even see him. Several more hours went by.

Then suddenly, I heard Lyall's and Esperanza's voices in the distance, echoing in the corridor. They were asking if the police knew anything of my whereabouts. I could hear the police answer clearly: they claimed they did not know who or where we were, or whom Lyall and Esperanza were talking about. They also claimed they had never even seen me or the guide, that there must be a mistake.

Now I was frozen with fear. If they denied our existence, how could they release us and make liars out of themselves? I was afraid to call out to Lyall and Esperanza because it might infuriate the police and cause another arrest. It was critical that Lyall remain by the ship and take action through the ship's radio if necessary. Soon the conversation stopped, and I figured that Lyall and Esperanza must have gone back to the ship.

At least three more hours passed, with nothing but the sound of muted voices in the background. It was futile to protest; it might have made matters even worse. I sat there in silence, not daring to create a disturbance, pondering the implication of the police denial of Moacir's and my existence. By doing so, they seemed to put us in the position of hostages who might better be liquidated, simply to prove they weren't lying. The stories of police deaths and brutality we had heard in São Paulo and Rio de Janeiro were vividly going through my mind.

Then I heard Lyall's voice again. Again the police denied they were holding us. Each time they denied it, it lessened our chances of ever being freed. I do not believe I have ever felt more terror. Again there was silence. It was now late in the evening. We had been in the cell block since early morning. If the police had not denied our existence, I would have felt some kind of hope that we would be released soon. This way, I didn't dare let myself think of the possible outcome.

After another couple of hours of intense mental stress, I heard the police coming down the corridor again. I had no idea what the verdict would be. It took only a few seconds for them to reach my cell, but it seemed hours. I had to expect the worst, but I was wrong. They opened the cell, and said that the matter had been settled from Brasília and I was free to go back to the ship with Moacir. I knew it was fruitless to protest their treatment of Moacir at the moment, but I hoped that some-day I would be able to. Meanwhile, I was grateful that we had both survived.

But there was a further indignity. Several officers insisted on coming aboard the ship to inspect it. It was obvious that they wanted "dash," the universal custom we always expect in remote ports of call, which requires us to hand out liquor and cigarettes to create a smooth landing and, usually, interference-free visits. Here at Santarém, I felt this was adding insult to usury. The thought of giving them liquor and cigarettes was repulsive. But we did it and were glad to be on our way to Manaus, 400 miles upriver. I had bad nightmares as I slept in my cabin that night—but also great relief.

We spent a pleasant two days in Manaus, where there was much to see in addition to the spectacular opera house. Rubber was still being processed, and the vestiges of the homes of the rubber barons still remained: elegant structures of French and Victorian style, some of which had been imported in pieces all the way from Europe. A few sky-scrapers defied the jungle that surrounded the city, and a few modern real estate developments contrasted with the rococo style of the 1800s. On the docks, we studied the stonework of the customhouse, imported from Liverpool, with marble from Italy and crystal from Paris. The market is embellished with the still-standing wrought-iron work designed by Alexandre Eiffel, of Eiffel Tower fame.

The Rio Negro and the Amazon join at Manaus. Here the Amazon is called the Solimões. Near a bend in the Solimões, we visited Coari, a center for jute, coca, and Brazil nuts, where there was excellent swimming and sport fishing from the Zodiacs. We didn't linger long, as the *Explorer* ploughed through the currents toward Leticia, a frontier outpost joining Brazil, Colombia, and Peru. Here some distressing evidence of the blatant destruction of wildlife came to my attention. I first noticed the symptoms when several members of the crew and passengers came back from a visit ashore with an assortment of wild animals and skins they had bought from the village markets. There were snakes, birds, ocelots, and even a jaguar. I had seen signs of this illegal activity back in Manaus, in warehouses full of jaguar and ocelot pelts for export all over the world. But this practice was not as obvious as in Leticia.

All the illegal animal dealers went about their work in the cruelest way. Live monkeys were collected by the thousands and sold to pet shops and research laboratories all over the world. To hunt for them, they would put out a barrel of water in a clearing, and the monkeys would come and drink from it. Then they would start lacing the water with rum, gradually increasing the amount. Finally the concentration would become so strong that the creatures would get dead drunk and fall asleep around the clearing. It was then a simple matter to pick them up and dump them into big sacks. Since the baby monkeys would not survive without their mothers, they were put away by breaking their necks. Some of the baby skulls were used to make necklaces.

The next step was to put them into holding cages, where another percentage of the monkeys died. When it came to shipping by air, they were crowded into even smaller cages, and more would die en route.

The same was true with birds; the bottoms of their cages were littered with dead. It is estimated that fifteen monkeys died for every one that reached its foreign destination. Fortunately, the United States has put a stop to this kind of importation, under pressure from the World Wildlife Fund.

The skin merchants went about their routine almost as cruelly. The animal dealer would give the Indian a knife, spade, or pot for one of the skins, but the skins had to be free of bullet holes or knife wounds to be marketable. Consequently, the animals had to be poisoned or trapped. One estimate of the annual kill of jaguars during the 1960s was 15,000. Ocelot estimates ran to 80,000. Skins of rare snakes went even higher. When this ruthless exploitation was outlawed in 1967, the number killed is estimated to have been cut in half, but it is still continuing, and the future is not bright.

None of this would be going on if there were not a market for the animals and their pelts, but of course there is. To me, a fur coat never looks as good on a woman as it does on a jaguar or an ocelot. The United States has passed an Endangered Species Act, but some European countries have not. As long as a market exists, the destruction is bound to continue.

The public in general knows little about wildlife and the importance of maintaining an ecological balance. In a study by the Interior Department's Fish and Wildlife Service, Dr. Stephen Kellert of Yale noted a great lack of understanding among large segments of the U.S. population about wildlife conservation and management. Of over 3000 adults interviewed, most were extremely weak in their knowlege of endangered species. Few knew about the practice of clubbing baby seals or the destruction of dolphins by tuna fishermen. Concern about wildlife is greater among groups with higher education.

Interestingly, the wholesale slaughter of wildlife is greatly diminished in Peru and Ecuador. The reason is that the Jivaro Indians there have a nasty habit of taking people's heads and shrinking them. They have a particular liking for white heads, so the hunters make it a point not to slip into Jivaro territory. Although the numbers of wildlife like bear, deer, and jaguar are generally on the decrease in Brazil and Colombia, they are actually on the increase in the territory of the remote Jivaro headhunters.

Wildlife conservation has come late to the Amazonas, or to South America in general for that matter. A spectacular feat was carried out by a good friend of mine, Felipe Benavides, a Peruvian diplomat whose great grandfather and grandfather had each in their times been president of Peru. Felipe was able to persuade his government to establish the Manu National Park, which became the largest protected rain forest and marine wetland in the world. His battle to save the vicuña from almost certain extinction was an outstanding feat. Like its close cousin, the llama, the vicuña's fleece and skins were so much in demand that the animal was fast disappearing as a species. Almost single-handedly, Benavides fought for its protection, even contacting the president of France to implore him to stop the importation of the skins there. Although poaching still continues, estimates are that their population has risen from a scattered few to 35,000, most of which are in Benavides's reserve. He is bitter about the animal exporters in both Peru and Leticia. His contention is that if the herds are allowed to be rebuilt, plenty of vicuña wool will be available. The killing of the animal and the taking of its skin have brought the threat of extinction.

At Leticia, the Amazon still runs wide and deep. But there are some passages that do not run deep at all. At times we would have to send out our Boston Whaler outboard, equipped with an echo sounder, about twenty-five yards ahead of the *Lindblad Explorer* as we sailed up the final leg of the journey to Iquitos, in Peru, passing through a small stretch of the Amazon in Colombia.

It is strange to find a major seaport more than 2000 miles away from the Atlantic, here at this city of 80,000 people. There are still touches of colonial elegance in Iquitos, along with more of Eiffel's wrought-iron structures, as in Manaus. Here our first successful trip up the Amazon ended, as we prepared to take aboard a new set of passengers, who had arrived in Iquitos by air for the downstream trip back to Belém.

The loss of revenue of a ship that is not kept moving every day of the year can mount astronomically. Nearly every ocean liner operates on a hairline schedule. The *Queen Elizabeth II* barely touches into a port before it turns around and is off on a new voyage. A full schedule for a year or more has to be plotted, down to the exact hour the ship will leave and arrive at various ports. In a one year-plus schedule, for instance, we plotted the *Lindblad Explorer*'s voyages to begin at 1800 hours at Lyttleton, New Zealand, on January 30, and to arrive back there at 0700 hours more than a year later, on February 23. In between those terminal stops, there would be over 355 ports of call, each keyed in carefully to maintain a thirteen-month synchronized schedule. For instance, the ship would put in at Lautoka, Fiji, on February 13 at 0700; at Madang in Papua New Guinea on February 27 at 0700; at Manila on March 15 at 0800; at Colombo, Sri Lanka, at 0700 on May 1; at Mahé, Seychelles, at 1800 hours on May 12; at Djibouti at 1800 hours on May 20; at Port Said, Egypt, on June 5 at 0700; at Reykjavík, Iceland, at 0700 hours on August 14; at Iquitos, Peru, at 0700 hours on October 18; and so on through the year-plus; and these are only a few of the ports.

The maintenance of a schedule like this leaves little room for error, because nearly a hundred passengers may be waiting at scores of out-of-the-way places with their own synchronized schedules to follow. We had already had the disastrous delay as a result of the Antarctic grounding; I could not afford any more.

To keep the *Lindblad Explorer*'s continuity going, it was urgent to set up, explore, and consolidate the South Pacific and Indonesia, an area that appears to cover half of the world when you look at it on the globe. Keeping in mind that only 10 percent of the areas scouted turn out to be of genuine interest to the intelligent traveler, I had my work cut out for me. Again I had the help of Lyall Watson, who was familiar with Indonesia and had a sound instinct for picking out the most interesting places. I had already scouted Australia, New Guinea, and many of the islands of the South Pacific four or five years before. I could tie this in with the projected Indonesia cruises. The problem was to complete the job on time to enable us to recover from the severe setback caused by laying up the *Lindblad Explorer* for months.

XIII

INDONESIA, NEW GUINEA, AND THE PACIFIC
Spice, Coral, and Headhunters

In the late 1960s, I had scanned the potential of the Pacific, in a broad band around the equator. I was wondering whether the wing safari concept might not lend itself to Australia. There were plenty of planes, with airstrips scattered all over. My friend Jimmy James of BOAC (now British Airways) was, as usual, enthusiastic about the idea, and we solicited the help of Reginald Ansett in Sydney to launch our random scouting trip. Ansett was founder and chief executive of the Australian airlines that bore his name, a pioneer in the Australian tourist industry, and he knew the Australian outback well. My thoughts were not on the *Lindblad Explorer* at this time; I would turn my attention to that later.

Ansett provided us with an Aero Commander that seated five passengers in comfort. We had no set itinerary, being content to probe the reaches of the continent in a random pattern. We set out from Melbourne at four in the morning because of the intense heat in the outback that reaches 100 to 115° F routinely.

We were heading for a town called Cooberpeddy, where Italian, Greek, and Yugoslav immigrants have been mining opal for many years. They had developed an ingenious way to survive in such unbearable heat by digging their homes into the ground, cutting away the soft rock to build up to ten rooms in a single "house." They had staked out their land and mined the opal industriously to provide a comfortable living.

On approaching the landing strip there, I saw a forest of mine ventilation stacks and little else. The entire town was underground. There was little visible to indicate there were any inhabitants at all. Even the town hall and stores were below the surface.

What interested me was that the success of the community arose from the energy and frugality of the immigrants. Many Australian old-timers had no taste for the hard work in the mines and in other menial jobs. The new immigrants had been suffering from social restraints and lack of opportunity in the Old World. Coming to Australia, they found opportunity everywhere, and with hard work there were practically no limitations to what they could do by their own efforts. Without the enterprise of these immigrants, Australia would be a poorer nation.

The cooperative spirit of the town was rare. Money was not given the highest priority. The Italian grocer in his underground store was lavish with his credit. Some of his accounts were three or four years old, but he was confident that if his customers kept searching, they would eventually hit opal and pay up. Cooberpeddy proved that when the incentive is right, every man will work to the limit of his capacity.

Interesting as it was, Cooberpeddy was too remote for part of an integrated tour program, and we continued on through the outback, over the Great Sandy Desert of Western Australia to Derby and Darwin at the far north of the continent on the Timor Sea. Then on to Arnhem Land, where herds of wild water buffalo roam. As on the Amazon island of Marajó, they sprang from shipwrecked stock. At the town of Catherine, we encountered a rather distressing situation. The favorite sport was to get into a car or Land-Rover at night and head out to the back country with headlights blazing. In the glare, the eyes of a buffalo would glow, making an easy target for the hunter. All this was done out of sheer boredom. There was no need for the meat or for thinning out the herds. The process was analagous to the destruction of the buffalo in America, where people would shoot at random out of the window of the train as it whisked across the plains. The same thing was now being done a hundred years later—mainly out of thoughtlessness, because the Australians are among the warmest and most congenial people in the world.

By the time we had finished our own wing safari, we had covered close to 15,000 miles and spent 80 percent of our time finding out what we couldn't really do. It became more apparent that the wing safari idea, at least, would not be workable for future projects. There were places of special beauty and fascinating interest, but the deep interior distances did not make them viable.

There was, however, the vast island of New Guinea, just north of Australia's Cape York Peninsula. Next to Greenland, New Guinea is the largest island in the world, with only a fraction of its landmass explored. An almost straight line splits the island down the middle of its 1500 mile length. The western half has been known as West Irian since the Indonesians took it over from the Dutch in 1969. The eastern half, then known as Papua New Guinea, was an Australian-administered territory. Along the entire length runs the spine of the Moake Mountains, including the Owen Stanley Range where the Allies pushed back the Japanese in the latter's attempt to take Port Moresby, the Papuan capital, with the intention of invading Australia.

The ranges are craggy and densely populated with narrow valleys. Forbidding slopes, more difficult to cross than the Alps, have kept the individual tribes isolated from one another for a millennium. Feuds and wars were continuous for many years; some still are. Head-hunting and cannibalism were slow to give way to Australian and Indonesian efforts to control them. Parts of the country still remain uncharted. Superstitions persist, and tribal traditions, including head-hunting, continue surreptitiously. The country harbors many tribes that live in a pure Stone Age, under prehistoric conditions.

We flew from Cape York Peninsula, uncertain of the best place to observe the more remote areas, where we hoped to get a genuine sense of a Stone Age civilization. The obvious place to get information was at Port Moresby on the southern shore, today a city of some 17,000. But our pilot had heard of an airstrip at Minj that sounded far more interesting. The landing strip, surrounded by ominous mountains, was barely visible in rain and fog. We made a precarious landing and were greeted by an officer from an Australian police post who was cordial but a little surprised at this strange plane and its passengers.

As we sat on the veranda of the officer's home, we discussed the many points of interest in the New Guinea highlands. Although the mountains in this area were rugged and the tribes isolated and often hostile, the region was of exceptional beauty and interest. Head-hunting was no idle rumor. It persisted, and there was little the police patrols could do about it.

As we talked with the officer, a large truck pulled up in front of us. The driver and his assistant jumped out, then unlocked the gate. With little ceremony, they dumped nine bodies out of the back. I couldn't help gasping when I looked at them: each body was headless.

But the chief officer was taking it all in stride. "Well," he said, "wait around for a few days and they'll be bringing nine more bodies in without heads. It's what the tribes call the payback system. One tribe will take a certain number of heads from a rival tribe. Before long, the rivals will raid the other village, and exact the same toll. It's inevitable."

I asked him what could be done about such savagery.

"Very little," he replied. "It's part of the culture, and it's as much ritual as it is revenge. It's not counted as cannibalism. They don't often eat the flesh. Most of them think that if they capture a head, they'll take on their enemy's strength. This still goes on, from the lowland along the coast to the high-altitude tribes. It's a fact of life."

We spent a week exploring the highlands, where there are over 400 different tribal languages, and where the people range from Pygmies to giants, and from pure black to almost white. The mountains and valleys are so difficult to cross that tribes remain unaware of other tribes less than a mile away. Except in warfare, there is little or no communication. I know of no other part of the world where this sort of condition exists.

We made many trips through the mountainous area by Land-Rover and our small plane, and found places where the Australians had encouraged neighboring tribes to come together in festivals they called, in pidgin English, sing-sings. These satisfied the longings of the tribesmen for their colorful ceremonies and enabled them to release their energies in a controlled environment. To sublimate their yearnings for war, highly realistic mock battles were set up, with designated warriors pretending to be killed in the battle. As we watched the mock battle, it was hard to believe that it wasn't real.

These annual affairs, one at the village of Goroka and another at Mount Hagen alternately, would create a rare feature for our future travel expeditions. Literally thousands of tribesmen would gather, even from remote villages several weeks of travel away. They would carry with them on litters the bodies of chiefs who had died that year, each in the fetal position. At the time the chiefs died, their bodies were put on wooden platforms and bracketed by arrows. The bodies were hoisted high above the fire and carefully smoked to preserve them until festival time. At the event itself, the dead chiefs would be honored by placing them in the front row, actually giving off the not unpleasant aroma of smoked meat. Later, the bodies were laboriously carried through the mountains to their villages, where they were put high on great cliffs in a sky funeral ceremony. As in Tibet and the Himalayas, the vultures and animals would then dispose of the bodies.

Another event in the area was called a pig killing festival. The villagers raised a large number of boarlike, semi-domestic pigs that needed little attention because they scavenged for their food. As many as 5000 or 6000 pigs were brought in at the pig festivals, where the tribesmen proceeded to club them and place them in giant pits. Here they were cooked and later eaten over the two-week fete. The problem was that all the pigs were cooked on the first day, which allowed plenty of time for spoilage. Some tribespeople died of food poisoning.

On a later trip, I discovered the courtship and marriage festivals that offered unrivaled pageantry. Here the tribespeople dressed magnificently from the neck up with elaborate headdresses, bones through the noses, war paint, and necklaces—with often nothing below the belt. The women wore a chunk of grass that they tied behind them, while the men wore penis sheaths that curled upward as high as the abdomen.

The Papuans were almost universally charming, including those who were still not averse to hunting a head or two if custom and ritual demanded it. Those who were exposed to the Aussies used an amusing form of pidgin English, forming words that became complete descriptive sentences. For instance, the word for piano was a sentence describing one: "A great big thing with black-and-white teeth." They had their own form of snobbery, calling anyone who had never come into contact with the white culture a *bush kanaka,* not a flattering term. For a flatterer or sycophant, the simple term "grease man" said it all.

While we were in Port Moresby, an unusual trial took place. A Papuan lady of considerable local stature had been raped and was presented with a photographic album that displayed some criminals, along with several totally innocent people as decoys to test her power of observation. In the court, she studied the pictures intently, and then pointed an accusing finger at the one she was certain was guilty. "There he is!" she exclaimed. "*This* one. He is the man who come up me." The problem was that she was pointing to the Catholic archbishop, who was totally innocent.

As we prepared to leave Port Moresby, I felt we had material for a more than exciting program in New Guinea. I had my eye now on the Great Barrier Reef off the west coast of Queensland, Australia, which I wanted to incorporate in future tours of the *Lindblad Explorer.*

We had not officially cleared our entry at Minj, and now there was a severe question as to whether we would be cleared for flying directly to the town of Cairns, near the northern section of the Great Barrier Reef. The officials were insisting that with only one pilot and the small size of the plane, we would have to make a way-stop for fuel at tiny Thursday Island in the Torres Strait. But like all the Australians we encountered in New Guinea, they were congenial and forgiving and cut the red tape for us.

It was a long flight for a small plane from Port Moresby to Cairns. From there we proceeded south toward Brisbane. In doing so we treated ourselves to the most gorgeous view of the Great Barrier Reef from fifty feet above the water. Here was the largest coral reef in the world, stretching for over 1200 miles, with islands and coral gardens and an extravagance of marine life. We saw sharks by the thousands, including the whale shark, the largest in the world. The reef stretches far out into the Coral Sea to create a natural breakwater for the Queensland shores. There are many little islands inside the reef, but not beyond.

There is a lot of talk about sharks in tropical waters not being dangerous because of the abundance of natural food supply. As I looked down on the swarming schools in the reef, I wasn't sure that this theory would always hold. The white shark will always attack. But any shark can be dangerous at any time. I think the theory of their benignity in warm waters was originated by some of the naturalists who study them so much that they practically fall in love with them. There do seem to be more human shark attacks in cooler waters where the food supply is less, and I have swum close to them in tropical waters without being molested—but I still am careful. The same theory has been applied to the crocodiles in Lake Rudolph in Africa: the heavy food supply is supposed to make them indolent. I have tested that and the theory has worked. But a man in Nairobi known as Half-Ass Singh decided to camp on one of the islands there, and only got halfway into the water for a swim before a crocodile did away with about 50 percent of his gluteus maximus.

I made a mental note that we would eventually bring the *Lindblad Explorer* to the Great Barrier Reef, along with stops at both eastern and western New Guinea. Later, after an avid study of maps and a visit to northern New Guinea's Sepik River, I planned to include that rich territory of masked warriors, ox-bowed lakes, and floating islands. The Sepik primitive art and masks are of rare beauty and the dances of the villagers overpowering.

But the problem was to figure out how tour groups could go up the river in relative comfort and safety from the tiny port of Wewak in the north of Papua New Guinea. I solved that by having a special riverboat built for us that would have accommodations for twenty people, plus the crew, and be sturdy enough to handle the great fluctuations of tide. Eventually, this cruise became one of the most compelling, even though at one time we ran into severe trouble. The ship was tied up to shore with strong hawsers, firmly secured to sturdy trees. But the tide went out and then came back with a vengeance. The ship tipped onto its side as the water flooded it. Another unscheduled bit of color took place on one of the cruises when the owner from whom we chartered the boat tried to shoot his girl friend as the passengers looked on help-lessly.

There were still many more new places to conquer in this fascinating region of the world. Basically, there are three major clusters of islands throughout the Pacific: Polynesia, Melanesia, and Micronesia. Polyne-sia includes the Hawaiian Islands, Samoa, Tonga, Tahiti, the Marquesas, and the isolated Easter Island. Melanesia includes islands in the south and southwest Pacific such as New Caledonia, New Hebrides, the Solomons, and the Fiji Islands, with people largely of Negroid stock speaking a mixture of Malayo-Polynesian. Micronesia lies north of the equator in the western Pacific, with people of Negroid and Mongoloid stock who speak a language like that of the Melane-sians.

The Australians themselves had staked out vacation retreats in the Pacific islands, just as in America the Caribbean islands offer similar havens with white beaches, blue water, and plenty of sun. I picked up considerable information about the likes and dislikes of Australians; the islands of New Hebrides, New Caledonia, and Fiji seemed to be among the favorites. Also not too far from Australia are the Solomons, New Britain, and New Ireland, all part of Melanesia; Samoa; and be-yond that, Tahiti. These were the popular main groups, but the lesser known island satellites seemed to stretch to infinity, and most peo-ple had never heard of them: Bellona, Viti Levu, Tana, Tikopia, Trobriand, Misima, Renard, Calvados, Gawa, Kitawa, Siasi, Deboyne—to name only a random selection. Each has its own charm and individuality.

To find out more about all this, I flew back to the south Pacific as soon as I could get free from the office. A commercial jet brought me to New Caledonia, some 800 miles east of the Australian coast, where I chartered a twin-engine Cessna and began my scouting trips for places to take the *Lindblad Explorer*.

James Michener wrote his book *Tales of the South Pacific* while living in the New Hebrides, a group of nearly eighty volcanic islands scattered over the Coral Sea roughly in the shape of a Y. Some are uninhabited, and nearly half are simply islets and volcanic outcrops. The rest, however, are lush, green, and mountainous, punctuated by volcanoes and home for nearly 100,000 people.

On Pentecost Island of the New Hebrides, the sport can be rugged. Once a year, the men and boys climb up a rickety bushtimber tower and dive headfirst toward the ground, fifty to a hundred feet below. All that breaks the fall is vines tied around the ankles that stop the jumper inches from the ground. On the island of Malekula, there are two main tribes—Little Namba and Big Namba—referring in pidgin English to the relative size of the male genitalia. The Big Nambas wrap the member in huge amounts of red bark cloth built up to reach the chest, and the Little Nambas wear a white penis sheath that looks rather forlorn. This is really the only difference between the two tribes, except that the Big Nambas in the highlands have a nasty habit of rewarding hardworking, virtuous women by knocking out their front teeth.

On Tana Island are members of the Cargo Cult, a religion shared with other tribes in New Britain and New Ireland. The cult started in World War II, when American troops poured in with equipment and supplies, and left surplus equipment everywhere. The religion is based on the belief that a messiah by the name of Jon From will come back with more supplies. He is supposed to be acting as the prophet for a god, who in turn is designated to be the U.S. president at the time. The islanders don't put up churches or crosses. They erect painted red doorways, complete with doors. It is through these doors that they expect Jon From to re-enter.

A considerable number of white Europeans, as well as Americans from the East and West Coasts, have settled in the New Hebrides Islands. They cluster together in colonies completely separate from the Stone Age village tribesmen, who rarely are seen among the colonists. In 1905 both the British and French had begun to colonize the New Hebrides, but they were on unusually good terms with each other. Winston Churchill, then with the British Admiralty, came up with a constitution for the territory in 1910 that would permit the citizen to live under either British or French law, as he desired.

The system worked surprisingly well up to the time of the territory's recent independence, when it was renamed Vanuatu. When I arrived there by chartered plane from New Caledonia, I was asked at the airport which flag I preferred to be registered under. There were duplicate customs and immigration desks. The one manned by slim and trim officers in pillbox hats, with short shorts and small moustaches, was obviously French. At the other desk were the British: big moustaches, large long shorts, and no hats. I opted for being under British law, and went through customs and immigration smoothly.

The joint rule was odd but relaxed. There were both French and English stamps. There was British money (the Australian pound) and French money (the Pacific franc). There were also French and British courts and penal systems. The joint high court was not functioning during my visit because of a strange twist in the constitution. The document called for the chief justice to be appointed by the king of Spain, and since there had been no king for many years, the court had been left vacant. The local people played no important role whatever. There were the French, English, Australians, and Chinese, but the native population was pushed out of everything and assumed to have no aspirations for independence at the time I arrived there in the late 1960s.

Far to the east in Tahiti, in the Society Islands, the Polynesians maintain their dignity and the illusion that they are masters of the islands and the French are there as guests. This attitude contrasts sharply with that in the Melanesian islands.

The Fiji Islands lie on the borderline between the benign Polynesian and the fiercer Stone Age tribes. When British missionaries arrived in 1835, the Fiji group was one of the few places in the world where pure cannibalism existed, as opposed to ritualistic head-hunting. Human meat was regarded as a staple food rather than a ritual. They actually raised people to eat them in cattle ranch style. The raiding of other islands was commonplace, and the prisoners were put in stockades for future consumption. When Captain Bligh was set adrift by Christian, he rowed right through the Fijis on his way to the island of Java, and in his log he showed that he was well aware that if he went ashore he would never escape alive.

In spite of their former penchant for human flesh, the Fijians are not Stone Age people by any means. In contrast to the tribesmen in the Melanesian islands, they have developed a royalty with princes and princesses conducting colorful ceremonies and rituals. But each society has a distinct culture that is extremely fragile in the face of the encroachment of the outside world. This fragility dramatizes the fact that tourism has to be carried out with tremendous thought and sensitivity, in order to avoid the critical problem of making zoos out of groups of people. As Westerners, we have come to think that we are more "civilized" than so-called primitive people. We say that it would be nice to preserve these other cultures. But we must also take into consideration their frustrations and aspirations for a higher standard of living. This is not easily accomplished.

The scattered islands all through the Pacific each had their own special kind of enchantment. The problem was to link each group with a practical series of cruises for the *Lindblad Explorer* that would be thematically attractive and compact enough to cover in separate voyages. One choice was a selected route through Micronesia that began in the Philippines and moved eastward through the Carolines, Marshalls, Gilberts, and eventually to Fiji. This would cover large colonies of coral islands and many kingdoms of men, from the Ponapean Saudeluers of the thirteenth century to the Gilbertese kings who ruled on the island of Abemama until the end of the nineteenth century.

The chain of Melanesian islands that stretches from Fiji westward to Madang in Papua New Guinea includes New Hebrides, the Solomons, and some Polynesian islands, and made another appealing cruise covering less than twenty days. By alternating various routes of the *Lindblad Explorer*, we were able to plan a rich variety of voyages for the years to come. Not the least interesting was among the 13,000 varied islands of Indonesia that could include everything from the Spice Islands like Banda, Komodo and its twelve-foot-long dragons, and the Asmat headhunters in West Irian, to the delicate art and culture of Bali.

To scout such an enormous territory properly was a major undertaking. The islands span one-eighth of the world's circumference, a distance equal to that from Anchorage to Bermuda, yet only 15 percent of the area is land. In the south, Sumatra, Java, and Timor form a crescent that points toward West Irian, the eastern half of New Guinea. Below the Philippines, two-thirds of Borneo, Sulawesi (once the Celebes), and the Moluccas were all scenes of colonial struggles between the Dutch, British, French, and Portuguese that culminated in the dominance of the Dutch East India Company, which for 200 years monopolized the spice trade. So powerful was Dutch control of the spice trade that the company eliminated all cloves on all the islands except Ambon and confined the production of nutmeg exclusively to Banda.

I was under the misconception that Indonesia consisted mainly of the old Dutch East Indies and little else. But I was soon made aware that this was a fallacy when I talked with Ambassador Suska, a retired Indonesian career diplomat and a personal friend of President Sukarno and of the regime that followed him. His wife was the sister of General Sutowo, founder and head of the huge Indonesian oil company, Pertamina.

Ambassador Suska was a gregarious, happy, and life-loving man. When I talked with him about our plans for bringing travelers to his country, he opened up many complicated doors within the government bureaucracy. Through Suska, I learned many things I had not realized before. Even though I had spent some time there, I wasn't aware, for instance, that all of Bali had not been administered by the Dutch until the early twentieth century. Bali had been ruled independently by its kings and queens until that time, when the Dutch moved in on some obscure pretext. I had not known that the islands of Aru, off the West Irian coast, were similar to the Galápagos, with Australian fauna such as the wallaby, Australian ostrich, cuscus, and bird of paradise—all vestiges of the time when the continental plates were fused together.

All this made the neglected islands east of Bali of singular interest for the *Lindblad Explorer*. There was fabulous animal life on almost every island, and fine unexplored reefs for snorkeling. Aru was ideal as nature's laboratory, but I discovered that man had reached out and practically destroyed the birds and animals, exporting them by the thousands both live and dead, especially over the previous fifteen years. The chief targets of the exploiters were the birds of paradise, along with parrots, parakeets, monkeys, salamanders, the smaller Komodo dragons, the cuscus (very similar to the raccoon), and wallabies. The dock at Aru presented a scene similar to that of the Amazon—packing cages full of the animals on the wharf, ready to be shipped to Ambon and then smuggled out of the country. Their laws against this were being ignored. There were high stakes here. The smugglers would kill one another in a squabble over a single bird.

Disheartening as this was, there were still endless scenes of beauty and interest to discover. We had to move fast in our 1972 survey because the *Lindblad Explorer* was scheduled to arrive soon, and the cruise plan would have to be established exactly to include the many relatively unexplored areas. This was a busy year for me, and I could not possibly cover such a large area alone. But Lyall Watson was again available. He joined with a knowledgeable Indonesian named Sutan Wiesmar, who would provide intimate information on many of the islands and also visit some places that had rarely been surveyed by Indonesian officials themselves.

Most interesting to all of us was the Asmat region, where Stone Age headhunters still live with little contact with the outside world or other Indonesians. There had been great trouble with the Asmats, with some 40,000 of them living a semi-nomadic life in the West Irian swamps. Most of the villages have little contact with each other, except in continual wars of revenge and the taking of heads in the "payback" system. Usually, the villages are hidden, set back from the coast up narrow muddy rivers that flow into shallow mud banks as they reach the ocean. The typical Asmat village rests on black mud in which it is easy to sink knee deep. Crude walkways of uncertain saplings are not too effective in keeping out of the mud.

When Lyall Watson and Wiesmar took on the big job of scouting the Asmat coast of West Irian, none of us knew quite what we might expect. Michael Rockefeller, on a search for the priceless art and wood carvings of the Asmats, disappeared in the area in 1961 and was thought to have been drowned, but was rumored to have been beheaded. Before the tragedy, he had been able to bring back to America a collection of wood carvings that are now the centerpiece of the new primitive art wing of the Metropolitan Museum of Art. Wiesmar was interested in trying to get Asmat relations with the Indonesian government straightened out. We were interested in exploring the sites for future visits there if the chaotic conditions permitted.

These are truly Stone Age people, and even the scattered missionaries have made little progress in persuading them to change their ways. About the only visible changes are the occasional wearing of trunks in place of penis sheaths, and an insatiable desire for cigarettes or tobacco introduced by the rare outside visitor. As recently as the summer of 1981, several missionaries were beheaded in the village of Agats. The reasons are still obscure.

Two weeks after this happened, a group of passengers from a *Lindblad Explorer* expedition cautiously visited the nearby village of Biwar by Zodiacs, over two hours up a narrow muddy river from its mouth. At considerable risk, Wiesmar and naturalist Jim Snyder went ahead of the passengers the night before to test the atmosphere of the village, because the mood of the Asmats is highly mercurial. On this occasion, the welcome for the Lindblad advance party was overwhelming. Seven years before, Wiesmar had been made an adopted son of the village, and he was not forgotten. As such, he had the obligatory privilege of sucking the breasts of the wives of the chief until milk came and kissing the armpits of the chief himself. Lyall and Wiesmar had had to go through this ceremony at Agats before, as I had done on my first visit to Biwar. It is a ritual not to be overlooked if you care to keep your head, and the ceremony must not be faked.

Even though the beheadings had taken place at Agats, Wiesmar and Jim Snyder were welcomed in nearby Biwar with a ceremonial dance that lasted through the night. The next day, over sixty passengers from the *Lindblad Explorer* were welcomed with the same ceremony as they arrived in their Zodiacs.

We have found that everything depends on the way the tribesmen are approached. Only two months before the *Lindblad Explorer* dropped anchor off the Asmat coast, a party of fifteen Germans had attempted to move up the Biwar River in small boats. The Asmat scouts spotted them, blocked the river in their war canoes, and drove off the Germans with a hail of arrows.

If the proper protocol is followed, there is nothing in the world of travel that equals a visit to an Asmat village. The approach from the sea in Zodiacs launched from the *Lindblad Explorer* is a long one, since the waters are shallow and the mud shoals treacherous, and the big ship must lie at anchor far offshore. Often, the situation requires a four-hour trip in the open sea in the Zodiacs before the small river mouth is located, usually across a mud flat over which the rubber boats have to be pushed. At this point, the Asmat warriors are usually seen at the river mouth—a dozen war canoes as long as thirty feet, their sides painted with stripes. Within minutes, the Zodiacs and passengers are surrounded by canoes, swiftly paddled by the warriors in full war paint, their noses punctured with bone ornaments. They paddle with intricately carved eleven-foot paddles tipped with white feathers, as they stand in the canoes with the balance of tightrope walkers.

With the Zodiacs surrounded, some of the warriors leap gracefully onto the Zodiacs, a cue for the Lindblad passengers to offer gifts of candy and cigarettes. But the ceremonies are just beginning. As the scout canoes escort the Zodiacs to the river mouth, an armada of some thirty war canoes suddenly appears, gliding down the river at full speed with up to ten warriors in each of the one-foot-wide crafts. They are chanting in rhythm with each stroke and moving as fast as an eight-oared scull. As soon as they have swept past the flotilla of Zodiacs, the canoes turn around at the river mouth and join to escort the Zodiacs for the hour-long ride up the river.

Halfway up the river, another armada of war canoes appears, manned by equally fierce-looking warriors. In minutes the two armadas are in mock combat, throwing white lime powder and palm-shoot spears at each other, and shouting war cries. By the time the village is reached, both passengers and tribesmen are emotionally exhausted. The mock battle is so realistic that it is a chilling thought to imagine what happens in an actual intervillage war, which is not an infrequent occurrence.

We have found that we have to be careful about which villages we visit because of tribal rivalries and jealousies. There is another village upriver from Biwar, and we make it a point to visit that on alternate expeditions to prevent any warfare resulting from one village being favored over the other. When I was there in 1974, the tribesmen were throwing real spears in their war games, which at times could break out into the real thing. The following year, we did not have time to get upriver to the next village as we had promised. Since Biwar had been visited twice in a row, we learned that the other village warriors had later swept down to Biwar, cut down their sago trees, and taken back with them some Biwar women and a few heads.

Two years later, in September 1976, John Clark, a retired physicist from La Jolla, and Alden Dickinson and his wife from Sun City, Arizona, shared a harrowing experience in Asmat territory, in Zodiacs from the *Explorer*. The Zodiacs were greeted at the mouth of the Euta River by Kokoi, the chief of the village Pirien, near the site where Michael Rockefeller had disappeared. Farther upriver was the village Otjenep, which was in the process of engaging in a blood feud with Kokoi's village.

To avoid exacerbating the conflict, the four Zodiacs from the *Lindblad Explorer* were loaded with equal gifts, with two of the rubber boats going to Pirien and two to Otjenep. Both Clark and the Dickinsons were in the Zodiacs assigned to Otjenep, but all four boats were boarded by Kokoi's naked warriors, who welcomed them with a grandiose tribal flourish. However, when the flotilla of Lindblad travelers and tribesmen reached Pirien, the atmosphere changed dramatically. Chief Kokoi learned that his brother had been killed that morning by a raiding party from Otjenep. The chief was stricken with grief, but he ordered the singing and dancing to go on as the funeral arrangements were made.

As Clark's and the Dickinsons' boats headed up the narrow river toward Otjenep, they saw a large Pirien war party with bows, arrows, and spears moving into the jungle in the same direction. The Lindblad group, totaling about thirty in the two Zodiacs, grew increasingly ap-

prehensive as they arrived at Otjenep to find a full funeral in progress—
the son of the second chief had been killed by the Piriens.

There was no welcoming ceremony, but Chief Ari of Otjenep
greeted the visitors and reassured them that the war was with Pirien, not
with them. The naked body of the slain warrior was laid on the ground
and smeared with ashes, as the other villagers wailed in grief and surrounded it. They touched and fondled every part of the body, as others
went down to the riverbank and wallowed in the thick black mud.

With the tide running out, the Zodiacs were quickly loaded for the
long trip down the river and back to the *Explorer,* several hours away in
the open ocean. The relief was great for all the passengers.

The villages are so separated from each other that the only real
means of communication between them is to raid and be raided. There
is really no regional network. You might have a pleasant reception in
one village, then go ten miles down a river and be killed. Yet for all the
fierceness of the Asmat headhunters, their carvings are among the most
sensitive and beautiful in the world of primitive art. Much of the carving relates to fertility and symbolizes the warrior's virility.

Interestingly, there are no antique pieces of this rare art. The damp-
ness and the mud, combined with the soft wood of the sago and mango
trees, make the carvings impossible to preserve for a long time in their
native environment. This does not diminish the value of the art, however. Museums value its rarity, regardless of its relative newness. Few
pieces were extant in the Western world as recently as thirty years ago.
In trading for the pieces, the missionaries at Agats tried to protect the
Asmats from exploitation, since money meant little or nothing to them.
A large ceremonial bis pole, worth thousands in the West, would be
sold for a pack of cigarettes. One wealthy American bought three poles
at $90 each. He sold one for $10,000, and having established the value,
deducted the other two on his income tax return for the same amount
after presenting them to a museum. Since the art is not made for public
consumption, it has remained above the tawdriness of tourist trinkets.

We had originally scouted the islands east of Bali mainly to concentrate on the wildlife. Finding it mostly decimated or entirely destroyed,

we were lucky to discover the varied kingdoms and cultures of even more fascinating interest.

We were able to open up new territories of lasting interest all throughout Indonesia. Dr. F. Wayne King of the New York Zoological Society, a foremost authority on the giant Komodo dragon, the carnivorous monitor lizard that can rapidly devour a goat or an unwary human, had set up a conservation research study on the creatures just before our first cruise.

The only possible ship we could find for our initial survey of the 13,000 islands of Indonesia was a large passenger ship with twenty-five staterooms, almost a quarter as large as the *Lindblad Explorer*. It was expensive and a big gamble because we still weren't sure what the reconnaissance would reveal as far as practical operations were concerned. The question was whether to pay out the more than $75,000 to charter the ship, or to cruise more or less blindly with the *Lindblad Explorer*. While Lyall and Wiesmar set sail in the large ship for the more distant islands, I took off by small boat and plane to cover nearer islands such as Komodo, Flores, Timor, and Sumba along the southern crescent formed by Java.

Here, too, I found that the wildlife was less interesting than the cultural contrasts. Most of the islands had their own structured society with considerable history, either written or handed down by word of mouth. When I arrived in Savu, the southernmost island of Indonesia, the scene was a complete revelation to me. The people were among the most cultured I had encountered. On an island some ten miles wide and twenty miles long, they had a fully functioning court, intricate traditional dances in elaborate costumes, and a special breed of small horses trained to do a delightful dance in honor of arriving visitors.

Few similarities exist among the islands since they have developed their isolated cultures on their own, and are like tiny medieval kingdoms. The Moluccas form the region of the Spice Islands, but the contrasts among the islands are many. Ceram is wild, but nearby Ambon is civilized, the result of the Dutch making Ambon the major shipping point for the spice trade. To the east of Ceram, tiny Banda, which had been turned into the exclusive source of nutmeg by the Dutch, is still the source of 80 percent of the world's production. Now the Dutch are gone without a trace, but their tidily laid-out houses are still there, now all in a state of decay.

The Moluccas are Christian, in contrast to the prevailing Hindu and Moslem population in Indonesia, and have a fierce desire for independence not only from their former Dutch rulers, but from Indonesia as well. The hijackers of a train in Holland a few years ago were Moluccan terrorists who were trying to force the Dutch to pressure the Indonesians to give them independence.

We have continued our Indonesian cruises with the *Lindblad Explorer* over the years with rewarding success. From our first visits in 1973, we have continually found new vistas, and we often land on islands whose inhabitants had never seen a large ship or a doctor before. On our first cruise, Roy Sexton and I disembarked at a remote island where the incidence of tropical diseases was even above the tragically high average. Among them were yaws, goiters, malaria, and leprosy, and we brought many sufferers back to the ship to give them treatment.

We made twelve voyages each year for the next two years, and at each stop we set up a clinic on our arrival. People eventually would get word of our stop and come in from the more remote neighboring islands for treatment for many illnesses, including leprosy. Before we sailed from each island, we would leave a supply of medicines with careful instructions on how to use them. We also took some of the ill to Bali for urgently needed operations. When we came back on a following voyage, we would return them to their home island. We invested over $150,000 in medicines, and one of the greatest pleasures was to come back to a small island to find the inhabitants remarkably improved.

On our first visit to Ambon in 1973, we encountered a most unusual dance ceremony involving a large ten-foot bamboo pole. Six strong men lift it, and suddenly the pole starts to writhe and jump, throwing the men to the ground. I studied the performance and ascribed the violent movement to the actions of the men themselves. I was then invited to try it myself. I joined the group, and again it began to writhe and jump uncontrollably, throwing me to the ground. I have no explanation for this phenomenon.

It is impossible to generalize about Indonesia, except to say that the people are warm and friendly, with strong and varied cultural backgrounds and a wide spectrum of beliefs, and they live on exquisite islands of captivating beauty. Every voyage I have taken there has been one of discovery.

At the village of Bau-bau on Butung Island in 1981, the ship was greeted with a charming folder titled "The Itinerary of the Coming Tourist," which reads as printed:

6.00 a.m.	M.S. Lindblad Explorer arrives at The Harbour.
6.30 a.m.	All The Tourists have been at The Pier; Accepted by Lawati Dance.
7.00 a.m.	The Veheckles are Ready to Kraton. All The Tourists are Pleased to get in the Bus.
7.30 a.m.	All The Tourists arrive at the gate of Kraton; Accepted by Galangi Dance.
8.00 a.m.	All the Tourists to Cultural-Hall with the Programme, as the following: 1. The presentation of Pekakande-kandea (having breakfast of traditional meals), 2. Performance of Bosu Dance, 3. Performance of Kalegoa Dance.
9.30 a.m.	Have a look of Souvenier, Have a look of Citerdal (fortress)
10.30 a.m.	All the Tourists leave Kraton toward The Regent Residence,
11.00 a.m.	All The Tourists arrive at The Regent Residence with programme as the following: 1. The opening Speech by The Announcer, 2. The speech by The Regent, 3. The impression by one of the Tourists,

12.00 a.m.   Closing Speech and All the Tourists leave The
                    Regent Residence to the ship.
                    Bau-bau,

                    The Committee.

With Indonesia well organized for the *Lindblad Explorer,* and tours
there ably conducted by Lyall Watson and expert naturalists, I turned
my attention to one of the most entrancing of the forbidden territories I
had always dreamed about visiting. It was almost as intriguing as
Tibet, which was my ultimate goal when opened up by the Chinese
government. The country was tiny Bhutan—sandwiched in the high
Himalayas between Tibet and eastern India—a truly hidden country of
mystery and enchantment. For centuries this royal feudal country of
towering mountains and forests had been almost sealed off from the
world, as its rulers sought to protect the kingdom from its powerful
neighbors. Between 1626 and 1921 only thirteen expeditions succeeded in penetrating this enigmatic land. Like its neighbors to the
west, Nepal and Sikkim, it sits on the roof of the world, but it has been
more isolated than either.

In 1974, I received word from my close friend and associate in India,
Gautam Khanna, that he had been working with government officials to
plan for the opening up of the country to tourism for the first time in its
history. Since the Bhutanese people had never been exposed to the outside world they were very vulnerable and the situation was tender.
Khanna, who had been working on the details of the coronation of
Bhutan's new king, had suggested to the officials that Lindblad Travel
would be just the right organization to work with them to avoid an
uncontrollable tourist invasion into an extremely fragile culture.

I immediately agreed to explore the idea with Khanna and Bhutanese
officials. I knew that the monasteries, chortens, temples, and palaces
of Bhutan were legendary; that the mountains and forests were among
the most beautiful; that the timeless folklore and cultural treasures were
among the richest. It was always fascinating to open up a new territory,
but Bhutan would be for me one of the most exciting.

XIV

BHUTAN
Forbidden Kingdom

IN 1958, India's Prime Minister Nehru decided to visit the kingdom of Bhutan. The only way he could get to the interior community of Paro Dzong was to go to Gangtok in neighboring Sikkim, where he had to transfer to a jeep for the journey to Natu La Pass on Bhutan's border. Here he transferred to ponyback. Joining a yak caravan, Nehru moved across the Chumbi Valley and then up to the high valley of Paro Dzong, where the meeting took place.

Bhutan had no airfields. Even the sites for primitive airstrips were limited. Up to the early 1970s, Bhutan remained a mountain fortress of ravishing beauty and strong resistance to industrial or cultural invasion. Not even foreign dignitaries had come to Bhutan in any numbers until the coronation of young king Jigme Singye Wangchuk in June 1974, a harbinger of the opening of the country to tourism. The coronation did not include tourists, however. Only statesmen and dignitaries from all over the world were invited to view for the first time a colorful pageantry, unspoiled by any taint of commercialism.

But the coronation was the beginning of the end of Bhutan's isolation. The new road from Phunchholing in the south, starting at the Sinchu La Pass and running to the capital of Thimphu, opened up 112 miles of twisting turns and climbing hairpins that formerly took a week or more to cross by mule and horseback. By 1974, it took less than five hours. It was now possible to fly from Baghdogra in West Bengal by small plane to an airstrip at Paro Dzong. Without these facilities, the lavish coronation would not have been possible. With them, it enabled countries from four different continents to bring in gifts for the new monarch, practical and unusual gifts, including buses and cars from Australia and Japan, and truckloads of White Horse Scotch to launch the inevitable westernization of the country.

Part of the reason for the long delay in the opening up of Bhutan had been India's policies. In spite of my love for India, it is hard for me to be charitable about how she treated the small neighboring countries to the north: Nepal, Sikkim, and Bhutan. She regarded them as vassals. Under the Indo-Bhutan Treaty of 1949, Bhutan agreed to be "guided by the advice" of India in its external affairs, as long as India kept her hands off the internal workings of the benevolent feudalism of the country.

And it was benevolent. The new king's late father, who died while on a safari in Africa, had given a high priority to land reform. Land-holdings were cut to a maximum of thirty acres, and the former king had redistributed all medicine, agriculture, and communications to bring the country into the twentieth century. By 1961, he had persuaded India to let Bhutan become a member of the United Nations, a giant step forward since India considered Bhutan's northern border with Tibet to be the first line of defense against the People's Republic of China.

India continued to hold a tight rein on Bhutan, and still does. But by the time of the 1974 coronation, the new king was ready to accept the idea of tourism—with reservations. When Bhutanese officials asked my friend Gautam Khanna to help set up the arrangements for the coronation, the fear of an open invasion by tourists was very pronounced. The officials told Khanna flatly: we must not let our country become another victim of destructive tourism.

They had every reason to be wary. The allure of a "forbidden" country always seems to bring with it an irresistible cachet for the tourist. In less than a single century, with the advent of high-speed travel and communications, more damage had been done to the rare cultures of the world than in all the previous centuries of history.

With the coronation over, the infrastructure for tourism was already there, thanks to the gifts and the training of local guides who had served for the ceremonies. Gautam Khanna had helped develop the three hotels in the country for the coronation's distinguished guests. They were charming and attractive in Bhutanese style, but did not have the sort of plumbing and heating that would eventually be required for an influx of visitors, even if limited.

With the exception of some islands in the Pacific and Indonesia, Bhutan was the least contaminated part of the civilized world. A country the size of Switzerland with mountains even more staggering, its one million people live in scattered communities that are rarely more than a cluster of houses. The larger of these settlements are built around a structure called a dzong—part fortress, part religious center, and part village administration center. Except for the Nepalese Hindu minority in the southern lowlands, the people are devoutly Buddhist, gentle, and civilized. Deciduous trees and evergreens cover the lower mountainsides, with rhododendrons exploding in color up to eighty feet in height. In the higher slopes, yaks serve farmers and their families in every possible way: transport, wool, meat, hides, glue—and butter and milk from the female version, called the nak.

It took courage, mixed with a certain amount of trepidation, for this little kingdom to open its doors to the world. The big question at the time I was called in in 1974 was: would the outside world have the perception to profit from the age-old wisdom of Bhutan? And further, would they respect the land, people, antiquities, customs, and religion enough to prevent a culture from being destroyed?

When Khanna and I met with Bhutanese officials, we discussed these problems at length. All of us were aware of what had happened in Nepal after it was opened up to tourism. The mani prayer walls had been destroyed systematically or stolen by dealers, tourists, and unscrupulous monks who sold them for a handful of money. Hundreds of these carefully carved prayer stones had disappeared.

I had now been invited as a representative of the travel industry to try to work out a viable plan that would prevent this from happening in Bhutan, but at the same time permit a limited number of visitors who would preserve the fragile and unprepared culture from the impact. There were two main problems: first, the sheer *amount* of traffic that would come in, and second, the sensitivity of the people who would be coming. These two factors would have to be considered one at a time.

The tourist demand in Bhutan was bound to be overwhelming. I knew that from the hundreds of requests we were getting from the moment it was announced that the kingdom was going to be opened up. Other travel operators were facing the same demand. How could you determine which visitors would respect the area and which might vandalize it? How was it possible to democratically screen those who wanted to visit there? It would be impossible to interview the thousands who were already banging at the door to get in. Yet the qualitative aspect of the problem was as important as the quantitative.

As a result of our meeting, it was decided that a stiff per diem price would be required for anyone applying for a tourist visa to Bhutan, a price that was set at $160 per day for each person visiting there. This would be an intentionally artificial barrier set for only one reason: to keep the traffic down and prevent Bhutan from being overrun. It would not be related to the actual cost, which would be far less. And the income would go directly to the government treasury, which in turn would be able to restore and maintain the temples, monasteries, stupas, and lands that had been untouched by outside hands for centuries.

I went along with this idea wholeheartedly. The setting up of artificial barriers appeared to be the only way to restrict the sheer numbers of tourists and save such rare places. Of course, it would be quite unconscionable if the tourist industry shared in the premium; that I made sure would not be done. But if the premium helped extend the life of Bhutan as it existed before tourism came, then the stiff assessment was worth it.

The unfairness in this practice bothers me, however. Many people, deserving people with knowledge and intelligence, would like to pay the price but simply can't. I don't have any pat answer. It is an almost imponderable question, one that people should think about so they can come up with alternative answers.

Aside from this major decision, there were technical problems in setting up the first tour groups to enter Bhutan. India, through which all groups had to come, was still touchy about the region, which lies within what India calls the "inner circle defense line," a line running south of Bhutan and Sikkim where India has thousands of troops stationed. It would take sixty days for each visitor to get the necessary permits even to reach the Bhutan border. These included a Transit Permit and a Restricted Area Permit that would often be held up for spurious reasons.

In the spring of 1974, I lined up the first three tours with those pioneering groups that are always ready to reach out and explore, just as I had done in Mongolia. I would be learning with them, since there had been no opportunity to research Bhutan in advance, except through books and extensive interviews. Our first route took us via New Delhi to Baghdogra in West Bengal. From there we motored through the tea-growing Dooar region of India to the gateway town of Phunchholing, where we would begin our journey into Bhutan. Before I left America with the first group of thirty travelers, there was no lack of others waiting to follow for the one-week stays that the Bhutanese permitted, in spite of the high price of $160 a day, plus extras.

At Phunchholing, the plains of India suddenly end, and the mountain fortress of Bhutan begins at the start of the new road to Paro and Thimphu. I was greeted at the administration building by the delightfully cordial Tseten Dorji, designated by the king to handle the new tourism. We bowed to each other as I placed the traditional white prayer scarf over his outstretched arms, and he returned the favor—an age-old custom in Buddhist tradition, which is never omitted. Following one of the few rules that the government lays down for its officials, he was wearing the national dress of Tibetan origin, a robe hitched up in the warm weather, with very long sleeves folded up for the summer. In winter, the robe is let down to provide the warmth of a cocoon.

The immigration officials were smiling and friendly as we turned over our passports to them—at the coronation, the process had been waived. At the customs office, I went in first to greet a cordial customs man, who asked me immediately, "How do we go about this?" It was plain that he needed guidance, and I shut the door to avoid any public display of his uncertainty.

He was eager to learn what questions he should ask, and I began making some up so that he would feel he was performing an essential function in his new capacity. I suggested he ask how much liquor was being carried, how many typewriters, how many cameras, how many animals, and other minor questions. He was very pleased. "Good idea," he said.

Later, I found that my informal and spontaneous routine had been printed up and became the process they continued to use. On the first journey, he passed everyone through without opening baggage, and with great courtesy.

However, the process was entirely different on our departure. Here the customs man fortunately knew exactly what to do. All the luggage was opened and examined because Bhutan was determined to prevent any precious treasures from being removed from the country. By Western standards even the poorest Bhutanese homes have sacred altars and priceless antiques. Without strict control, Bhutan could be easily stripped of these treasures. At our meetings to design the practices of the new tourism, I had emphasized the importance of preventing the sales of antiques of any kind; I was glad to see the restriction was being followed.

The very narrow road from Phunchholing to Thimphu is cut out of rock. It twists through an abundance of forests that have been spared because of Bhutan's small population, in contrast to those of Nepal, which have been decimated. The road weaves up and down through valleys and ranges, with sheer drops of 3000 feet off the side. Occasionally, you see a crowd gathered, peering down at a hapless truck that continued straight instead of making a hairpin turn.

En route, the traditional Bhutanese houses are seen, with thick stone walls and wooden second stories that are carved with precision and care. In the Paro Valley, less than twenty miles from Thimphu, are the Kyichu Monastery and the Paro Dzong sitting high up as a fortress and devotional Buddhist center, part of a pattern seen all through the countryside. Many monks are evident in the monasteries, for Buddhism is at the root of the nature of all the people. The dzongs are reminiscent of the burgs of Germany, with the village around the castle to which the peasants retreated under attack.

There are eight major monasteries throughout Bhutan and 200 smaller shrines, or gompas, all of graceful beauty. The magnificent Tashichodzong in Thimphu serves not only as a lamasery but also as the seat of the royal government. The Taktshang Monastery in the Paro Valley, called "the tiger's lair," is where Padmasambhava, the mystic who brought Buddhism from India, is supposed to have flown on the back of a flying tiger. All the monks and clerics belong to the Drukpa branch of the Kagyutpa sect of Tibetan Buddhism, called the "Red Hat" sect.

Life on the whole in Bhutan is happy. There is no hunger or malnutrition, in sharp contrast to India. There are also no beggars, and the people refuse to accept tips. There is little disease, too, and no apparent poverty. Not even the monks carry begging bowls, as they move reverently about in their burgundy robes, in contrast to the saffron robes of the lowland Buddhists. There is very little crime, and what there is seems to be mainly crimes of passion.

By the fall of 1976, our travel operations were running smoothly in Bhutan, with a new group arriving there each week during the travel season. The reactions were consistently enthusiastic. I became good friends with Tseten Dorji, who conducted the internal operations of the tours with great expertise. In the spring of 1977, he was kind enough to invite my new wife, Cary, and me to the first temple festival to which a foreigner had been invited, and we welcomed the chance. It was to be held at the large dzong at Punakha, the summer capital, situated at the confluence of two great rivers that tumble down from the high ranges to the north. The Machu is called the female river, coming in from the northwest; the Pachu, the male river from the northeast. The source of the latter is the 25,000-foot-high glacier at the highest point in the land.

It was March, and the cold was penetrating when we arrived in Thimphu en route to Punakha. Dorji had made all the arrangements for us at the Hotel Motithang, where we were greeted royally. It was a visually beautiful hotel, with lavishly hand-painted walls and traditional Bhutanese furniture. We were ushered into an elegant suite with living room and bedroom that was most inviting except for one thing: there was no heat. The heating system, imported from India, simply did not work. In fact, it was slightly warmer outside. We asked as politely as we could for a smaller room with a space heater, a request that was turned down equally politely, since they apparently felt that nothing less than a suite was suitable for important foreign visitors. We sat down in the living room of the suite with Dorji to go over the plans of our visit to the temple festival. Even Dorji, as a hardy Bhutanese, was shivering.

We had not talked long before we heard a tremendous crash in the bedroom. We rushed to the doorway to find that several tons of water were pouring through the ceiling onto the bed, the furniture, and the floor. A large water tank on the roof had burst open and dumped its contents to flood the bedroom.

With great apologies from the manager, we were whisked to an identical suite on the floor below, complete with dressing room, bath, and hot water buckets. Still there was no space heater, and even if there had been, it would have been impossible to heat the large rooms. But we were too tired to complain again, and our hosts were trying to do everything they could to please us in face of the disaster in the rooms above.

The problem was that it was so cold we couldn't undress or even take off our boots. We lay down on the bed and fell asleep immediately. It must have been about four when I woke up and noticed the floor. It was a solid sheet of ice, at a higher level than the carpet. When I got up to investigate further, I skidded across the room and into the wall. The water from the room above had seeped down during the night and turned our floor into a frozen lake.

Fortunately, we were already dressed. We skated out to the hall and down to the lobby, and waited for the sun to come up. By six-thirty in the morning it rose, but there was little warmth from it outside. We did, however, manage to commandeer a taxi that would take us up to the 15,000-foot-high Dochu La Pass, which was a scheduled stop on our way to Punakha, where we found a fire burning so we could warm up. We huddled close until Tseten Dorji arrived later on a motorcycle to join us.

The fire raised both our temperatures and our spirits. For the first time we could look around us with a sense of enjoyment. The view was ravishing. Far to the north, we could see the towering white peak of Chomulari, the highest peak in the eastern Himalayas. The valley below was a medley of colors, with a profusion of azaleas, rhododendrons, camellias, orchids, and magnolias. Around us were high-altitude coniferous trees that created a sort of Disneyland landscape. The view was worth all our trouble and inconvenience.

The approach to Punakha by the new road took us down to a Shangri-la valley, where citrus trees and apple blossoms joined in a blaze of color. When we reached the campgrounds at Punakha, the village people were swarming down from the high mountain valleys by the thousands for the festival. They included various remote tribes of Tibetan stock, some swarthy, some light-skinned, some half-naked and primitive. Villagers were selling Buddhist artifacts, and jugglers and magicians displayed their talents.

It was warmer now, and we were a lot happier. A large tent was set up for us where we relaxed for a while, and then we visited the dzong, with its tinkling bells and chanting monks. By nightfall it was cold again, but not as bad as the night before. We were given an oil lamp to use in the tent, and it didn't take us long to get into bed to warm up and read for a few moments in the dim light of the lantern.

We must have dropped off to sleep with the lantern still burning, because when I woke up and looked over at Cary, I couldn't believe what I saw. The lamp had smoked up during the night and left a thick veneer of oily soot over everything in the tent—including Cary. Her face was totally blackened by the soot in a smooth, even layer. It was hard to recognize her. Then I noticed that she was laughing at me and drew the obvious conclusion that my face was in the same condition.

We were on the bank of a river where the water was so cold it was useless to try to wash in it. One of the boys who were assigned to us brought boiling water that was so hot that it, too, was useless. We finally mixed the water to a compromise temperature and were able to get ourselves almost presentable. Cary remained at our campsite while I climbed up to a smaller monastery on the mountainside.

When I returned I found that Cary's adventures had continued. It seemed that she had heard shots outside the tent and had gone out to find a young Bhutanese man shooting cormorants in the river. When he claimed he was shooting ducks, Cary corrected him in no uncertain terms, pointing out that they were cormorants and were totally inedible. She gave him a lecture on wildlife conservation, and he apologetically slipped away.

Later, while we were resting by the tent, a young man appeared with a large mountain trout as a gift. With it was a note bearing greetings from the king, who turned out to be the bird hunter Cary had so vigorously bawled out.

We felt very privileged to be the only Westerners at the temple festival among the thousands of pilgrims who had come from throughout the country to watch and participate. The dances and pantomimes depicted the ancient struggle between good and evil, centuries old in tradition and originating in Tibet, where the festivals had stopped with the Chinese occupation.

The exquisite handmade costumes are blindingly colorful. The Bhutanese dance with explosive joy and acrobatic skill, with masks designed to frighten the most hardy. Bells, drums, horns, and cymbals punctuate the subtle movements, all of religious significance. At the yearly festival of Paro Dzong, an enormous silk appliquéd tanka picturing Padmasambhava is brought out for display. Nearly a hundred feet long and over fifty feet high, it is unfolded and placed over the entire face of the monastery. It depicts the inscrutable guru who brought Buddhism to Bhutan in serene contemplation. So revered is it that it is protected from the light even when on display for a few hours each year. On one occasion it was threatened by fire, and twelve monks risked their lives to save it.

Archery is the national sport in Bhutan, and two days later back in Thimphu we were able to watch the contest where the amazing skill of the archers is sometimes balanced by shaky marksmanship. At the coronation, an Australian ambassador had ended up with an arrow through his leg. Generally, however, the contest is an event of beauty whether the king, royal family, or villagers are competing. The bows are graceful, of ancient design, and the target stands 160 yards away.

While we watched the archers getting ready for the contest, an emissary from the king approached us, bearing what looked like two balls of fur. A closer look proved they were tiny Tibetan Apso puppies, that rare breed of dog which originated in the lamaseries near Lhasa in Tibet. With a heavy coat and a tail that curls upward over the back, they grow to only two feet in length, yet make splendid watchdogs.

We were startled when they offered both puppies to us as gifts from the king—at least that was what we thought at the time. It turned out that only one was being offered, but after our mistake was discovered both dogs were generously pressed on us. They turned out to be the first breeding pair to leave Bhutan, and only two other males were in America at the time. We named ours Scubi and Dubi, and they are very much a part of the family now.

The whole region of the Himalayas, from the Hindu Kush in the west to Bhutan in the east, has become the location of a favorite series of tours that have continued in popularity to the present: from Tiger Tops and Kathmandu in Nepal to Tenzing Norgay's trekking tours out of Darjeeling, and on to Kashmir.

Except for its barren landscape, Ladakh has much in common with Bhutan. It honors Padmasambhava, and its monasteries and lamaseries are of the Drukpa Kagyutpa order of Tibetan Buddhism. There are castles, like the dzongs of Bhutan, and the festivals are of the same rich energy and brilliance.

Those trips all came later. In planning our arrangements for the Himalayan countries, I had the privilege of entertaining the Karmapa from the Gangtok Monastery in Sikkim at my home in Connecticut. He was a Tibetan refugee, greatly revered as the leader of the Yellow Hat sect and as the reincarnation of a famous high lama of the past. His stature matched that of the Dalai Lama.

The Karmapa had been traveling around the world for five or six years, more or less as a missionary, in his quiet and dignified way. He greatly influenced the thinking of men like Senator Charles Percy and Buckminster Fuller.

The Karmapa and I were sitting by the pool, in the summer of 1979, discussing my interest in birdlife. He interrupted me to ask if I had seen a special eagle of Tibet—a very strange one. After I asked him what was strange about the bird, he replied, "Often when the female lays an egg, it hatches into a tiny dog, so small that it can fit into a teacup. What's more, it has no hair and barks ferociously."

I looked at the great lama with utter amazement. He was totally serious. Finally I asked, "Have you ever seen one?"

"No," he said solemnly, "but many of my lamas have."

Frankly, I didn't know what to make of it. The legend and lore of the Himalayas are rich and embroidered. The problem was that the Karmapa left the story at that and was obviously not sharing a little joke with me.

A year later, I brought the subject up to Tseten Dorji and his assistant, a gentleman named Sangey. Sangey was one of the few Bhutanese who was very worldly and had traveled extensively. Curious as to why the Karmapa had told me such a story with a straight face, I asked Dorji how such a myth had ever become circulated.

But Dorji was very solemn. "The Karmapa was absolutely correct. There *is* an eagle who lays just such an egg. It is well known."

"Have you ever seen one?" I asked.

"No, but I know many people who have seen them."

Then he turned to Sangey and said, "When we come back to Bhutan, why don't you get one of those little dogs for Lars." Like the Karmapa, he continued to be very serious.

But Sangey was wryly humorous in his reply. "I suppose you want me to send him a yeti, too."

Dorji nodded without a smile. "Of course," he said. "That would be a very good idea."

"Very well," Sangey said with a twinkle, "I will do that. But then I'm going to quit my job in Bhutan, and Mr. Lindblad and I are going to travel around the world and make a million dollars."

I am still puzzled about how this story got started, but then many mysteries in the Himalayas will never be solved. The region's beauty and culture are so rare that it is not enough for *most* trekkers and visitors who go there to have a love for the wilderness and the fragile civilization; *all* of them have to have such a love, or what they come to visit will disappear before their eyes.

Throughout my life I had dreamed of going to China, where my relatives had been missionaries and in which my interest had always been intense. Tibet was even more alluring. My explorer-hero Sven Hedin had opened up the vast lands of central Asia, Siberia, China, and Tibet for me, and I had devoured all his books. Any man who could survive in the burning Gobi Desert by burying himself in the sand during the day and trekking at night for weeks on end had all the attributes of the classical explorer I would have liked to have been.

Hedin lived in Stockholm. When I was fourteen I knocked on his door one day. I couldn't believe it when he invited me in for a chat and spoke of his experiences. The visit set up my dreams for years to come.

They remained just as vivid all during the time I was doing my own explorations throughout the world. The problem was that China remained inaccessible. The political situation was anything but benign, and for years the United States felt it necessary to ignore the existence of the one billion people in the People's Republic of China. Along with many others, I had trouble understanding why this had to be, even though there were obvious great political and ideological differences and internal abuses that were hard to swallow.

Taiwan was certainly not any shining example, with a corrupt and unpopular government that we were pretending was the official government representing the one billion people on the mainland. When I arrived in Taipei in 1959, each person in the customs and immigration line was asked if he was going to vote for Nixon or Kennedy. It became immediately apparent that the pro-Kennedy luggage was searched from top to bottom, while the pro-Nixon luggage was whisked through without being touched. Several of us toward the rear of the line got wise and switched our vote over, and the line suddenly became all Nixon.

But Nixon was the one who broke through the Chinese wall for the first time since 1949, and I was very happy about that. From the moment it became apparent that China was going to open up to visitors, I determined to be among the first to bring in touring groups. As I began to plan the Lindblad Travel program for 1973, I got in touch with the China International Travel Service, where I ran into my first disappointment. They stated politely that they were not set up in any way to accommodate any numbers of American tourists, and that they planned to simply continue with small special interest groups.

I tried in vain to persuade them that by bringing the *Lindblad Explorer* to the China coastal cities, we could supply our own accommodations while our passengers would visit on shore on foot, with no problems of hotel or transportation for them and no inconvenience for the Chinese. I kept up a constant stream of communications with the travel service, but seemed to get nowhere.

In February 1974, I was aboard the *Lindblad Explorer* moving up the coast of Chile. We were returning from a successful Antarctic cruise and were about halfway up the South American coast between the Strait of Magellan and Santiago. The coastline is rugged and beautiful here, dotted with inland waterways and fjords.

We were heading toward a small port called Puerto Montt, situated just west of the Andes that separate Chile from Argentina, when I received a radiogram in the ship's radio room. It was from my good friend Hans Winter of Ethiopian Airlines who had obtained an invitation for me from the China International Travel Service to come immediately to the People's Republic of China to discuss future tourist possibilities. It was the breakthrough I had been waiting for for years, and especially over the previous year when all my attempts to make headway had run into a stone wall.

It was a magic moment. But there was a great problem. The radiogram specified that I had to pick up my visa in Ethiopia in just four days. Puerto Montt was a good day's sail away from our ship's position. From there I faced the problem of getting over the Andes to a remote and barren region of Argentina, and then attempting to get a flight to Buenos Aires, from where I could fly to Paris, where there was a chance of connecting with Ethiopian Airlines to reach Addis Ababa within the limited time.

I studied charts, maps, and airline schedules. We couldn't be in a more difficult location. It was impossible to fly directly from Chile to Argentina for political reasons, and the only option was to cross over the Andes by land to an airport at Bariloche in central Argentina. To reach Bariloche, I would have to travel by lake steamer, transfer to private car to climb over the mountain passes, and change roughly six times in doing so. It was a journey that involved moving halfway across South America, across the Atlantic to Europe, then down to Ethiopia, covering half of the world to reach China on a continuous stop-and-go journey.

XV

CHINA
Breaking Through the Wall

IT was a novel way to get halfway around the world. There wasn't just one Chilean lake to cross by boat; there were several. They were interspersed with what seemed endless auto stretches across the mountains, where we crawled at the pace of a Galápagos tortoise. When I finally reached Bariloche on the other side of the Andes, over 200 tortuous miles away, I was able to make a plane connection to Buenos Aires without too long a wait. Miraculously, there was a flight from there to Paris that same night, with a reasonably good connection to Addis Ababa on Ethiopian Airlines.

I took off from Ethiopia with five colleagues from the travel industry who had also been invited by the China International Travel Service, known as CITS. I was excited but bone tired. The trip through South America and the transatlantic flight, plus the leg to Africa, all in continuous motion, had sapped most of my energy. But I had waited for this journey for years. From 1949 to 1974 the gate to China had been firmly shut. I had had only one vicarious peek at the country through the eyes of my Swedish aunt, who had been allowed to visit in 1954.

My colleagues and I arrived in China at a time when the political climate was thawing. The period of the Cultural Revolution and the great purges of the Red Guards were still running their course. In 1974, Mao and Chou En-lai were still alive, and the era called "The Criticism of Lin Piao and Confucius" was extant. The whole country was involved in frantic discussions about the "crimes" of Lin Piao, once the apparent heir to Mao Tse-tung, and the ethical philosopher, Confucius. Factories, schools, and community groups were being forced to hold meetings at which these men were denounced roundly.

I remember one really terrifying scene in a kindergarten class, with several little tots of four or five sitting around a table. Suddenly, a cute little girl in a fresh, clean dress stood up and gave a long speech that ended with her raising her left arm with a closed fist and saying, "Down with Confucius, down with Lin Piao!" Immediately, all the other fists went up and the same shout was repeated. The girl was followed by another tot, who rose and denounced in a piping voice some of the things her mother and father had told her about the times before "liberation."

We saw this sort of thing nearly everywhere we went, confirming the ideological pressures. But this was 1974. There was also factional infighting that would eventually result in the return of many purged officials to office to bring new reforms and the eradication of the Gang of Four and its abuses.

There was not much evidence of the reforms when we first arrived, however. There was a lot of fear on the part of the officials, especially fear of talking with foreigners. All officials dressed exactly the same, in their simple Mao jackets and pants, and there was no way you could tell the difference between those in authority and those who were not. The very idea of giving us their names was taboo. They referred to themselves as anonymous representatives of CAAC, the Chinese airline, or the CITS, whichever service they represented. We were never able to knowingly meet the decision makers.

At our first meeting, I outlined in detail the advantages of our plan to bring the *Lindblad Explorer* to the coastal ports. I didn't know whether I was talking to anyone who could make a decision. When the meeting was over it was still unclear. We were, however, allowed to travel to Shanghai, Hangzhou, Canton, and other cities before returning to

Beijing, more familiar to the Westerner as Peking, the capital city. My travel colleagues and I were joined by a group of French physicians, one of the specialized groups that the People's Republic was permitting to tour under restricted conditions.

There was a considerable amount of controversy among the members of our travel group as we discussed the various places we visited. Our program included a lot of propaganda and indoctrination as we were taken to sewing machine and bicycle factories, housing developments, agricultural communes, and nurseries. But we were taken to very few places of visual beauty. With our group of French doctors we were required to visit a hospital to watch operations where the patients were anesthetized by acupuncture, which was little known in the Western world at that time. I don't know how effective this method is. I can only report that when the incisions were made, the faces of the patients were contorted in pain. It was fascinating to watch, however.

Everywhere was the blind allegiance to the words of Mao. A religious fervor seemed to grip even the most intelligent. Mao's book was the Bible. People lived by it, quoting it in every possible situation. To them, the words of Mao created miracles. They could solve problems, create jobs, make women pregnant, and find husbands for girls who wanted to be married. At the sewing machine factory, the solemn-faced manager said that thanks to the wise leadership and good example of Mao, his factory had been able to raise production many times over. At one time, he said, they had worked very hard at trying to create a machine that would sew three different kinds of stitches instead of the one stitch their ordinary machines could create. "We retired to our chambers," the manager told me, "and studied the words of Mao. When we completed our studies, we were immediately able to create the proper machine, where we had failed before."

We were dealing here with the less intellectual sort, but even among the highly educated, the reverence for Mao was overwhelming. At one large hospital, I talked to two surgeons. Both had been educated and trained abroad, one at Harvard and Massachusetts General Hospital and the other at the University of Edinburgh. I was amazed when the surgeon from Harvard told me, "We had been having great difficulty

in the technique of rejoining limbs that had been amputated in an accident. The problem was that the rejoined limbs would swell, and we
would have to make deep cuts to reduce the swelling. This was not very
effective. So we retired to our studies and read the words of Mao.
Thanks to this inspiration, we were able to develop techniques to rejoin
the veins and arteries, and now we are able to help people from all over
the country who come to us with limbs packed in ice.''

The words seemed out of place for such a highly trained medical scientist, but the prevalence of that same blind fervor was all-embracing.
In later years, I have talked with other members of the Chinese intelli-
gentsia, who have confessed that they find such blind faith abhorrent
now, but that during the Cultural Revolution they went through a period of religious extremism. On reflection they came to realize its hyp-
notic irrationality. They had accepted it first as perhaps 70 percent
good, then perhaps 50 percent, and finally, zero.

When I arrived there in 1974, the so-called Gang of Four had not yet
been exposed. With Mao and Chou En-lai still alive, the new forces of
pragmatism and reform were just beginning to emerge, and the reaction
against the severe repression and mass torture was just setting in. Later,
with the deaths of Mao and Chou En-lai, the new ruling forces quickly
began to change Mao's policies in nearly every field: education, industry, culture, and religion. With the change, the barriers to non-
Communist countries began to fall.

The Gang of Four consisted of Mao's widow, Chiang Ching, and
three unrelenting officials on the extreme Left. Their eventual exposure
brought reassurance to many people. There was still a great fear of that
sort of repression returning, however. The people were not entirely
free, but they were measurably better off than before. Symbolically,
the conformity that had been forced on them as far as dress was concerned was liberalized. The women, especially, liberalized their fash-
ions so that they have become more attractive every year. I have noticed in many socialist countries that if it were not for women, things
would be a lot worse. Men are more likely to accept the camaraderie of
dress equality, while women will not accept it so easily. If women see
their children underdressed, they use more creativity in dressing

them—one of the few areas in which they are allowed to avoid conformity.

One of the big differences between China and the Soviet Union is that now, at the beginning of the 1980s, the people in China do not have an obsessive fear of their government. Nor are they afraid to talk with foreigners about it. The new Chinese regime tries to reason with the people. Furthermore, a large mass of the Chinese people is reasonably informed about the rest of the world, especially the United States. Their general knowledge of us is considerably greater than ours of them. Many of them know about our politics and politicians, whereas in America, knowledge of the political goings-on in China is slight. This tendency toward reasoning rather than coercion seems to spring from a willingness of Chinese officials to admit their mistakes of both past and present. This system filters down from the top echelons through the communes, housing units, factories, towns, and cities.

The torture and the beatings have long been stopped. This is not to say that if someone disagrees with the official policies and criticizes them, the local secretaries will not try to convince him that he is wrong. The prevalent custom of ''criticism and self-criticism'' continues, and the Chinese are adept at it. At the local communes, they will criticize their own actions. The meetings are for all the world like a meeting of Alcoholics Anonymous. They stand up, criticize or confess, or both. Because both people and officials are willing to admit their mistakes, it is possible for them to like something one day and hate it the next.

In the United States this attitude is not acceptable. You express an opinion and you stand by it, right or wrong. Our culture does not permit changing your mind. The Chinese take the time to analyze thoughts and attitudes in accordance with official lines laid down by the high authorities. In America, it is difficult for a politician to alter his basic political views; if he does he risks political death. To have admitted, for example, to past Marxist beliefs at a period of one's youth almost surely would finish a political career.

The practice of admitting errors, past or present, is part of the Chinese system. It is behind the quite frequent policy shifts of the Chinese government. The period from 1949, when the People's Republic was proclaimed, to the present has been marked by a bewildering zigzag course.

Our understanding of the Chinese Revolution was influenced by George Meany's statement in an early 1950 speech when he said that "10 million had been killed" in the early purges. He later admitted that he had no factual basis for that remark and had pulled this figure out of the air. The actual number was only a small percentage of this. Although the death of even that number is certainly not laudable, the misstatement caused revulsion among Americans and a rejection of the Chinese Revolution.

Unquestionably, many large landowners were killed during the Communist takeover. The reaction against this group was severe because the landowners had had the power of life and death over the peasants, who were abused and mistreated, raped and enslaved. In 1949 hundreds and thousands of landlords had to stand trial, but very often the charges against them were for acts the Western world would also have regarded as crimes. The People's Court moved swiftly and probably unfairly in many cases, but most of those who were found guilty were so.

The Chinese believed in Leninist rather than Stalinist theory. They never engaged in purges as Stalin did. There were few political executions, Stalin-style, and the fact that many political leaders emerged at the end of the Cultural Revolution was evidence of this. Members of the opposition were not shot, but rather were put out to graze and rest in innocuous desuetude. The new leadership consists of many old men in their seventies and eighties who have survived all the changes.

My efforts to open up China for conventional tourism in 1974 were fruitless, even though I emphasized that our tours would be done very simply. We would pay substantial fees for the *Lindblad Explorer* to visit up and down the coast, and would not put any pressure or burden on the new and inexperienced China International Travel Service.

The travel officials seemed to listen politely, but their faces were inscrutable, and it was almost impossible to know if they were really listening or not. I furnished them with two long reports on our suggested program, written in both English and Chinese. They accepted the reports graciously—but I never heard another word from them for the next three years.

It was a bitter disappointment. To me, the opening up of China would be a landmark in the modern travel industry. None of the other travel representatives who flew there with me in 1974 made any progress either. The situation remained a complete stalemate. But in October 1977, I received another cable from China. It asked me to come there to discuss tourism and allowed only ten days for me to get there, very little lead time to prepare another proposal. I was to fly via Ethiopian Airlines—consistently used by China because of cordial relations between the two countries—and to pick up my visa in New Delhi. After such a long period of silence, it was hard to believe that they were still interested, and again my hopes rose.

Cary and I arrived in Beijing and were taken to the Peking Hotel—then the best in China—where we were met by a charming gentleman named Gian Ping Kwei, an official of the China International Travel Service. I felt it was a heartening sign that he actually gave us his name, a great change from 1974 when all the officials were cloaked in anonymity. At the hotel, we spent a couple of days cooling our heels because things never move swiftly in China.

Eventually we were summoned to the offices of CITS to meet an equally charming gentleman named Chao Wei. I was completely surprised when he pulled out the two reports I had filed three years before and thought for sure had been delegated to the dustbin. But Chao Wei was fully conversant with their contents and seemed to know every detail about the *Lindblad Explorer,* which would be the centerpiece of our first tours in China.

The only tourist visas that had been granted up to this time in 1977 were issued under carefully controlled quotas offered to certain airlines. These included airlines from Pakistan, Yugoslavia, Romania, Ethiopia, and other countries that had had cordial relations with the People's Republic for many years. But the problem was that the planes were now flying empty to Beijing, and losing money on the operation.

Although these airlines had the coveted visas available, they were unable to fill the quotas.

Our meeting represented the first direct serious negotiations between China and an American travel operation. It culminated in their giving us permission to bring the *Lindblad Explorer* to the ports of Shanghai and Canton in 1978, the following year. But more than that, they offered us an extensive land tour program as well. This was an unexpected bonus, and we were happy to be the first American tourist agency to operate in the country.

I was so enthusiastic about the news, I began to tell them about the features of the *Lindblad Explorer,* making a point of explaining how we did special scientific work on board, and that it was truly an expedition ship above all. At this point I began to notice a sharp change of expression in Chao Wei's face. Where before it had been smiling and pleasant, I noticed what looked like a scowl. He began shaking his head from side to side and said, "I am very, very sorry, Mr. Lindblad. But if it is an expedition ship, we positively cannot allow it to come in our waters. I am sorry."

I was speechless. He rose as if to dismiss us, and I could see our whole program going down the drain. But Cary, who was sitting next to me in silence, suddenly spoke up. "Sir," she said, "my husband has given you the wrong idea. He didn't explain it properly to you. The ship is purely a pleasure vessel. There are no scientists aboard, just passengers who have a hobby of studying nature. That's what he meant by 'expedition' ship. He didn't mean it was a scientific ship."

He must have been charmed by Cary, because he relaxed at once and let her explain the situation in detail. She finally won out, and I was able to breathe more easily again.

Once the crisis was over, we settled down to an exchange of ideas about tourism. Chao Wei explained that tourism in China would not be for the purpose of making money, but to create peace and understanding among people. It would become a big business, he recognized that, but the income revenues would be regarded as a by-product. Most important would be the promotion of understanding between the people of the United States and the People's Republic of China.

What emerged from our meeting was, to me at least, the importance of understanding Oriental thought. It is quite different from ours, and often difficult for the Westerner to comprehend. I have many friends in Japan and elsewhere in the Orient, and have come to a gradual understanding of it, which was to be helpful in establishing Lindblad Travel as the primary travel operation in China.

Orientals are reluctant to say "no." They will find many excuses to avoid saying it. In the United States and Europe, when two parties discuss a subject, they are likely to state their positions and then sit back and have a dialogue. In China or Japan, you have to give a monologue and tell everything about your position in detail. Meanwhile, it seems as if you are talking to a blank wall wearing an inscrutable smile and an impassive face. A meeting can go on for two days with little or no response.

It is very disconcerting and even dangerous not to be aware of this. I have known some who have presented a program to Chinese officials, and who think that because of this silence the project has been approved. They may wait at their hotel for a day or so and find that although the officials have made careful note of everything said, the program has been turned down. But the "no" is well cushioned. It is in there, but terribly hard to detect.

Thanks to Cary, I had overcome the resistance to bringing the *Lindblad Explorer* to China, but there was another project I was keenly interested in establishing. Our program in Outer Mongolia had continued to be a fascinating one, but to bring groups there we had to deal with the Soviet travel organization, which is probably the most inefficient in the world. I wanted very much to see if we could arrange to reach Outer Mongolia through the Chinese region of Inner Mongolia and thus eliminate our problems. Culturally, traveling through China to Mongolia made more sense because of the ethnic similarities of the people.

I explained this to Chao Wei and waited for an answer. But there was none. The meeting was over, and we were politely dismissed. We went on to another meeting, followed by a banquet given by CITS officials. At the banquet, I was called aside and told that we could now go to Outer Mongolia through China, in addition to receiving the permission for bringing in the *Explorer.* I have an idea that the second request was granted so swiftly because there was no love lost between the Soviet Union and China.

China without a banquet would be no China at all, and by definition, banquets are very expensive. Most important is the return of the favor; you must not accept a banquet without giving one in return. Many foreigners don't realize that to fail in this is very bad manners, and manners to the Chinese have been deeply rooted for centuries. They are sometimes of a different type from ours. I have seen high officials burp out loud or even spit on the floor. But it is gross bad manners to tell an off-color joke or fail to return a banquet.

Sometimes this leads to difficult situations. On one occasion, I had only one day to spend in China and was tendered an official banquet at noon. As is customary, there were roughly fifteen courses and the festivities didn't end until four in the afternoon. I had already planned my reciprocal banquet for six that evening, when we had to face another barrage of fifteen courses. Although the food on both occasions was delicious, the digestion suffered. But failure to return the favor would have been disastrous.

The final negotiations for a travel project can be done only by the top representatives of both parties concerned. This meant that I had to commute to China many times in a long series of negotiations, during which there was much room for misunderstanding. But in the process, I made very good friends and observed the Chinese code for good manners scrupulously. One thing they seemed to like was that Cary and I worked as a team, because it was an unusual procedure. The result of all our negotiations was that in 1978 we were permitted to carry out a full series of tours with the *Lindblad Explorer* and twelve other departures for Mongolia in the summer of 1978. Literally within days after these tours were announced back in the United States, they were fully booked as the first American tours to visit the country.

We now had to build up an industry in a country that was changing so fast it was hard to keep up with the policies. What we told our Lindblad tour leaders in March was not holding true in July. It wasn't long before we were conducting sixteen tours a month. Today, we are operating eleven groups a week, or close to taking as many as 1000 persons a month to China. Prices range from $2500 for sixteen days on a land tour to $7900 for a twenty-nine day coastal cruise on the *Lindblad Explorer*. Since experienced tour leaders were not available, we had to set up an intensive training program.

What was most gratifying was the reception our tours received in China, in every location visited. What excited the American groups was the outpouring of genuine affection for the visitor. It seemed as if the Chinese were saying: you have come a long way to visit us; we will return your favor with love. In shops and on the streets, the faces of the people would light up when they recognized Americans, yet only a few years earlier the reaction had been exactly the opposite. It was surprising to be stopped in the street and asked to talk about politics. This would be unthinkable in Russia.

There were other contrasts to the Soviet Union. Chinese officials make no attempt to screen off the visitor from Western news or comment. In many of the hotels, shortwave radios explain how to tune in on the Voice of America, the BBC, or the U.S. Armed Forces radio. There doesn't seem to be the fear of political contamination encountered in many countries of the Soviet bloc.

Since 1978 there has been a continuing dialogue in regard to the Cultural Revolution that hit the nation brutally all the way to the far reaches of Tibet. Mao's policy was that the revolution had to be constantly renewed with the intensity of a religious revival. The fear of this revival still lurks.

One terrible and incomprehensible thing about the Cultural Revolution was the destruction of beauty. If a writer wrote or a painter painted with beauty, their minds were assaulted mercilessly, and they were sometimes physically beaten. The places of beauty were also subjected to the same process. The temples, monasteries, palaces, pavilions—everything esthetically beautiful—were destroyed or burned to the ground. One of the exceptions was the Forbidden City of Beijing.

The thrust was that the people were to be taught to have the "right mind." People who worked in offices, in hospitals, and in advanced skills were sent to work in the fields for one to five years, while their

superior talents went to waste. The officials with whom I was dealing—
the Harvard surgeon, the factory managers—all had just returned from
the fields and hard manual labor when I first met them back in 1974.
Families had been split up, and even a ban on love existed. It was
strictly prohibited to hold hands with a girl.

During the Cultural Revolution a United Nations conference on birth
control was held in Romania. China was vetoing all the resolutions presented, because it was convinced that artificial birth control was a
method for the developed countries to keep down the populations of the
developing countries. But China's birthrate was not increasing measurably because they had an extraordinary method of birth control. A man
was not supposed to marry until he was twenty-nine and a woman could
not do so until she was twenty-eight. Before 1949 mothers used to bear
children at the age of sixteen. Late marriages became the rule of the
day, which fit in with the idea that children are expensive and in a sense
a drain on production.

With Mao and the Gang of Four gone, the new leaders could concentrate on restoring what the Red Guards had destroyed. When I first saw
the Forbidden City in 1974, large placards announced that these elegant structures had been built by slave labor and were only vestiges of
the corrupt past. The followers of the Cultural Revolution claimed that
the destruction had been carried out because esthetic beauty was
"counter-revolutionary." It was supposed to pervert and divert attention away from productivity. The monotonous dress was also imposed
because of this theory. Women were made to look ugly in order to keep
the minds of both men and women on production.

But by 1978, China was taking tremendous pride in the restoration
work, although at tremendous cost. Their whole outlook had changed.
I believe that the Chinese are the only people in the world who can ab-
sorb this rapid change without experiencing a sort of emotional case of
the bends. Again the capacity for criticism and self-criticism comes up.
The blame was placed directly on the Gang of Four, and once they had
been removed from power, restoration could be carried out.

I have met many people who lived in terror under the Cultural Revolution and were almost destroyed by it. But now they say that they have

to forgive their oppressors. They excuse them because they believe the oppressors were acting on the theory that they "were doing the right thing" at the time. I think this extraordinary ability to analyze and reflect is impossible in the United States. If your neighbor came and destroyed your house and took your furniture and burned it in front of your eyes, you could never forgive or forget. In China, the lack of polarization between victim and perpetrator is astounding. But without it, the tension throughout the country would be untenable.

Another amazing phenomenon is that religion, including Confucius, is back. Just a few years ago, the constitution was rewritten to safeguard freedom of religion, and China is experiencing a definite religious revival. Excluded, however, are the former abuses of the Tibetan monasteries, where serfdom and exploitation were integral parts of the system.

In 1979, during a visit to Chengdu in Sichuan, I had a discussion with some friends from CITS about religion. They spoke of the cliché that religion was something for the older people only and that the young would have little or nothing to do with it. I pointed out that the absence of the younger people at temples and churches was based on repression only. When that was lifted, the people of China would be ready to accept the new constitutional approval of religious freedom. My friends in Chengdu were reluctant to admit that my comments were probably true.

In 1981 the same friends happened to be with me in Beijing at Easter. They joined me at the Easter service at the Catholic cathedral, and our conversation of two years earlier was brought back to mind. The cathedral was filled to capacity with worshippers, mostly young people. The same is true in the Buddhist temples and monasteries. Young people are engaging in meditation, although many are doing so underground.

In the years after the Cultural Revolution, many felt that it would take a long time for China to recover. But the Third Reich under Hitler, with its unbelievable intensity, lasted only a dozen or so years—not even for a full generation. The Third Reich and the Cultural Revolution both reveal how quickly the human mind can turn around. To travel and observe the recovery of the post-Mao China is an intellectual adventure. Travel in China is not a holiday trip. But as a learning experience, the visit there cannot be equaled. You find yourself in contact with a political phenomenon that is mind boggling.

What we have tried to do in our programs is to help the Western mind understand the underlying reasons for this fantastic turnaround. It is extraordinary to see that the Americans who return home from the visit most impressed are the politicians and executives. They come back to the United States with a new outlook, a changed mind. None has been unmoved by what he has seen.

I asked my Chinese friends one time why they had been so generous in setting up so many Lindblad programs. They went out of the way to favor us, it seemed, and of course this was much appreciated. They answered very frankly by saying that much of Lindblad clientele represented the so-called establishment, or opinion makers. "This is what we need," I was told. "These are the people who will go back to the United States with the most influence. We can't think of a better way to promote understanding and peace. We are not interested in the radical Left."

The extremes and excesses of the Cultural Revolution did great damage because all initiative was stifled, and still is for the most part. Basically, there is still little difference in pay between a Harvard surgeon or a 747 pilot and a workman in a bike factory. Even the higher salaries amount to under $100 a month, while the top range is $120 to $150. The factory workman makes around $60, so there is not much reward for higher skill and training. As a result, the Chinese labor force today is not hardworking.

However, with the shedding of the vestiges of the Cultural Revolution, the necessity of incentives, bonuses, and better pay for more work is becoming clear to the Chinese leadership. More and more China is beginning to apply Western methods, with more incentive pay for mental work and skills, so much so that American businessmen come back visibly impressed. They see a country with a great deal of discipline. Although too many people are still required to carry out a single job, to some degree capitalist methods are beginning to be applied, with the new regime much more pragmatic than the old.

No one tries to pretend that a Westerner's visit to China is a luxury experience, although great strides have been made over the past few years to improve accommodations. If a traveler doesn't enter into that intellectual experience, he may be unhappy. In our first 1978 programs, we invariably froze in winter and baked in summer. The Chinese idea of cold differs considerably from ours. They dress in many layers, the most effective way of insulation, and are able to cope with it better than we can. But the necessity of good heat and air conditioning was quickly recognized, and complaints have fallen off dramatically.

In our first year, the American traveler proved himself able to take the bad with the good. In spite of many inconveniences, there were few complaints. The insufficient accommodations were compensated by the richness of the experience. To me, the American traveler is the best in the world, and I have seen few prototypes of the "ugly American" on our tours. As a group, I feel Americans rank above French, Italian, or German tourists. If an American is interested, he'll put up with anything.

There were few if any problems with the programs that involved the *Lindblad Explorer* because we carried our own accommodations with us. The ship had just completed an Alaskan cruise that ended in July 1978 and was making its way down to Yokohama, where the passengers would board for the inaugural cruise to China. We were cleared to put in at Shanghai on August 21, with a promised one-day excursion by air to Beijing and the Forbidden City. In Shanghai, where the ship was docked close to the center of the city, we were permitted to visit nearby farm communes; attend a ballet; study housing projects, schools, and hospitals; and attend an acrobatic show. This was followed by side trips to Soochow, one of the most beautiful cities in China, with visits to its gardens and temples. From there, we moved by train to Wu Xi, bordering one of China's lakes, the Tai Hu. This in turn was followed by visits to Kweilin and Canton. Compared to our later tours to the most remote corners of China, Tibet, and Inner Mongolia, this trip was of somewhat limited scope. But the excitement of our first visit and the cooperation of the travel officials made the occasion memorable.

The greeting of the *Lindblad Explorer*, the first cruise ship of the era to arrive in Shanghai, was overwhelming. Flags and banners were everywhere—except that there was a small problem. Somehow word must have gotten around about my partnership with the Swedish-American Lines, and all the banners read: WELCOME TO THE LINDBLAD EXPLORER AND ALL OUR SWEDISH FRIENDS. Except for our captain and many of the crew, no other Swedes were aboard, but I'm sure it made them swell with pride.

Most amusing was our flight from Shanghai to Beijing for the one-day visit. We were accompanied on the hour-and-a-half plane trip by a congenial gentleman named Mr. Lu, who was a guide for our Beijing visit. He suggested that we fasten our seat belts after the plane had already taken off, and then turned to the passengers and said, "Now I want to tell you about the little paper bag in front of you. If you feel like throwing up, please use it. It is not polite to throw up on your neighbor."

He paused a minute, then continued. "Our flight today will be very short because I know the captain, he's a good friend of mine, and he knows the direct route. Most of the captains don't know the direct route. Now I also must tell you that this is my first flight and I am scared to death!"

He was no more reassuring as we made our final approach. He suddenly jumped up and said, "We're going down! We're going down! Fasten your seat belts!"

He was even more charming when we got to the Great Wall. Before we started out he turned to the group and announced, "You have to be very careful, because we have a long way to walk. I am looking at you people and know that some of you shouldn't do it. I am looking at you again now, and I think there are many of you who will never come back to China!"

There were several guides like this, all of them with an endearing naiveté.

After our first year's program, my rapport and good friendship with the officials I worked with in the CITS grew rapidly. Because of their genuine desire for anonymity, I cannot mention their names here, but I am deeply in debt to them for the extraordinary help they have been and are continuing to be.

But one problem is that they often fail to provide enough lead time to prepare for a program. For example, we were very much interested in setting up a cruise on the Yangtse River. It is the longest river in China, plunging over 3200 miles down from the interior, and navigable for much of the way. Traditionally, the river is considered the borderline between North and South China, the scene of many battles and wars, and the final hurdle when the Chinese Communist troops crossed it to capture Chiang Kai-shek's capital at Nanjing. From Zhenjiang, near Shanghai, to Chungqing is nearly a thousand miles through the three famous gorges where the Yangtse narrows into a canyon. Here the current rushes through at more than ten knots, and navigational skill is all important. Through the entire voyage, a cross section of China's life and culture can be viewed along the shores in the most colorful panorama.

At a cocktail party in September 1979 in Hong Kong, Cary and I heard a rumor that Mao Tse-tung once had built a luxurious ship for himself and distinguished visitors which would make an ideal vessel for the Yangtse River program if the existence of such a ship could be confirmed and its location determined. This intrigued me. Shortly afterward, we were guests of CITS on another riverboat cruising on the Yangtse called *The East is Red Number 46*. It was smaller than the *Lindblad Explorer* yet it carried 1000 passengers. It was frankly not an appealing ship, and I determined to keep on trying to find this mythical boat of Mao's.

When we reached the port of Wuhan, I ran into an official of the Yangtse River Shipping Company, and I was sure that if anyone knew about the mystery ship, he would. All the other queries we made brought only blank stares. The same was true of the shipping official. He also added that Mao would never have commissioned such a ship to be built: it was not egalitarian to do so.

I finally had to concede that the ship was nothing more than a legend, although I was convinced that a leisurely trip up the Yangtse in the relative comfort of a large riverboat would be one of the most appealing programs we could offer. I had no sooner got back to the United States than I received a cable from CITS reading in effect: WE FOUND THE SHIP YOU TALKED ABOUT. Cary and I made our way back to China and inspected the ship carefully. Oddly enough, the M.S. *Kun Lun* was all it was rumored to be. She was graceful, modern, and luxurious, all 2300 tons of her. There were eighteen exquisite cabins, with state-rooms ranging from 230 to 630 square feet. There were even two grand pianos on board.

She had not been built for Mao, however, but for visiting heads of state and distinguished foreign visitors arriving on official business. The problem was that she could accommodate only thirty-six passengers, which would be extremely expensive. But with accommodations sparse all over China, we knew that premium space like this would justify the cost. We concluded the deal immediately, and since then the M.S. *Kun Lun* has been a successful part of our program.

As our tours increased, hotel space was still a problem. The Peking Hotel was the most popular, but with a cumbersome assignment system, we never were sure where any of our groups would end up. It was very awkward for a large group to arrive after a long air trip and face uncertainty in lodging.

On the way to the airport after concluding the arrangements for the *Kun Lun,* I brought up the hotel problem with one of my CITS friends. He told me, "Lars, I think I can solve your problem. We have a national state guesthouse, the place where Nixon stayed when he was here. Actually, we pass it on our way to the airport. It will cost a bit more than ordinary hotel accommodations, but I think it will fit your needs."

I told him that cost was no object when it came to having secure arrangements for the Lindblad groups. Since we were going to pass it I asked, "Can we see it now?"

"We will pass the wall that surrounds it," he said. "It will be in view soon."

"But can we examine it now?"

"I'm sorry," he said, "but we can't." Then he pointed through the window of the car. "There's where it is, however. Right there."

It was a beautiful wall. But it was very frustrating to pass by the guesthouse without seeing it, because making arrangements to use it would entail another trip to China almost as soon as we got back to the United States.

But this was the mood and tempo of the Chinese travel industry and constant adjustment to them was necessary. The trip back to China was well worth it, for the Angler's Rest House, as it is called, is a complex of superbly beautiful houses with large living rooms, antique furniture, lovely paintings, king-sized beds, and closed-circuit television with 625-line screens that present a sharp, clear definition. The Angler's Rest presented all the amenities that had been lacking and assured us of confirmed reservations in advance, a critical necessity.

To say that China became one of my greatest interests is an understatement. But to me, Tibet was the icing on the cake. With Sven Hedin's indelible imprint on my mind since childhood, I could sense Tibet's beauties and wonders long before I allowed myself to dream of the chance to go there. I had brought tours and trekkers to the borders of Tibet on the other side of the Himalayas in Nepal, Sikkim, and Bhutan, but had never been able to step over the border. With China now opened up, the dream could become a reality. To bring the first tour to Tibet would be the culmination of all my years in the tourist industry.

But permission from China still remained elusive. I did everything but get down on my hands and knees to get it, but seemed to make little progress. I had to keep reminding myself that frustration was part of the game. Finally, however, I had a banquet meeting with CITS in April 1980 to discuss general topics and I bluntly said, ''There are two things that I would like above everything you've been so kind to help me with. One is that someday you must let me see a panda in its natural environment. The other is that you *must* let me go to Tibet.''

This was not quite the usual way of dealing with Chinese officials, but I guess my frustrations had gotten the better of my good judgment. After the banquet, however, one CITS official called me aside for a quiet talk. I was afraid that I had ruined my chances by being so blunt, but waited expectantly for what he had to say.

"The managing director of CITS tells me that you would like to go to Tibet," he said.

"I'd give anything to do so," I told him.

"Very well," he replied, "I'll arrange it."

It was that simple. But there was the usual problem. No immediate arrangements were made, and with other pressures pending, I had to return to the United States and wait. But the wait was short. Two weeks later, I received word that I could plan a trip immediately to Tibet with a small group of travelers.

I was now faced with another quick turnaround to return to China and gather a group on short notice. I knew I would have no trouble in forming an ad hoc group, but the problem was the timing. My mind flashed back to two conversations I had had in previous years with two gentlemen who had been with me in China. One was Melvin Belli, the attorney who had made quite a name for himself with landmark cases. He came up to me in Beijing and introduced himself. Tall and heavy, he spoke with a commanding voice.

"You are Lars Lindblad," he said. "You have to promise me that on the first trip to Tibet you will take me along." I promised.

The other was Jay Pritzker, of the Hyatt Hotel chain. I had lunch with him at "21" one time, where he said, "Can you get me to Tibet?"

I promised him that on the first tour there, I would make sure he could come along.

When the cable arrived to clear the way for Tibet, I called both Belli and Pritzker and they accepted immediately. It didn't take long to gather a few others, and in May 1980 we were off to Tibet, moving from New York to Beijing to Sichuan and on toward Lhasa, the once forbidden city of this high, hidden country resting on a 12,000-foot plateau and surrounded by the highest mountains in the world.

We left Chengdu in Sichuan early in the morning, flying in an Ilyushin 18 four-engine turboprop, with the sharp white Himalayas in the distance to our left. It was comforting to know that three or four flights a day are made to the nearest airstrip to Lhasa, and there has never been an accident. When Lhasa finally appeared on the horizon, you could barely make out the Potala, a white shimmering wedding cake that seemed like a chimera. It was hard to keep my enthusiasm under control. This was a miracle, a dream coming true—a feeling that I hope I never lose.

The plane swept down over the mountains and the bare brown plateau beneath us, and touched down on the airstrip. Lhasa was a full three hours away by four-wheel vehicle, and we began sweeping along the Lhasa River, winding and twisting toward Lhasa at last, surrounded by frosted white mountains. I was surprised at the number of terns, gulls, and other birds along the route.

Because we had come suddenly from lower altitudes, there was the possibility of altitude sickness, but I have never found it bothersome and feel that the more you think about it, the more you are likely to get it. It's like putting a finger on a sore; you can make it worse. But I did feel exhilarated the nearer we got to Lhasa. On the way, prayer flags fluttered, white shreds of salutations to the Buddha, and suddenly we came upon a giant bas-relief of Buddha himself, thirty feet high, carved into the wall of a mountain, and gazing serenely into space, his carved robe painted in bright saffron. Other rocks on the mountain were carved with the eternal scripture O MANI PADME UM, the constant salute to Buddha as the "jewel in the eye of the lotus."

A few wandering Tibetans appeared along the road, probably on the pilgrimage to Lhasa, often requiring several weeks of walking. Then suddenly we rounded a curve, and there was the Potala, once the home of the Dalai Lama, from a ground view, sprawled across the top of a high hill overlooking the city. It was bathed in the bright sunlight, looking as if it were floating on air, fading in and out like an apparition. It remained more of a mirage than a reality, yet there were a thousand rooms in it, and thousands of monks once chanted in its temples.

I had no idea what to expect in the way of accommodations for our group. Our Chinese lady guide was as ill-informed about Lhasa as any of us. No officials of CITS had been in Lhasa since the 1950s. There were all kinds of rumors. One was that we would all have to sleep in one room. There were twelve of us, which might have led to a little crowding. But no one worried about the idea. The enchantment of being the first bona fide tourists to visit Tibet was all that we needed.

However, we were driven to the charming compound of a government guesthouse. There were rooms for all and private baths. We learned that it was a special VIP guesthouse, equipped with all the appropriate amenities.

Tibet is very much like Bhutan in that it has been a country entirely steeped in religion, so much so that everything the people do in their daily lives is somehow connected with it. Buddhism has endured in spite of years of depression. Practically all the people —even members of the Communist Party—are Buddhists, unlike in the rest of China. On everybody's lips was the possible return of the Dalai Lama, rumored as a distinct possibility after his long years of exile.

I learned much about the current scene in Tibet at one of our first receptions in Lhasa. I was introduced to the Chinese General Ren Ron, who looked familiar to me when I first saw him across the room. Then I realized that I had seen him on the TV screen during the cease-fire negotiations of the Korean War. He had then been the commanding general of the Chinese forces in Korea and was now governor-general of Tibet. Like most of the Chinese he was a Han, the primary ethnic group that makes up 94 percent of the population. He was a charming man, and I spent most of the evening talking with him.

As senior representative in Tibet of the central Beijing government, he told me China had recognized that its previous policies in Tibet had failed, that they had to be changed, and that the issue of religious freedom was critical here. He said that a program had been laid out to give the land back to the Tibetans, and that most of the Han Chinese would be leaving the region. The Han Chinese had done a number of good things, however. Health care, schools, roads, electricity, and distribution of goods had all been vastly improved. The money spent by the central government in relation to the number of people was actually greater than in the rest of China.

As the general confessed that mistakes had been made, and that they had to be redressed, the reflection of the criticism and self-criticism philosophy arose again. The central point in the redress was to be the return of the Dalai Lama. In fact, I learned that the Dalai Lama's sister was in Tibet at the time, working with a special commission in serious negotiations.

I asked the general, if the Dalai Lama returned, would he again be the religious leader? The general replied that he would not only be that, but there was hope that he would also become the political leader, as he had been before 1959 when he fled the country. Hopefully, however, the general added, there would be no return of the severe abuses which had been carried out in the name of religion.

There was no question that the exploitation of the people by the monks and lamas had matched the abuses of the Cultural Revolution. Serfdom had been an indisputable fact: slaves could actually be bought and sold. The religious leaders held the power of life or death over the people.

It's impossible to say too much about the Potala and the monasteries in and near Lhasa that still remain in spite of the purge. The Potala, a blend of palace and fortress, dominates everything from its 700-foot-high perch above the city. Pure white, with an upper midsection of red-dish brown, with irregular jutting roofs and walkways, its splendor is imposing but its grace is simple. Its 1000 rooms, 10,000 altars, and 200,000 statues have been left the way they were when the Dalai Lama fled the country. It is a museum now that had very few visitors after the revolution and before our visit. A maintenance crew of a hundred Tibetans works to preserve it through the Chinese Cultural Relics Commission at a cost of over $60,000 a year. It was built mostly during the last half of the seventeenth century, but today only the ghosts of the thousands of monks and lamas who lived and worshipped there remain.

A fifteen-minute walk away from the Potala is the Jokhang monastery, regarded as the holiest place in Tibet. Built in the seventh century, it has been the mecca of Tibetan Buddhists since that time. It had only been reopened for worshippers a few months before we arrived, and only a few hundred pilgrims had come to pray there. At one time, 6000 or more monks resided there. On our arrival, there were barely more than a dozen, and they were wearing ordinary Tibetan costumes, not the burgundy red robes of their order. Their heads, however, were shaved according to custom. In front of the ancient monastery was a large iron fence, and the pilgrims had to pay a small entrance fee to get in on the few days a week it was open.

But inside were some of the most astounding treasures of Tibet. There were statues of the Buddha weighing tons, not of gold leaf, but of solid gold. I had never seen the likes of this anywhere. Inside the central hall the altars were rimmed with constellations of yak butter candles, giving off an overpowering waxlike aroma and illuminating exquisite paintings and tapestries.

Northwest of Lhasa is the Drepung monastery and its temples, once harboring over 9000 monks. On the day we visited there were only fourteen. Its sacred buildings made up a small city housing priceless ancient treasures.

The Red Guard, in its ruthless campaign of destruction, burned and leveled over 2000 monasteries throughout Tibet. But the Potala, Jokhang, and Drepung were spared when Chou En-lai sent a telegram to the invading forces that these three shrines were to be protected at all costs. One other monastery was included in the order, but the telegram failed to arrive in time to save it.

Later, when we returned for another visit to Lhasa in 1981, there was a remarkably different scene at Jokhang. The iron fence had been removed. Instead of a few hundred pilgrims a week, there was an average of 6000 every day. Many would circle the monastery by prostrating themselves full length on the ground, bringing their feet up to where their arms had extended and then moving forward, body length by body length. Some would do so sideways on the ground, a much slower process. Those who walked spun their prayer wheel cylinders constantly, mumbling O MANI PADME UM.

The number of monks at Jokhang also had increased dramatically, from fifteen to nearly 250. By the end of the year, the total was expected to be a thousand. There was an amazing relaxation of religious oppression. But the independent shopkeeper was beginning to rise again, too. Not only were shops open, but local Tibetans would pull trinkets out from under their robes to offer to the visitors.

We also had a chance to visit the Dalai Lama's summer palace in

Lhasa. The interior, our guide told us, had never been disturbed. We saw an old wind-up phonograph in its open case, a Victor record still on it, and a roll-index calendar on the Dalai Lama's chest of drawers, marked with the date MONDAY 31 —the day he had left. The bedclothes on his simple iron bed were still in disarray, unmade from the day of his abrupt departure. "You see," our guide said, "everything is just as he left it, so that he can return and continue just as before."

We moved on to an agricultural commune outside Lhasa. For centuries, Tibetans have been nomadic, roaming the grasslands, raising yaks, cattle, and horses in great numbers. They are magnificent horsemen and demonstrate their skill often at festivals where they gallop at full speed, shooting arrows as they do so, or bending down to pick up a handkerchief at the same speed. At the collective farm communes, much of this color is lost, but food production is dramatically improved. Cabbages, turnips, and potatoes are being buttressed by Chinese-style tomatoes and apples.

We were the first tourists to visit a commune, and everyone turned out to have a look at us foreign devils. They were as intrigued by us as we were by them. We noticed fishing in the nearby river, and since Cary and I love to fish, we asked if we could give it a try. They quickly agreed and brought out two strange long sticks with a steel wire loop at one end, somewhat like a lasso. We were completely mystified. Then they brought out long wires, unrolled them, and attached them to our poles. We were more puzzled than ever. At last, they brought the wires back to a big generator near the pond and attached them there.

We finally learned the mystery. We were to stand by the edge of the river, poles in hand, then place the loops in the water. When we were ready we raised our hands to signal to the generator man to turn on the current, and soon all kinds of electrocuted fish were floating to the top of the water. We then gave the hand signal to stop. I must confess it was quite a haul in a fraction of the time ordinary fishing would require. When I asked them how they fished in the large lakes, they told me dynamite was most efficient.

All kinds of misinformation about Tibet distort the Westerner's thinking. Tibet was historically part of China in the form of an autonomous region, even before the takeover by Mao Tse-tung's government. When the present Dalai Lama was installed, his confirmation had to be approved in Beijing, a tradition that has always prevailed, including during Chiang Kai-shek's rule.

Tibet has never been actually independent of China. When the Han Chinese came to Tibet in 1949, their purpose was to eliminate the manifest serfdom and slavery being carried out by the monks and lamas. They undertook to change this feudal system. At the same time, they permitted the Dalai Lama and the nobility to remain. The Dalai Lama also continued to serve as both the religious and temporal leader of the region.

In 1959, however, the Tibetans staged an armed rebellion. There is no question that the Han Chinese put this down ruthlessly. On the heels of that came the unleashed irrationality of the Cultural Revolution, including the execrable actions of the Red Guards. The Tibetans were clearly in rebellion, but historically they have been against every type of Chinese regime, from the warlords to Chiang Kai-shek to the Communist rule.

In the violence, the Dalai Lama fled the country, but the uprising continued long after he had left. However, the possibility remains strong that the spiritual leader will return, and with the Oriental capacity for forgiveness so strong, there is also the chance that the serene religion of Buddhism can exist side by side with the material productivity that new China has brought about—and without the ancient serfdom that was totally in conflict with the truths that Buddha taught.

The Tibetans utilize the process of Sky Funerals for the disposal of the dead, a custom that is pervasive throughout the Himalayas—and also in the far away mountain regions of New Guinea. The reason for the custom is obvious: the hard rocky landscape makes it next to impossible to dig graves; there is little other choice, except cremation, a firmly imbedded Hindu custom in India and elsewhere, but ignored by the highland Buddhists for the most part. The Sky Funeral practice in Tibet is carried out in the mountains around Lhasa and is rather complicated.

First, the body is carried to the higher slopes, where it is undressed and washed. Then all the soft parts of the body are sliced off, while the bones are ground in water to make a paste that is rolled into balls. The flesh is fine-chopped, hamburger style. The bone paste, including the teeth, is scattered around a wide area of the mountain. This is the least attractive morsel for the vultures, and only after they have devoured this are the favored flesh portions put out. A special group of holy men are engaged and the job passes from father to son. It is not a pretty sight. I have seen films of it shown by the Consul General of Nepal in Tibet, but I politely declined an invitation to attend one of the Sky Funerals. In other parts of Tibet where there are large lakes, the head is cut off and ground up, then the body is sliced and placed in the water where hundreds of fish dispose of the flesh as the bones sink to the bottom.

Tibetan people are fiercely individualistic, with faces of great and fascinating character. The women's headdresses are as elaborate and colorful as those in India and Nepal. They are garnished with solid gold ornaments that are incredibly expensive, especially in light of the frugal existence. There is some native gold in Tibet, but most of it has come in over the centuries from India, along with turquoise, having been shipped through India from faraway lands.

As in China, the Tibetans are always ready with a cheerful smile, a most engaging custom. They also greet you by sticking out their tongues, a sign of affection. The food is a little harder to take. The basic staple everywhere is tsampa, a paste made of roast barley flour, blended with rancid clarified yak butter and tea. Tea is also usually mixed with the yak butter and salt, which I would call an acquired taste at best. A visit to a monastery invariably requires the sipping of the tea, which is sometimes difficult to get past the palate.

Life in Tibet is not the easiest. There is still a long way to go to eliminate poverty and hardship in a harsh climate with vast stretches of desert and mountains. I talked to many who had spent long years in jail after the coming of the Red Guards, simply because they were lovers of beauty, or writers and artists who were creative and sensitive. Many of them had remained in jail until 1980 because they had been forgotten.

Almost everyone who was jailed during that time, however, has now been released.

In spite of these gross injustices, most Tibetans you meet will say that life is better today than it was before, that there is surprising improvement. What they are most interested in now is the possible return of the Dalai Lama as the great spiritual leader in a basically spiritual land.

Normally, the traveler abroad is not concerned primarily with the political scene of the places of great history or natural beauty he visits. But understanding history and politics is of primary importance in visiting China. Thousands of Americans are seeing the country of a billion people for the first time. The Chinese people are inordinately friendly to Americans, but the Americans in turn must come with their minds in gear, not in neutral. They must come not to be converted to Communism, but to understand something very important that is happening in China today. China is searching for an alternative to the previous corruptions of the warlords, the wars with Japan, and the internal poisoning by the Cultural Revolution and the Red Guards. It is now seeking peace and understanding through the tourist. To me, this search—in countries everywhere—could be the most vital function that tourism could perform.

By 1982, the demand for our China and Tibet tours had grown to such an extent that we were able to offer eleven weekly departures on a wide variety of programs that included Glimpses of China, Wonders of China, Classical China, Along the Grand Canal, Ancient Cities, Explorer's Tour, Tibet, and the Yangtse River and China Coastal cruises on the *Lindblad Explorer*. The tours run from sixteen to twenty-eight days each.

The success in opening up China and Tibet was the culmination of all the pioneer work done elsewhere in the world by Lindblad Travel in over a quarter of a century, and is of deep personal satisfaction to me. In spite of our covering most of the world, from top to bottom, I have no intention of resting on the oars. There are still new worlds to conquer in China and elsewhere. But just as important is the course that the travel industry as a whole follows over the next five or ten years. To me this is critical, and of great concern to people all over the world.

XVI

TRAVEL
Future Shock

LOOKING back over the years, I've come to certain conclusions. One is that people do not *want* to be tourists: they want to *know;* they want to *do.* Looking is passive. It's action that counts. In Antarctica, for instance, we match our wits with nature in finding our way through pack ice and in braving storms and rough seas. We experience the difficulty of travel.

If I could have been a discoverer, I would have been. The age of discovery on this planet may be over. But for the average person, it has hardly begun. I try to appeal to people who are not just idly curious, and who can afford to pay to have their whims satisfied. I like them to have some scientific background or special interest—or at least the intelligence to take part in the special programs we arrange. I urge them to go through the books on our special reading lists so they can feel and participate in the places we visit. I've found that sophisticated American travelers who think they are roughing it in Paris if they don't stay at the George V are happy to sleep under the stars if they are seeing and understanding new and important things—and if they are in action.

Out of my travels I've developed a certain credo, a very simple one: I believe in freedom, creativity, and conversation. And further, I be-

284

lieve that tourism is the handmaiden of them all. I believe in complete individual freedom—freedom in literature, the arts, film, theater. I believe in freedom of clothing—in bikinis, topless dresses, or no dresses at all, if you like. I believe in the freedom of a professor to express unpopular views and in the freedom of students to edit their own publications. I believe that only restrictions cause excesses. Excesses are boring and fade away in the light of freedom.

I believe that out of freedom comes creativity. I don't believe in merely specializing in offbeat travel, for instance. I believe in creating new possibilities for human experience and understanding. If I couldn't do that, I wouldn't be in this business; it wouldn't be very much fun. I want to have fun, and at the same time I want to leave my mark on the world.

I've been criticized for putting thousands of dollars of my own money into the restoration of one church in Peru. Why? Because I don't have that kind of money. But it's more important to me to revive something that is disappearing than to build something that can be duplicated. In this way, I can reawaken in people a sense of pride in their ancient ways. Without tourism and what it represents in buying power and taste, none of this would be possible.

There is a sign that greets travelers when they arrive by small airplane at an airstrip deep in the Serengeti Plain of Kenya. It reads: THIS LAND IS HELD BY US IN TRUST FOR OUR CHILDREN AND FOR OUR CHILDREN'S CHILDREN AND WE MUST TREAT IT ACCORDINGLY.

The sign was installed by the Serengeti Game Department, and it sums up a theme that should be applied not only to Africa but to the entire world. All the animals and land throughout the planet are held in trust by us. We have no right to destroy or change this heritage so that it becomes unrecognizable. We have a duty to pass the planet along to future generations in as unspoiled a way as possible. This requires intelligence, foresight, understanding, and creative effort.

The big question is how we can go about keeping the world's balance and beauty in trust. To accomplish this, we depend on organizations like the World Wildlife Fund, the International Council of Bird Preservation, the Audubon Society in the private sector, and several international agencies under the United Nations aegis. Concerted efforts in co-ordinating many of these organizations are being made by the International Union for Conservation of Nature and Natural Resources (IUCN), which has recently completed a comprehensive project in conjunction with the World Wildlife Fund and the United Nations Environment Program called World Conservation Strategy. Its purpose is to present a global strategy for two of the most critical problems the world faces: the need to supply the economic wants of the people, and the need to conserve nature and natural resources. Oddly enough, these two goals are not in opposition to each other, as many people think. Conservationists are just as interested in making the resources of the world available as they are in preserving them.

The heart of the matter lies in the lack of awareness by the general public of the direct and indirect benefits of conservation for the continuing existence of life everywhere. The World Conservation Strategy points out that ecosystems and species are being destroyed because people do not see that it is in their interest not to destroy them. The benefits of protecting natural ecosystems and their component plants and animals are regarded by all but a few as trivial and dispensable. If we don't know what can happen and what is happening, we can never understand how important conservation is to us directly.

A lobsterman knows that if he doesn't respect the mating cycle he won't have any more lobsters. He also knows that he'd better throw back the small ones into the sea to keep his catches profitable. He does this because he is in intimate contact with the environment, and his economy depends on his respecting it.

The situation becomes less obvious when it comes to the preservation of the coastal wetlands. Here the barely visible ecosystem comes into play. If a high-rise hotel is built on a landfill, the average observer shrugs it off. But a shrimp fisherman knows better. That filled-in land has destroyed the nutrients and nurseries for the shrimp supply that affects his living. The shrimp eggs are laid offshore. The larvae move inshore, toward the wetlands. But the juvenile and adolescent shrimp have to have the nutrients to feed on or they will die. Only after they mature can they return to the sea. Without the haven of the wetlands, the shrimp crop will die off. The cost of damage to U.S. fisheries alone by wetland destruction is estimated to be $86 million a year.

A similar process exists through the entire global ecosystem. It is less obvious, more subtle, hard to trace, and therefore hard to understand. But if we don't understand, there is danger ahead for all of us in both developed and developing countries. Conservation and economic development are mutually dependent. The conservationist isn't in love with insects, for instance. He sees their *need*. Beneficial insects serve as predators and parasites of more serious pests. If they are indiscriminately wiped out by pesticides, the results can be catastrophic. The number of pesticide-resistant insects and mites has doubled in twelve years.

The studies of the World Conservation Strategy point up other dramatic facts with directly traceable consequences. The livelihood of half the world depends on the way the watershed ecosystems of the world are preserved. Yet the watershed forests are being widely devastated by logging, clearance for agriculture, overgrazing, and inept road building. Argentina has to spend $10 million a year simply to dredge silt, once part of the forest lands, from the estuary of the Río de la Plata to keep Buenos Aires open to shipping. India has to spend up to $750 million for the repair of damage caused by floods resulting from overuse of mountainous areas. In Sri Lanka, the destruction of corals for the production of lime has wiped out some local fisheries and productive coconut groves. In other parts of the world, the construction of dams has blocked the passage of migrating fish and destroyed the habitats of others.

People often wonder why the destruction of an obscure species is important. There are several reasons, from the point of view of both insurance and investment. A major one is that we cannot predict what species may become useful to us, as the World Conservation Strategy points out. Everything in life is linked. The food chain and the subtle differences of genetic diversity play an important part in the life-support systems we depend on. Certain varieties of wheat and cereals last as little as five to fifteen years. Pests and diseases suddenly spring up to destroy one variety, and without a new strain of crop coming along to resist them, disaster can follow. New varieties of wild plants are the best insurance to protect a food supply source.

A most dramatic example of destruction happened in the mid-1800s, when almost every vineyard in Europe was destroyed by a North American insect called the *Phylloxera.* The entire production of Europe's wine was saved only by grafting the resistant American rootstocks onto European vines, a practice that is still going on today. We cannot depend on a few varieties of plants that may become vulnerable to certain pests and diseases. Some estimates indicate that up to a million species of animals may become extinct by the end of the century because their habitats are being destroyed. The point is that conservation is not limited to wildlife or the soil. It governs the production and development of life-sustaining elements that are needed for human existence. It is urgent that people understand why ecosystems and species must be protected.

The future of the travel industry is heavily involved with the efforts of global conservation. We have to examine where we stand in relation to people and their cultures, to animal life, and to places of great natural beauty. In my lifetime, I've had the opportunity to see many different peoples in many different cultures, some of them regarded as primitive. In all probability, these cultures and peoples will be lost in the future because the Western version of civilization is so powerful that it has taken over even in the remote parts of the world. The lure is irresistible because civilization provides comforts that primitive people have not known before. Through the opening up of remote areas by trade, there is no longer the pressing need to spin, weave, dye, and print by hand. Factory-made textiles of synthetic fibers are less expensive and eventually become easily available to wipe out the indigenous arts and crafts.

Music that has come from the souls of people in different cultures is now being replaced by the transistor radio or tape deck, with folk dancing and ancient drumbeats being pushed out of the picture. It is not at all unusual, for instance, to see a Sherpa in the highest Himalayas trekking with a portable radio up to his ear, listening to rock music. The oldest instrument in the world is the nose flute. It goes as far back as we can trace civilization. Tribes in the Middle East, Troy, and India played this instrument in ancient times, and some of the tribes in South America still do. Five years from now, it will be hard to find anyone who can play it, and the instrument will regrettably disappear.

Even languages are becoming severely eroded; it is much more convenient to use a single lingua franca. I went to a business meeting in Sweden recently where the entire group was Swedish, but the language used was English. One of the official languages of India is English, spoken at the expense of the other rich tongues used there. Although tongues and traditions are still fighting to stay alive in Asia, Africa, and South America, their retention may become a losing battle.

More than forty multilateral conventions deal with the management of living resources. One of them is the World Heritage convention for UNESCO members that works toward the protection of natural and cultural areas of such international value that they are part of the heritage of all humankind. The convention is attempting to make sure that areas of global importance are not lost because of the lack of local money and skills. Along with other international conventions for the protection of wetlands, flora and fauna, and migratory species, their objective is to establish international laws and action for this protection.

The majority of people in the world do not want to see the world destroyed. Only through a law can the individual who is bent on destruction be stopped. It was because of lack of legislation that Waikiki was destroyed by its junk stores, condominiums, and high-rises that dwarfed the palms, coconut trees, and beaches.

The same problem is reflected in Switzerland in places like Davos or Cranz-Montana. When I was young these were places of incredible beauty. They now have suffered the same fate as Waikiki. Overbuilding has made them not only ugly but incredibly ugly. I can't see anyone wanting to visit them anymore. The same is true of Majorca, Toremolinos, and the Côte d'Azur. Along the Mediterranean coast, you can find only a string of parked cars from the Spanish border to the south of Italy, with the accompanying pollution.

Prudent and intelligent people will realize that the unlimited exploitation of tourist resorts is not progress. One generation becomes rich at the expense of impoverishing future generations. That inevitable day will come when people will open their eyes and say, ''God, what an awful sight.''

There is a place for tourist development, but it cannot be done blindly, and greed cannot be the main ingredient. Such development requires research, knowledge, and a love for nature and cultures. Tourist facilities must be created in cooperation with local people, drawing on the knowledge of experts on traditions, music, and history in order to safeguard the trust in which all places must be held.

Fortunately, I do not see an immediate invasion of those places that have a natural defense, those harsh paradises that have teeth. The Antarctic is fraught with danger, and the greedy entrepreneur is not likely to take the risk. All of the Antarctic's seabirds, penguins, seals, and sea life will probably remain inviolate for years to come. The Himalayas require effort to reach, and the exploiter may find that, too, an obstacle.

Places like Easter Island, the Galápagos, and the remote atolls may survive well in spite of their fragility. In addition to the many safeguards that have been established for them, other defenses have turned their fragility into strength: the distance to them is great, and it is time-consuming and expensive to reach them so that they will not be easily overrun. As with China, they cannot be visited with the mind in neutral. They are not vacation wonderlands; they are intellectual wonderlands.

It is the benign paradises that are going to be under increasing attack, islands like Bali, Tahiti, Ponape, and Palau. These are ''soft'' places—relatively easy to reach, easy to build on, and easy to live on. Without proper legislation, they are helpless and vulnerable to the tourist traffic that is bound to increase rapidly over the next five to ten years, as the workweek is reduced and vacation time is increased for more and more people. This has been a historical trend. There is no reason that it should not continue in spite of economic cycles and setbacks.

With a greater number of people having time and money that they never had before, the potential destruction of the soft paradises will be imminent. Yet everyone should have a chance to have a relaxing vacation in places of beauty. There is no justice in suggesting that people should be denied attractive vacations simply because the potential for destruction is there. The burden is on local planning and control officials to prevent that destruction, to hold the land and waters in trust for present and future generations. To do this, there must be strong international help.

Every farmer knows that in planting, cultivating, and harvesting, the soil must be fertilized and husbanded so that future crops are assured. The case of the tourist industry is similar. In creating attractive resorts, we must find a way to develop them with care and love and with an eye to the future. We have to have such places; they are badly needed.

The problem today is the speed of destruction. It continues like a runaway horse. We have very little time to act, whether the damage is taking place in local towns, big cities, state and national forests, or remote vacation places. They are all linked, from the metropolis to the wilderness. Once the damage is done, it is irreversible.

I don't believe anything makes this point more movingly than a letter written by an Indian chief in 1854, when President Franklin Pierce offered to buy some of his lands in the northwest part of the United States. Chief Seattle of the Duwamish League gave this reply to the president:

How can you buy or sell the sky, the warmth of the land? The idea is strange to us. Yet we do not own the freshness of the air or the sparkle of the water. How can you buy them from us? . . .

But if we sell you our land, you must remember that the air is precious to us, that the air shares its spirit with all the life it supports. The wind that gave our grandfather his first breath also receives his last sigh. . . .

If we decide to accept, I will make one condition. The white man must treat the beasts of this land as his brothers. I am a savage and do not understand any other way. I have seen a thousand rotting buffalo on the prairie, left by the white man who shot them from passing trains. I am a savage and I do not understand how the smoking iron horse can be more important than the buffalo that we kill only to stay alive. . . .

If all the beasts were gone, men would die from a great loneliness of spirit. For whatever happens to the beast soon happens to man. All things are connected. . . .

So if we sell you our land, love it as we've loved it. Care for it as we've cared for it. Hold in your mind the memory of the land as it is when you take it. And with all your strength, with all your might and with all your heart preserve it for your children, and love it as God loves us all. . . .

Nothing could express what I've tried to say in this book more simply and more beautifully than these words of Chief Seattle written more than a century ago.

4-30-76

INDEX